HOW TO WRITE SHORT STORIES

Ring W. Lardner

HOW TO WRITE SHORT STORIES

[WITH SAMPLES]

BY

RING W. LARDNER

Fredonia Books
Amsterdam, The Netherlands

How to Write Short Stories:
With Samples

by
Ring W. Lardner

ISBN: 1-4101-0785-X

Reprinted from the 1924 edition

Fredonia Books
Amsterdam, The Netherlands
http://www.fredoniabooks.com

PREFACE

HOW TO WRITE SHORT STORIES

A glimpse at the advertising columns of our
leading magazines shows that whatever else this
country may be shy of, there is certainly no lack
of correspondence schools that learns you the
art of short-story writing. The most notorious
of these schools makes the boast that one of their
pupils cleaned up $5000.00 and no hundreds dollars
writing short stories according to the system
learnt in their course, though it don't say if that
amount was cleaned up in one year or fifty.

However, for some reason another when you
skin through the pages of high class periodicals,
you don't very often find them cluttered up with
stories that was written by boys or gals who had
win their phi beta skeleton keys at this or that
story-writing college. In fact, the most of the
successful authors of the short fiction of to-day
never went to no kind of a college, or if they did,
they studied piano tuning or the barber trade.
They could of got just as far in what I call the literary game if they had of stayed home those four
years and helped mother carry out the empty
bottles.

The answer is that you can't find no school in

Preface

operation up to date, whether it be a general institution of learning or a school that specializes in story writing, which can make a great author out of a born druggist.

But a little group of our deeper drinkers has suggested that maybe boys and gals who wants to take up writing as their life work would be benefited if some person like I was to give them a few hints in regards to the technic of the short story, how to go about planning it and writing it, when and where to plant the love interest and climax, and finally how to market the finished product without leaving no bad taste in the mouth.

Well, then, it seems to me like the best method to use in giving out these hints is to try and describe my own personal procedure from the time I get inspired till the time the manuscript is loaded on to the trucks.

The first thing I generally always do is try and get hold of a catchy title, like for instance, "Basil Hargrave's Vermifuge," or "Fun at the Incinerating Plant." Then I set down to a desk or flat table of any kind and lay out 3 or 4 sheets of paper with as many different colored pencils and look at them cock-eyed a few moments before making a selection.

How to begin—or, as we professionals would say, "how to commence"—is the next question. It must be admitted that the method of approach

Preface

("L'approchement") differs even among first class fictionists. For example, Blasco Ibañez usually starts his stories with a Spanish word, Jack Dempsey with an "I" and Charley Peterson with a couple of simple declarative sentences about his leading character, such as "Hazel Gooftree had just gone mah jong. She felt faint."

Personally it has been my observation that the reading public prefers short dialogue to any other kind of writing and I always aim to open my tale with two or three lines of conversation between characters—or, as I call them, my puppets—who are to play important rôles. I have often found that something one of these characters says, words I have perhaps unconsciously put into his or her mouth, directs my plot into channels deeper than I had planned and changes, for the better, the entire sense of my story.

To illustrate this, let us pretend that I have laid out a plot as follows: Two girls, Dorothy Abbott and Edith Quaver, are spending the heated term at a famous resort. The Prince of Wales visits the resort, but leaves on the next train. A day or two later, a Mexican reaches the place and looks for accommodations, but is unable to find a room without a bath. The two girls meet him at the public filling station and ask him for a contribution to their autograph album. To their amazement, he utters a terrible oath, spits

Preface

in their general direction and hurries out of town. It is not until years later that the two girls learn he is a notorious forger and realize how lucky they were after all.

Let us pretend that the above is the original plot. Then let us begin the writing with haphazard dialogue and see whither it leads:

"Where was you?" asked Edith Quaver.

"To the taxidermist's," replied Dorothy Abbott.

The two girls were spending the heated term at a famous watering trough. They had just been bathing and were now engaged in sorting dental floss.

"I am getting sick in tired of this place," went on Miss Quaver.

"It is mutual," said Miss Abbott, shying a cucumber at a passing paper-hanger.

There was a rap at their door and the maid's voice announced that company was awaiting them downstairs. The two girls went down and entered the music room. Garnett Whaledriver was at the piano and the girls tiptoed to the lounge.

The big Nordic, oblivious of their presence, allowed his fingers to form weird, fantastic minors before they strayed unconsciously into the first tones of Chopin's 121st Fugue for the Bass Drum.

From this beginning, a skilled writer could go most anywheres, but it would be my tendency to

Preface

drop these three characters and take up the life of a mule in the Grand Canyon. The mule watches the trains come in from the east, he watches the trains come in from the west, and keeps wondering who is going to ride him. But she never finds out.

The love interest and climax would come when a man and a lady, both strangers, got to talking together on the train going back east.

"Well," said Mrs. Croot, for it was she, "what did you think of the Canyon?"

"Some cave," replied her escort.

"What a funny way to put it!" replied Mrs. Croot. "And now play me something."

Without a word, Warren took his place on the piano bench and at first allowed his fingers to form weird, fantastic chords on the black keys. Suddenly and with no seeming intention, he was in the midst of the second movement of Chopin's Twelfth Sonata for Flute and Cuspidor. Mrs. Croot felt faint.

That will give young writers an idea of how an apparently trivial thing such as a line of dialogue will upset an entire plot and lead an author far from the path he had pointed for himself. It will also serve as a model for beginners to follow in regards to style and technic. I will not insult my readers by going on with the story to its obvious

Preface

conclusion. That simple task they can do for themselves, and it will be good practice.

So much for the planning and writing. Now for the marketing of the completed work. A good many young writers make the mistake of enclosing a stamped, self-addressed envelope, big enough for the manuscript to come back in. This is too much of a temptation to the editor.

Personally I have found it a good scheme to not even sign my name to the story, and when I have got it sealed up in its envelope and stamped and addressed, I take it to some town where I don't live and mail it from there. The editor has no idea who wrote the story, so how can he send it back? He is in a quandary.

In conclusion let me warn my pupils never to write their stories—or, as we professionals call them, "yarns"—on used paper. And never to write them on a post-card. And never to send them by telegraph (Morse code).

Stories ("yarns") of mine which have appeared in various publications—one of them having been accepted and published by the first editor that got it—are reprinted in the following pages and will illustrate in a half-hearted way what I am trying to get at.

RING LARDNER.

"THE MANGE,"
    Great Neck, Long Island, 1924.

CONTENTS

THE FACTS

A sample story of life in the Kentucky mountains. An English girl leaves her husband, an Omaha policeman, but neglects to obtain a divorce. She later meets the man she loves, a garbage inspector from Bordeaux, and goes with him "without benefit of clergy." This story was written on top of a Fifth Avenue bus, and some of the sheets blew away, which may account for the apparent scarcity of interesting situations.

How to Write Short Stories

I

THE FACTS

I

The engagement was broken off before it was announced. So only a thousand or so of the intimate friends and relatives of the parties knew anything about it. What they knew was that there had been an engagement and that there was one no longer. The cause of the breach they merely guessed, and most of the guesses were, in most particulars, wrong.

Each intimate and relative had a fragment of the truth. It remained for me to piece the fragments together. It was a difficult job, but I did it. Part of my evidence is hearsay; the major portion is fully corroborated. And not one of my witnesses had anything to gain through perjury.

So I am positive that I have at my tongue's end the facts, and I believe that in justice to everybody concerned I should make them public.

Ellen McDonald had lived on the North Side

How to Write Short Stories

of Chicago for twenty-one years. Billy Bowen had been a South-Sider for seven years longer. But neither knew of the other's existence until they met in New York, the night before the Army-Navy game.

Billy, sitting with a business acquaintance at a neighboring table in Tonio's, was spotted by a male member of Ellen's party, a Chicagoan, too. He was urged to come on over. He did, and was introduced. The business acquaintance was also urged, came, was introduced and forgotten; forgotten, that is, by every one but the waiter, who observed that he danced not nor told stories, and figured that his function must be to pay. The business acquaintance had been Billy's guest. Now he became host, and without seeking the office.

It was not that Billy and Miss McDonald's male friends were niggards. But unfortunately for the b. a., the checks always happened to arrive when everybody else was dancing or so hysterical over Billy's repartee as to be potentially insolvent.

Billy was somewhere between his fourteenth and twenty-first highball; in other words, at his best, from the audience's standpoint. His dialogue was simply screaming and his dancing just heavenly. He was Frank Tinney doubling as Vernon Castle. On the floor he tried and accom-

The Facts

plished twinkles that would have spelled catas-
trophe if attempted under the fourteen mark, or
over the twenty-one. And he said the cutest
things—one right after the other.

II

You can be charmed by a man's dancing, but
you can't fall in love with his funniness. If you're
going to fall in love with him at all, you'll do it
when you catch him in a serious mood.

Miss McDonald caught Billy Bowen in one at
the game next day. Entirely by accident or a
decree of fate, her party and his sat in adjoining
boxes. Not by accident, Miss McDonald sat in
the chair that was nearest Billy's. She sat there
first to be amused; she stayed to be conquered.

Here was a different Billy from the Billy of
Tonio's. Here was a Billy who trained his gun
on your heart and let your risibles alone. Here
was a dreamy Billy, a Billy of romance.

How calm he remained through the excitement! How indifferent to the thrills of the game!
There was depth to him. He was a man. Her
escort and the others round her were children,
screaming with delight at the puerile deeds of
pseudo heroes. Football was a great sport, but
a sport. It wasn't Life. Would the world be
better or worse for that nine-yard gain that Ele-

5

phant or Oliphant, or whatever his name was, had
just made? She knew it wouldn't. Billy knew,
too, for Billy was deep. He was thinking man's
thoughts. She could tell by his silence, by his
inattention to the scene before him. She scarcely
could believe that here was the same person who,
last night, had kept his own, yes, and the neighboring tables, roaring with laughter. What a
complex character his!

In sooth, Mr. Bowen was thinking man's
thoughts. He was thinking that if this pretty
Miss McDowell, or Donnelly, were elsewhere, he
could go to sleep. And that if he could remember which team he had bet on and could tell
which team was which, he would have a better
idea of whether he was likely to win or lose.

When, after the game, they parted, Billy ral-
lied to the extent of asking permission to call.
Ellen, it seemed, would be very glad to have him,
but she couldn't tell exactly when she would have
to be back in Chicago; she still had three more
places to visit in the East. Could she possibly
let him know when she did get back? Yes, she
could and would; if he really wanted her to, she
would drop him a note. He certainly wanted
her to.

This, thought Billy, was the best possible arrangement. Her note would tell him her name
and address, and save him the trouble of 'phoning

to all the McConnells, McDowells, and Donnellys on the North Side. He did want to see her again; she was pretty, and, judging from last night, full of pep. And she had fallen for him; he knew it from that look.

He watched her until she was lost in the crowd. Then he hunted round for his pals and the car that had brought them up. At length he gave up the search and wearily climbed the elevated stairs. His hotel was on Broadway, near Forty-fourth. He left the train at Forty-second, the third time it stopped there.

"I guess you've rode far enough," said the guard. "Fifteen cents' worth for a nickel. I guess we ought to have a Pullman on these here trains."

"I guess," said Billy, "I guess——"

But the repartee well was dry. He stumbled down-stairs and hurried toward Broadway to replenish it.

III

Ellen McDonald's three more places to visit in the East must have been deadly dull. Anyway, on the sixth of December, scarcely more than a week after his parting with her in New York, Billy Bowen received the promised note. It informed him merely that her name was Ellen McDonald, that she lived at so-and-so Walton Place, and that she was back in Chicago.

How to Write Short Stories

That day, if you'll remember, was Monday. Miss McDonald's parents had tickets for the opera. But Ellen was honestly just worn out, and would they be mad at her if she stayed home and went to bed? They wouldn't. They would take Aunt Mary in her place.

On Tuesday morning, Paul Potter called up and wanted to know if she would go with him that night to "The Follies." She was horribly sorry, but she'd made an engagement. The engagement, evidently, was to study, and the subject was harmony, with Berlin, Kern, and Van Alstyne as instructors. She sat on the piano-bench from half-past seven till quarter after nine, and then went to her room vowing that she would accept any and all invitations for the following evening.

Fortunately, no invitations arrived, for at a quarter of nine Wednesday night, Mr. Bowen did. And in a brand-new mood. He was a bit shy and listened more than he talked. But when he talked, he talked well, though the sparkling wit of the night at Tonio's was lacking. Lacking, too, was the preoccupied air of the day at the football game. There was no problem to keep his mind busy, but even if the Army and Navy had been playing football in this very room, he could have told at a glance which was which. Vision and brain were perfectly clear. And he had been getting his old eight hours, and, like the

The Facts

railroad hen, sometimes nine and sometimes ten, every night since his arrival home from Gotham, N. Y. Mr. Bowen was on the wagon.

They talked of the East, of Tonio's, of the game (this was where Billy did most of his listening), of the war, of theatres, of books, of college, of automobiles, of the market. They talked, too, of their immediate families. Billy's, consisting of one married sister in South Bend, was soon exhausted. He had two cousins here in town whom he saw frequently, two cousins and their wives, but they were people who simply couldn't stay home nights. As for himself, he preferred his rooms and a good book to the so-called gay life. Ellen should think that a man who danced so well would want to be doing it all the time. It was nice of her to say that he danced well, but really he didn't, you know. Oh, yes, he did. She guessed she could tell. Well, anyway, the giddy whirl made no appeal to him, unless, of course, he was in particularly charming company. His avowed love for home and quiet surprised Ellen a little. It surprised Mr. Bowen a great deal. Only last night, he remembered, he had been driven almost desperate by that quiet of which he was now so fond; he had been on the point of busting loose, but had checked himself in time. He had played Canfield till ten, though the bookshelves were groaning with their load.

How to Write Short Stories

Ellen's family kept them busy for an hour and a half. It was a dear family and she wished he could meet it. Mother and father were out playing bridge somewhere to-night. Aunt Mary had gone to bed. Aunts Louise and Harriet lived in the next block. Sisters Edith and Wilma would be home from Northampton for the holidays about the twentieth. Brother Bob and his wife had built the cutest house; in Evanston. Her younger brother, Walter, was a case! He was away to-night, had gone out right after dinner. He'd better be in before mother and father came. He had a new love-affair every week, and sixteen years old last August. Mother and father really didn't care how many girls he was interested in, so long as they kept him too busy to run round with those crazy schoolmates of his. The latter were older than he; just at the age when it seems smart to drink beer and play cards for money. Father said if he ever found out that Walter was doing those things, he'd take him out of school and lock him up somewhere.

Aunts Louise and Mary and Harriet did a lot of settlement work. They met all sorts of queer people, people you'd never believe existed. The three aunts were unmarried.

Brother Bob's wife was dear, but absolutely without a sense of humor. Bob was full of fun, but they got along just beautifully together. You never saw a couple so much in love.

The Facts

Edith was on the basket-ball team at college and terribly popular. Wilma was horribly clever and everybody said she'd make Phi Beta Kappa.

Ellen, so she averred, had been just nothing in school; not bright; not athletic, and, of course, not popular.

"Oh, of course not," said Billy, smiling.

"Honestly," fibbed Ellen.

"You never could make me believe it," said Billy.

Whereat Ellen blushed, and Billy's unbelief strengthened.

At this crisis, the Case burst into the room with his hat on. He removed it at sight of the caller and awkwardly advanced to be introduced.

"I'm going to bed," he announced, after the formality.

"I hoped," said Ellen, "you'd tell us about the latest. Who is it now? Beth?"

"Beth nothing!" scoffed the Case. "We split up the day of the Keewatin game."

"What was the matter?" asked his sister.

"I'm going to bed," said the Case. "It's pretty near midnight."

"By George, it is!" exclaimed Billy. "I didn't dream it was that late!"

"No," said Walter. "That's what I tell dad —the clock goes along some when you're having a good time."

Billy and Ellen looked shyly at each other, and then laughed; laughed harder, it seemed to Wal-

11

ter, than the joke warranted. In fact, he hadn't thought of it as a joke. If it was that good, he'd spring it on Kathryn to-morrow night. It would just about clinch her.

The Case, carrying out his repeated threat, went to bed and dreamed of Kathryn. Fifteen minutes later Ellen retired to dream of Billy. And an hour later than that, Billy was dreaming of Ellen, who had become suddenly popular with him, even if she hadn't been so at Northampton, which he didn't believe.

IV

They saw "The Follies" Friday night. A criticism of the show by either would have been the greatest folly of all. It is doubtful that they could have told what theatre they'd been to ten minutes after they'd left it. From wherever it was, they walked to a dancing place and danced. Ellen was so far gone that she failed to note the change in Billy's trotting. Foxes would have blushed for shame at its awkwardness and lack of variety. If Billy was a splendid dancer, he certainly did not prove it this night. All he knew or cared to know was that he was with the girl he wanted. And she knew only that she was with Billy, and happy.

On the drive home, the usual superfluous words

The Facts

were spoken. They were repeated inside the storm-door at Ellen's father's house, while the taxi driver, waiting, wondered audibly why them suckers of explorers beat it to the Pole to freeze when the North Side was so damn handy.

Ellen's father was out of town. So in the morning she broke the news to mother and Aunt Mary, and then sat down and wrote it to Edith and Wilma. Next she called up Bob's wife in Evanston, and after that she hurried to the next block and sprang it on Aunts Louise and Harriet. It was decided that Walter had better not be told. He didn't know how to keep a secret. Walter, therefore, was in ignorance till he got home from school. The only person he confided in the same evening was Kathryn, who was the only person he saw.

Bob and his wife and Aunts Louise and Harriet came to Sunday dinner, but were chased home early in the afternoon. Mr. McDonald was back and Billy was coming to talk to him. It would embarrass Billy to death to find such a crowd in the house. They'd all meet him soon, never fear, and when they met him, they'd be crazy about him. Bob and Aunt Mary and mother would like him because he was so bright and said such screaming things, and the rest would like him because he was so well-read and sensible, and so horribly good-looking.

13

How to Write Short Stories

Billy, I said, was coming to talk to Mr. McDonald. When he came, he did very little of the talking. He stated the purpose of his visit, told what business he was in and affirmed his ability to support a wife. Then he assumed the rôle of audience while Ellen's father delivered an hour's lecture. The speaker did not express his opinion of Tyrus Cobb or the Kaiser, but they were the only subjects he overlooked. Sobriety and industry were words frequently used.

"I don't care," he prevaricated, in conclusion, "how much money a man is making if he is sober and industrious. You attended college, and I presume you did all the fool things college boys do. Some men recover from their college education, others don't. I hope you're one of the former."

The Sunday-night supper, just cold scraps you might say, was partaken of by the happy but embarrassed pair, the trying-to-look happy but unembarrassed parents, and Aunt Mary. Walter, the Case, was out. He had stayed home the previous evening.

"He'll be here to-morrow night and the rest of the week, or I'll know the reason why," said Mr. McDonald.

"He won't, and I'll tell you the reason why," said Ellen.

"He's a real boy, Sam," put in the real boy's

14

The Facts

mother. "You can't expect him to stay home every minute."

"I can't expect anything of him," said the father. "You and the girls and Mary here have let him have his own way so long that he's past managing. When I was his age, I was in my bed at nine o'clock."

"Morning or night?" asked Ellen.

Her father scowled. It was evident he could not take a joke, not even a good one.

After the cold scraps had been ruined, Mr. McDonald drew Billy into the smoking-room and offered him a cigar. The prospective son-in-law was about to refuse and express a preference for cigarettes when something told him not to. A moment later he was deeply grateful to the something.

"I smoke three cigars a day," said the oracle, "one after each meal. That amount of smoking will hurt nobody. More than that is too much. I used to smoke to excess, four or five cigars per day, and maybe a pipe or two. I found it was affecting my health, and I cut down. Thank heaven, no one in my family ever got the cigarette habit; disease, rather. How any sane, clean-minded man can start on those things is beyond me."

"Me, too," agreed Billy, taking the proffered cigar with one hand and making sure with the other that his silver pill-case was as deep down in his pocket as it would go.

"Cigarettes, gambling, and drinking go hand in hand," continued the man of the house. "I couldn't trust a cigarette fiend with a nickel."

"There are only two or three kinds he could get for that," said Billy.

"What say?" demanded Mr. McDonald, but before Billy was obliged to wriggle out of it, Aunt Mary came in and reminded her brother-in-law that it was nearly church time.

Mr. McDonald and Aunt Mary went to church. Mrs. McDonald, pleading weariness, stayed home with "the children." She wanted a chance to get acquainted with this pleasant-faced boy who was going to rob her of one of her five dearest treasures.

The three were no sooner settled in front of the fireplace than Ellen adroitly brought up the subject of auction bridge, knowing that it would relieve Billy of the conversational burden.

"Mother is really quite a shark, aren't you, mother?" she said.

"I don't fancy being called a fish," said the mother.

"She's written two books on it, and she and father have won so many prizes that they may have to lease a warehouse. If they'd only play for money, just think how rich we'd all be!"

The Facts

"The game is fascinating enough without adding to it the excitements and evils of gambling," said Mrs. McDonald.

"It is a fascinating game," agreed Billy.

"It is," said Mrs. McDonald, and away she went.

Before father and Aunt Mary got home from church, Mr. Bowen was a strong disciple of conservativeness in bidding and thoroughly convinced that all the rules that had been taught were dead wrong. He saw the shark's points so quickly and agreed so whole-heartedly with her arguments that he impressed her as one of the most intelligent young men she had ever talked to. It was too bad it was Sunday night, but some evening soon he must come over for a game.

"I'd like awfully well to read your books," said Billy.

"The first one's usefulness died with the changes in the rules," replied Mrs. McDonald. "But I think I have one of the new ones in the house, and I'll be glad to have you take it."

"I don't like to have you give me your only copy."

"Oh, I believe we have two."

She knew perfectly well she had two dozen.

Aunt Mary announced that Walter had been seen in church with Kathryn. He had made it his business to be seen. He and the lady had

17

come early and had manœuvred into the third
row from the back, on the aisle leading to the
McDonald family pew. He had nudged his aunt
as she passed on the way to her seat, and she had
turned and spoken to him. She could not know
that he and Kathryn had "ducked" before the
end of the processional.

After reporting favorably on the Case, Aunt
Mary launched into a description of the service.
About seventy had turned out. The music had
been good, but not quite as good as in the morning. Mr. Pratt had sung "Fear Ye Not, O
Israel!" for the offertory. Dr. Gish was still
sick and a lay reader had served. She had heard
from Allie French that Dr. Gish expected to be
out by the middle of the week and certainly
would be able to preach next Sunday morning.
The church had been cold at first, but very comfortable finally.

Ellen rose and said she and Billy would go out
in the kitchen and make some fudge.

"I was afraid Aunt Mary would bore you to
death," she told Billy, when they had kissed for
the first time since five o'clock. "She just lives
for the church and can talk on no other subject."

"I wouldn't hold that against her," said Billy
charitably.

The fudge was a failure, as it was bound to be.
But the Case, who came in just as it was being

18

The Facts

passed round, was the only one rude enough to say so.

"Is this a new stunt?" he inquired, when he had tested it.

"Is what a new stunt?" asked Ellen.

"Using cheese instead of chocolate."

"That will do, Walter," said his father. "You can go to bed."

Walter got up and started for the hall. At the threshold he stopped.

"I don't suppose there'll be any of that fudge left," he said. "But if there should be, you'd better put it in the mouse trap."

Billy called a taxi and departed soon after Walter's exit. When he got out at his South Side abode, the floor of the tonneau was littered with recent cigarettes.

And that night he dreamed that he was president of the anti-cigarette league; that Dr. Gish was vice-president, and that the motto of the organization was "No trump."

Billy Bowen's business took him out of town the second week in December, and it was not until the twentieth that he returned. He had been East and had ridden home from Buffalo on the same train with Wilma and Edith McDonald. But he didn't know it and neither did they. They could not be expected to recognize him from Ellen's description—that he was horribly good-looking. The dining-car conductor was all of that.

Ellen had further written them that he (not the dining-car conductor) was a man of many moods; that sometimes he was just nice and deep, and sometimes he was screamingly funny, and sometimes so serious and silent that she was almost afraid of him.

They were wild to see him and the journey through Ohio and Indiana would not have been half so long in his company. Edith, the athletic, would have revelled in his wit. Wilma would gleefully have fathomed his depths. They would both have been proud to flaunt his looks before the hundreds of their kind aboard the train. Their loss was greater than Billy's, for he, smoking cigarettes as fast as he could light them and playing bridge that would have brought tears of compassion to the shark's eyes, enjoyed the trip, every minute of it.

Ellen and her father were at the station to meet the girls. His arrival on this train had not been heralded, and it added greatly to the hysterics of the occasion.

Wilma and Edith upbraided him for not knowing by instinct who they were. He accused them of recognizing him and purposely avoiding him. Much more of it was pulled in the same light vein, pro and con.

The Facts

He was permitted at length to depart for his office. On the way he congratulated himself on the improbability of his ever being obliged to play basket-ball versus Edith. She must be a whizz in condition. Chances were she'd train down to a hundred and ninety-five before the big games. The other one, Wilma, was a splinter if he ever saw one. You had to keep your eyes peeled or you'd miss her entirely. But suppose you did miss her; what then! If she won her Phi Beta Kappa pin, he thought, it would make her a dandy belt.

These two, he thought, were a misdeal. They should be reshuffled and cut nearer the middle of the deck. Lots of other funny things he thought about these two.

Just before he had left Chicago on this trip, his stenographer had quit him to marry an elevator-starter named Felix Bond. He had 'phoned one of his cousins and asked him to be on the look-out for a live stenographer who wasn't likely to take the eye of an elevator-starter. The cousin had had one in mind.

Here was her card on Billy's desk when he reached the office. It was not a business-card visiting-card, at $3 per hundred. "Miss Violet Moore," the engraved part said. Above was written: "Mr. Bowen—Call me up any night after seven. Calumet 2678."

21

How to Write Short Stories

Billy stowed the card in his pocket and plunged into a pile of uninteresting letters.

On the night of the twenty-second there was a family dinner at McDonald's, and Billy was in on it. At the function he met the rest of them—Bob and his wife, and Aunt Harriet and Aunt Louise.

Bob and his wife, despite the former's alleged sense of humor, spooned every time they were contiguous. That they were in love with each other, as Ellen had said, was easy to see. The wherefore was more of a puzzle.

Bob's hirsute adornment having been disturbed by his spouse's digits during one of the orgies, he went up-stairs ten minutes before dinner time to effect repairs. Mrs. Bob was left alone on the davenport. In performance of his social duties, Billy went over and sat down beside her. She was not, like Miss Muffet, frightened away, but terror or some other fiend rendered her temporarily dumb. The game Mr. Bowen was making his fifth attempt to pry open a conversation when Bob came back.

To the impartial observer the scene on the davenport appeared heartless enough. There was a generous neutral zone between Billy and Flo, that being an abbreviation of Mrs. Bob's given name, which, as a few may suspect, was Florence. Billy was working hard and his face was flushed with

22

The Facts

the effort. The flush may have aroused Bob's suspicions. At any rate, he strode across the room, scowling almost audibly, shot a glance at Billy that would have made the Kaiser wince, halted magnificently in front of his wife, and commanded her to accompany him to the hall.

Billy's flush became ace high. He was about to get up and break a chair when a look from Ellen stopped him. She was at his side before the pair of Bobs had skidded out of the room.

"Please don't mind," she begged. "He's crazy. I forgot to tell you that he's insanely jealous."

"Did I understand you to say he had a sense of humor?"

"It doesn't work where Flo's concerned. If he sees her talking to a man he goes wild."

"With astonishment, probably," said Billy.

"You're a nice boy," said Ellen irrelevantly.

Dinner was announced and Mr. Bowen was glad to observe that Flo's terrestrial body was still intact. He was glad, too, to note that Bob was no longer frothing. He learned for the first time that the Case and Kathryn were of the party. Mrs. McDonald had wanted to make sure of Walter's presence; hence the presence of his crush.

Kathryn giggled when she was presented to Billy. It made him uncomfortable and he thought for a moment that a couple of studs had fallen out.

How to Write Short Stories

He soon discovered, however, that the giggle was permanent, just as much a part of Kathryn as her fraction of a nose. He looked forward with new interest to the soup course, but was disappointed to find that she could negotiate it without disturbing the giggle or the linen.

He next centred his attention on Wilma and Edith. Another disappointment was in store. There were as many and as large oysters in Wilma's soup as in any one's. She ate them all, and, so far as appearances went, was the same Wilma. He had expected that Edith would either diet or plunge. But Edith was as prosaic in her consumption of victuals as Ellen, for instance, or Aunt Louise.

He must content himself for the present with Aunt Louise. She was sitting directly opposite and he had an unobstructed view of the widest part he had ever seen in woman's hair.

"Ogden Avenue," he said to himself.

Aunt Louise was telling about her experiences and Aunt Harriet's among the heathen of Peoria Street.

"You never would dream there were such people!" said she.

"I suppose most of them are foreign born," supposed her brother, who was Mr. McDonald.

"Practically all of them," said Aunt Louise.

Billy wanted to ask her whether she had ever

The Facts

missionaried among the Indians. He thought possibly an attempt to scalp her had failed by a narrow margin.

Between courses Edith worked hard to draw out his predicated comicality and Wilma worked as hard to make him sound his low notes. Their labors were in vain. He was not sleepy enough to be deep, and he was fourteen highballs shy of comedy.

In disgust, perhaps, at her failure to be amused, the major portion of the misdeal capsized her cocoa just before the close of the meal and drew a frown from her father, whom she could have thrown in ten minutes, straight falls, any style.

"She'll never miss that ounce," thought Billy.

When they got up from the table and started for the living-room, Mr. Bowen found himself walking beside Aunt Harriet, who had been so silent during dinner that he had all but forgotten her.

"Well, Miss McDonald," he said, "it's certainly a big family, isn't it?"

"Well, young man," said Aunt Harriet, "it ain't no small family, that's sure."

"I should say not," repeated Billy.

Walter and his giggling crush intercepted him.

"What do you think of Aunt Harriet's grammar?" demanded Walter.

"I didn't notice it," lied Billy.

"No, I s'pose not. 'Ain't no small family.' I s'pose you didn't notice it. She isn't a real aunt like Aunt Louise and Aunt Mary. She's just an adopted aunt. She kept house for dad and Aunt Louise after their mother died, and when dad got married, she just kept on living with Aunt Louise."

"Oh," was Billy's fresh comment, and it brought forth a fresh supply of giggles from Kathryn.

Ellen had already been made aware of Billy's disgusting plans. He had to catch a night train for St. Louis, and he would be there all day tomorrow, and he'd be back Friday, but he wouldn't have time to see her, and he'd surely call her up. And Friday afternoon he was going to South Bend to spend Christmas Day with his married sister, because it was probably the last Christmas he'd be able to spend with her.

"But I'll hustle home from South Bend Sunday morning," he said. "And don't you dare make any engagement for the afternoon."

"I do wish you could be with us Christmas Eve. The tree won't be a bit of fun without you."

"You know I wish I could. But you see how it is."

"I think your sister's mean."

Billy didn't deny it.

"Who's going to be here Christmas Eve?"

The Facts

"Just the people we had to-night, except Kath-ryn and you. Why?"

"Oh, nothing," said Billy.

"Look here, sir," said his betrothed. "Don't you do anything foolish. You're not supposed to buy presents for the whole family. Just a little, tiny one for me, if you want to, but you mustn't spend much on it. And if you get anything for any one else in this house, I'll be mad."

"I'd like to see you mad," said Billy.

"You'd wish you hadn't," Ellen retorted.

When Billy had gone, Ellen returned to the living-room and faced the assembled company.

"Well," she said, "now that you've all seen him, what's the verdict?"

The verdict seemed to be unanimously in his favor.

"But," said Bob, "I thought you said he was so screamingly funny."

"Yes," said Edith, "you told me that, too."

"Give him a chance," said Ellen. "Wait till he's in a funny mood. You'll simply die laughing!"

V

It is a compound fracture of the rules to have so important a character as Tommy Richards appear in only one chapter. But remember, this isn't a regular story, but a simple statement of what occurred when it occurred. During Chapter Four, Tommy had been on his way home from the Pacific Coast, where business had kept him all fall. His business out there and what he said en route to Chicago are collateral.

Tommy had been Billy's pal at college. Tommy's home was in Minnesota, and Billy was his most intimate, practically his only friend in the so-called metropolis of the Middle West. So Tommy, not knowing that Billy had gone to St. Louis, looked forward to a few pleasant hours with him between the time of the coast train's arrival and the Minnesota train's departure.

The coast train reached Chicago about noon. It was Thursday noon, the twenty-third. Tommy hustled from the station to Billy's office, and there learned of the St. Louis trip. Disappointed, he roamed the streets a while and at length dropped into the downtown ticket office of his favorite Minnesota road. He was told that everything for the night was sold out. Big Christmas business. Tommy pondered.

The coast train reached Chicago about noon. It was Thursday noon, the twenty-third.

"How about to-morrow night?" he inquired.

"I can give you a lower to-morrow night on the six-thirty," replied Leslie Painter, that being the clerk's name.

"I'll take it," said Tommy.

The Facts

He did so, and the clerk took $10.05.

"I'll see old Bill after all," said Tommy.

Leslie Painter made no reply.

In the afternoon Tommy sat through a vaudeville show, and at night he looped the loop. He retired early, for the next day promised to be a big one.

Billy got in from St. Louis at seven Friday morning and had been in his office an hour when Tommy appeared. I have no details of the meeting.

At half-past eight Tommy suggested that they'd better go out and h'ist one.

"Still on it, eh?" said Billy.

"What do you mean?"

"I mean that I'm off of it."

"Good Lord! For how long?"

"The last day of November."

"Too long! You look sick already."

"I feel great," averred Billy.

"Well, I don't. So come along and bathe in vichy."

On the way "along" Billy told Tommy about Ellen. Tommy's congratulations were physical and jarred Billy from head to heels.

"Good stuff!" cried Tommy so loudly that three pedestrians jumped sideways. "Old Bill hooked! And do you think you're going to celebrate this occasion with water?"

How to Write Short Stories

"I think I am," was Billy's firm reply.

"You think you are! What odds?"

"A good lunch against a red hot."

"You're on!" said Tommy. "And I'm going to be mighty hungry at one o'clock."

"You'll be hungry and alone."

"What's the idea? If you've got a lunch date with the future, I'm in on it."

"I haven't," said Billy. "But I'm going to South Bend on the one-forty, and between now and then I have nothing to do but clean up my mail and buy a dozen Christmas presents."

They turned in somewhere.

"Don't you see the girl at all to-day?" asked Tommy.

"Not to-day. All I do is call her up."

"Well, then, if you get outside of a couple, who'll be hurt? Just for old time's sake."

"If you need lunch money, I'll give it to you."

"No, no. That bet's off."

"It's not off. I won't call it off."

"Suit yourself," said Tommy graciously.

At half-past nine, it was officially decided that Billy had lost the bet. At half-past twelve, Billy said it was time to pay it.

"I'm not hungry enough," said Tommy.

"Hungry or no hungry," said Billy, "I buy your lunch now or I don't buy it. See? Hungry or no hungry."

The Facts

"What's the hurry?" asked Tommy.

"I guess you know what's the hurry. Me for South Bend on the one-forty, and I got to go to the office first. Hurry or no hurry."

"Listen to reason, Bill. How are you going to eat lunch, go to the office, buy a dozen Christmas presents and catch the one-forty?"

"Christmas presents! I forgot 'em! What do you think of that? I forgot 'em. Good night!"

"What are you going to do?"

"Do! What can I do? You got me into this mess. Get me out!"

"Sure, I'll get you out if you'll listen to reason!" said Tommy. "Has this one-forty train got anything on you? Are you under obligations to it? Is the engineer your girl's uncle?"

"I guess you know better than that. I guess you know I'm not engaged to a girl who's got an uncle for an engineer."

"Well, then, what's the next train?"

"That's the boy, Tommy! That fixes it! I'll go on the next train."

"You're sure there is one?" asked Tommy.

"Is one! Say, where do you think South Bend is? In Europe?"

"I wouldn't mind," said Tommy.

"South Bend's only a two-hour run. Where did you think it was? Europe?"

How to Write Short Stories

"I don't care where it is. The question is, what's the next train after one-forty?"

"Maybe you think I don't know," said Billy. He called the gentleman with the apron. "What do you know about this, Charley? Here's an old pal of mine who thinks I don't know the time-table to South Bend."

"He's mistaken, isn't he?" said Charley.

"Is he mistaken? Say, Charley, if you knew as much as I do about the time-table to South Bend, you wouldn't be here."

"No, sir," said Charley. "I'd be an announcer over in the station."

"There!" said Billy triumphantly. "How's that, Tommy? Do I know the time-table or don't I?"

"I guess you do," said Tommy. "But I don't think you ought to have secrets from an old friend."

"There's no secrets about it, Charley."

"My name is Tommy," corrected his friend.

"I know that. I know your name as well as my own, better'n my own. I know your name as well as I know the time-table."

"If you'd just tell me the time of that train, we'd all be better off."

"I'll tell you, Tommy. I wouldn't hold out anything on you, old boy. It's five twenty-five."

"You're sure?"

The Facts

"Sure! Say, I've taken it a hundred times if I've taken it once."

"All right," said Tommy. "That fixes it. We'll go in and have lunch and be through by half-past one. That'll give you four hours to do your shopping, get to your office and make your train."

"Where you going while I shop?"

"Don't bother about me."

"You go along with me."

"Nothing doing."

"Yes, you do."

"No, I don't."

But this argument was won by Mr. Bowen. At ten minutes of three, when they at last called for the check, Mr. Richards looked on the shopping expedition in an entirely different light. Two hours before, it had not appealed to him at all. Now he could think of nothing that would afford more real entertainment. Mr. Richards was at a stage corresponding to Billy's twenty-one. Billy was far past it.

"What we better do," said Tommy, "is write down a list of all the people so we won't forget anybody."

"That's the stuff!" said Billy. "I'll name 'em, you write 'em."

So Tommy produced a pencil and took dictation on the back of a menu-card.

How to Write Short Stories

"First, girl's father, Sam'l McDonald."

"Samuel McDonald," repeated Tommy. "Maybe you'd better give me some dope on each one, so if we're shy of time, we can both be buying at once."

"All right," said Billy. "First, Sam'l McDonal'. He's an ol' crab. Raves about cig'rettes."

"Like 'em?"

"No. Hates 'em."

"Sam'l McDonald, cigarettes," wrote Tommy. "Old crab," he added.

When the important preliminary arrangement had at last been completed, the two old college chums went out into the air.

"Where do we shop?" asked Tommy.

"Marsh's," said Billy. "'S only place I got charge account."

"Maybe we better take a taxi and save time," suggested Tommy.

So they waited five minutes for a taxi and were driven to Marsh's, two blocks away.

"We'll start on the first floor and work up," said Tommy, who had evidently appointed himself captain.

They found themselves among the jewelry and silverware.

"You might get something for the girl here," suggested Tommy.

"Don't worry 'bout her," said Billy. "Leave her till las'."

The Facts

"What's the limit on the others?"

"I don't care," said Billy. "Dollar, two dollars, three dollars."

"Well, come on," said Tommy. "We got to make it snappy."

But Billy hung back.

"Say, ol' boy," he wheedled. "You're my ol'st frien'. Is that right?"

"That's right," agreed Tommy.

"Well, say, ol' frien', I'm pretty near all in."

"Go home, then, if you want to. I can pull this all right alone."

"Nothin' doin'. But if I could jus' li'l nap, ten, fifteen minutes—you could get couple things here on fir' floor and then come get me."

"Where?"

"Third floor waitin'-room."

"Go ahead. But wait a minute. Give me some of your cards. And will I have any trouble charging things?"

"Not a bit. Tell 'em you're me."

It was thus that Tommy Richards was left alone in a large store, with Billy Bowen's charge account, Billy Bowen's list, and Billy Bowen's cards.

He glanced at the list.

"'Samuel McDonald, cigarettes. Old crab,'" he read.

He approached a floor-walker.

"Say, old pal," he said. "I'm doing some shopping and I'm in a big hurry. Where'd I find something for an old cigarette fiend?"

"Cigarette-cases, two aisles down and an aisle to your left," said Old Pal.

Tommy raised the limit on the cigarette-case he picked out for Samuel McDonald. It was $3.75.

"I'll cut down somewhere else," he thought. "The father-in-law ought to be favored a little."

"Charge," he said in response to a query. "William Bowen, Bowen and Company, 18 South La Salle. And here's a card for it. That go out to-night sure?"

He looked again at the list.

"Mrs. Samuel McDonald, bridge bug. Miss Harriet McDonald, reverse English. Miss Louise McDonald, thin hair. Miss Mary Carey, church stuff. Bob and Wife, 'The Man Who Married a Dumb Wife' and gets mysteriously jealous. Walter McDonald, real kid. Edith, fat lady. Wilma, a splinter."

He consulted Old Pal once more. Old Pal's advice was to go to the third floor and look over the books. The advice proved sound. On the third floor Tommy found for Mother "The First Principles of Auction Bridge." and for Aunt Harriet an English grammar. He also bumped into a counter laden with hymnals, chant books, and Books of Common Prayer.

The Facts

"Aunt Mary!" he exclaimed. And to the clerk: "How much are your medium prayer-books?"

"What denomination?" asked the clerk, whose name was Freda Swanson.

"One or two dollars," said Tommy.

"What church, I mean?" inquired Freda.

"How would I know?" said Tommy. "Are there different books for different churches?"

"Sure. Catholic, Presbyterian, Episcopal, Lutheran——"

"Let's see. McDonald, Carey. How much are the Catholic ones?"

"Here's one at a dollar and a half. In Latin, too."

"That's it. That'll give her something to work on."

Tommy figured on the back of his list.

"Good work, Tommy!" he thought. "Four and a half under the top limit for those three. Walter's next."

He plunged on Walter. A nice poker set, discovered on the fourth floor, came to five even. Tommy wished he could keep it for himself. He also wished constantly that the women shoppers had taken a course in dodging. He was almost as badly battered as the day he played guard against the Indians.

"Three left besides the queen herself," he

How to Write Short Stories

observed. "Lord, no. I forgot Bob and his missus."

He moved down-stairs again to the books.

"Have you got 'The Man Who Married a Dumb Wife'?" he queried.

Anna Henderson looked, but could not find it.

"Never mind!" said Tommy. "Here's one that'll do."

And he ordered "The Green-Eyed Monster" for the cooing doves in Evanston.

"Now," he figured, "there's just Wilma and Edith and Aunt Louise." Once more he started away from the books, but a title caught his eye: "Eat and Grow Thin."

"Great!" exclaimed Tommy. "It'll do for Edith. By George! It'll do for both of them. 'Eat' for Wilma, and the 'Grow Thin' for Edith. I guess that's doubling up some! And now for Aunt Louise."

The nearest floor-walker told him, in response to his query, that switches would be found on the second floor.

"I ought to have a switch-engine to take me round," said Tommy, who never had felt better in his life. But the floor-walker did not laugh, possibly because he was tired.

"Have you anything to match it with?" asked the lady in the switch-yard.

The Facts

"No, I haven't."

"Can you give me an idea of the color?"

"What colors have you got?" demanded Tommy.

"Everything there is. I'll show them all to you, if you've got the time."

"Never mind," said Tommy. "What's your favorite color in hair?"

The girl laughed.

"Golden," she said.

"You're satisfied, aren't you?" said Tommy, for the girl had chosen the shade of her own shaggy mane. "All right, make it golden. And a merry Christmas to you."

He forgot to ask the price of switches. He added up the rest and found that the total was $16.25.

"About seventy-five cents for the hair," he guessed. "That will make it seventeen even. I'm some shopper. And all done in an hour and thirteen minutes."

He discovered Billy asleep in the waiting-room and it took him three precious minutes to bring him to.

"Everybody's fixed but the girl herself," he boasted. "I got books for most of 'em."

"Where you been?" asked Billy. "What time is it?"

"You've got about thirty-three minutes to get

How to Write Short Stories

a present for your lady love and grab your train. You'll have to pass up the office."

"What time is it? Where you been?"

"Don't bother about that. Come on."

On the ride down, Billy begged every one in the elevator to tell him the time, but no one seemed to know. Tommy hurried him out of the store and into a taxi.

"There's a flock of stores round the station," said Tommy. "You can find something there for the dame."

But the progress of the cab through the packed down-town streets was painfully slow and the station clock, when at last they got in sight of it, registered 5.17.

"You can't wait!" said Tommy. "Give me some money and tell me what to get."

Billy fumbled clumsily in seven pockets before he located his pocketbook. In it were two fives and a ten.

"I gotta have a feevee," he said.

"All right. I'll get something for fifteen. What'll it be?"

"Make it a wrist-watch."

"Sure she has none?"

"She's got one. That's for other wris'."

"I used your last card. Have you got another?"

"Pocketbook," said Billy.

The Facts

Tommy hastily searched and found a card. He pushed Billy toward the station entrance.

"Good-by and merry Christmas," said Tommy.

"Goo'-by and God bless you!" said Billy, but he was talking to a large policeman.

"Where are you trying to go?" asked the latter.

"Souse Ben'," said Billy.

"Hurry up, then. You've only got a minute."

The minute and six more were spent in the purchase of a ticket. And when Billy reached the gate, the 5.25 had gone and the 5.30 was about to chase it.

"Where to?" inquired the gateman.

"Souse Ben'," said Billy.

"Run then," said the gateman.

Billy ran. He ran to the first open vestibule of the Rock Island train, bound for St. Joe, Missouri.

"Where to?" asked a porter.

"Souse," said Billy.

"Ah can see that," said the porter. "But where you goin'?"

The train began to move and Billy, one foot dragging on the station platform, moved with it. The porter dexterously pulled him aboard. And he was allowed to ride to Englewood.

Walking down Van Buren Street, it suddenly occurred to the genial Mr. Richards that he would have to go some himself to get his baggage and catch the 6.30 for the northwest. He thought of it in front of a Van Buren jewelry shop. He stopped and went in.

Three-quarters of an hour later, a messenger-boy delivered a particularly ugly and frankly inexpensive wrist-watch at the McDonald home. The parcel was addressed to Miss McDonald and the accompanying card read:

"Mr. Bowen: Call me up any night after seven. Calumet 2678. Miss Violet Moore."

There was no good-will toward men in the McDonald home this Christmas. Ellen spent the day in bed and the orders were that she must not be disturbed.

Down-stairs, one person smiled. It was Walter. He smiled in spite of the fact that his father had tossed his brand-new five-dollar poker set into the open fireplace. He smiled in spite of the fact that he was not allowed to leave the house, not even to take Kathryn to church.

"Gee!" he thought, between smiles, "Billy sure had nerve!"

Bob walked round among his relatives seeking to dispel the gloom with a remark that he thought apt and nifty:

"Be grateful," was the remark, "that he had one of his screamingly funny moods before it was too late."

The Facts

But no one but Bob seemed to think much of the remark, and no one seemed grateful.

Those are the facts, and it was quite a job to dig them up.   But I did it.

SOME LIKE THEM COLD

This story is an example of a story written from a title, the title being a line from Tennyson's immortal "Hot Cross Buns." A country-bred youth, left a fortune, journeys to London "to become a gentleman." Adventures beset him, not the least of them being that he falls out of a toy balloon.

II

SOME LIKE THEM COLD

N. Y., Aug. 3.

DEAR MISS GILLESPIE: How about our bet now as you bet me I would forget all about you the minute I hit the big town and would never write you a letter. Well girlie it looks like you lose so pay me. Seriously we will call all bets off as I am not the kind that bet on a sure thing and it sure was a sure thing that I would not forget a girlie like you and all that is worrying me is whether it may not be the other way round and you are wondering who this fresh guy is that is writeing you this letter. I bet you are so will try and refreshen your memory.

Well girlie I am the handsome young man that was wondering round the Lasalle st. station Monday and "happened" to sit down beside of a mighty pretty girlie who was waiting to meet her sister from Toledo and the train was late and I am glad of it because if it had not of been that little girlie and I would never of met. So for once I was a lucky guy but still I guess it was time I had some luck as it was certainly tough luck for you and I to both be liveing in Chi all that time and never get together till a half hour before I was leaveing town for good.

47

How to Write Short Stories

Still "better late than never" you know and maybe we can make up for lost time though it looks like we would have to do our makeing up at long distants unless you make good on your threat and come to N. Y. I wish you would do that little thing girlie as it looks like that was the only way we would get a chance to play round together as it looks like they was little or no chance of me comeing back to Chi as my whole future is in the big town. N. Y. is the only spot and specially for a man that expects to make my liveing in the song writeing game as here is the Mecca for that line of work and no matter how good a man may be they don't get no recognition unless they live in N. Y.

Well girlie you asked me to tell you all about my trip. Well I remember you saying that you would give anything to be makeing it yourself but as far as the trip itself was conserned you ought to be thankfull you did not have to make it as you would of sweat your head off. I know I did specially wile going through Ind. Monday P. M. but Monday night was the worst of all trying to sleep and finely I give it up and just layed there with the prespiration rolling off of me though I was laying on top of the covers and nothing on but my underwear.

Yesterday was not so bad as it rained most of the A. M. comeing through N. Y. state and in the

Some Like Them Cold

p. m. we road along side of the Hudson all p. m.
Some river girlie and just looking at it makes a
man forget all about the heat and everything else
except a certain girlie who I seen for the first
time Monday and then only for a half hour but
she is the kind of a girlie that a man don't need
to see her only once and they would be no danger
of forgetting her. There I guess I better lay
off that subject or you will think I am a "fresh
guy."

Well that is about all to tell you about the trip
only they was one amuseing incidence that come
off yesterday which I will tell you. Well they
was a dame got on the train at Toledo Monday
and had the birth opp. mine but I did not see
nothing of her that night as I was out smokeing
till late and she hit the hay early but yesterday
a. m. she come in the dinner and sit at the same
table with me and tried to make me and it was
so raw that the dinge waiter seen it and give me
the wink and of course I paid no tension and I
waited till she got through so as they would be
no danger of her folling me out but she stopped on
the way out to get a tooth pick and when I come
out she was out on the platform with it so I tried
to brush right by but she spoke up and asked me
what time it was and I told her and she said she
geussed her watch was slow so I said maybe it
just seemed slow on acct. of the company it was in.

49

How to Write Short Stories

I don't know if she got what I was driveing at or not but any way she give up trying to make me and got off at Albany. She was a good looker but I have no time for gals that tries to make strangers on a train.

Well if I don't quit you will think I am writeing a book but will expect a long letter in answer to this letter and we will see if you can keep your promise like I have kept mine. Don't dissapoint me girlie as I am all alone in a large city and hearing from you will keep me from getting home sick for old Chi though I never thought so much of the old town till I found out you lived there. Don't think that is kidding girlie as I mean it.

You can address me at this hotel as it looks like I will be here right along as it is on 47th st. right off of old Broadway and handy to everything and am only paying $21 per wk. for my rm. and could of got one for $16 but without bath but am glad to pay the differents as am lost without my bath in the A. M. and sometimes at night too.

Tomorrow I expect to commence fighting the "battle of Broadway" and will let you know how I come out that is if you answer this letter. In the mean wile girlie au reservoir and don't do nothing I would not do.

Your new friend (?)

CHAS. F. LEWIS.

Some Like Them Cold

Chicago, Ill., Aug. 6.

MY DEAR MR. LEWIS: Well, that certainly was a "surprise party" getting your letter and you are certainly a "wonder man" to keep your word as I am afraid most men of your sex are gay deceivers but maybe you are "different." Any way it sure was a surprise and will gladly pay the bet if you will just tell me what it was we bet. Hope it was not money as I am a "working girl" but if it was not more than a dollar or two will try to dig it up even if I have to "beg, borrow or steal."

Suppose you will think me a "case" to make a bet and then forget what it was, but you must remember, Mr. Man, that I had just met you and was "dazzled." Joking aside I was rather "fussed" and will tell you why. Well, Mr. Lewis, I suppose you see lots of girls like the one you told me about that you saw on the train who tried to "get acquainted" but I want to assure you that I am not one of those kind and sincerely hope you will believe me when I tell you that you was the first man I ever spoke to meeting them like that and my friends and the people who know me would simply faint if they knew I ever spoke to a man without a "proper introduction."

Believe me, Mr. Lewis, I am not that kind and I don't know now why I did it only that you was so "different" looking if you know what I

How to Write Short Stories

mean and not at all like the kind of men that usually try to force their attentions on every pretty girl they see. Lots of times I act on impulse and let my feelings run away from me and sometimes I do things on the impulse of the moment which I regret them later on, and that is what I did this time, but hope you won't give me cause to regret it and I know you won't as I know you are not that kind of a man a specially after what you told me about the girl on the train. But any way as I say, I was in a "daze" so can't remember what it was we bet, but will try and pay it if it does not "break" me.

Sis's train got in about ten minutes after yours had gone and when she saw me what do you think was the first thing she said? Well, Mr. Lewis, she said: "Why Mibs (That is a pet name some of my friends have given me) what has happened to you? I never seen you have as much color." So I passed it off with some remark about the heat and changed the subject as I certainly was not going to tell her that I had just been talking to a man who I had never met or she would of dropped dead from the shock. Either that or she would not of believed me as it would be hard for a person who knows me well to imagine me doing a thing like that as I have quite a reputation for "squelching" men who try to act fresh. I don't mean anything per-

Some Like Them Cold

sonal by that, Mr. Lewis, as am a good judge of
character and could tell without you telling me
that you are not that kind.

Well, Sis and I have been on the "go" ever
since she arrived as I took yesterday and today
off so I could show her the "sights" though she
says she would be perfectly satisfied to just sit in
the apartment and listen to me "rattle on." Am
afraid I am a great talker, Mr. Lewis, but Sis
says it is as good as a show to hear me talk as I
tell things in such a different way as I cannot
help from seeing the humorous side of everything
and she says she never gets tired of listening to
me, but of course she is my sister and thinks the
world of me, but she really does laugh like she
enjoyed my craziness.

Maybe I told you that I have a tiny little apartment which a girl friend of mine and I have together and it is hardly big enough to turn round
in, but still it is "home" and I am a great home
girl and hardly ever care to go out evenings except occasionally to the theatre or dance. But
even if our "nest" is small we are proud of it and
Sis complimented us on how cozy it is and how
"homey" it looks and she said she did not see
how we could afford to have everything so nice
and Edith (my girl friend) said: "Mibs deserves
all the credit for that. I never knew a girl who
could make a little money go a long ways like

she can." Well, of course she is my best friend
and always saying nice things about me, but I
do try and I hope I get results. Have always
said that good taste and being careful is a whole
lot more important than lots of money though
it is nice to have it.

You must write and tell me how you are getting along in the "battle of Broadway" (I laughed
when I read that) and whether the publishers
like your songs though I know they will. Am
crazy to hear them and hear you play the piano
as I love good jazz music even better than classical, though I suppose it is terrible to say such a
thing. But I usually say just what I think
though sometimes I wish afterwards I had not of.
But still I believe it is better for a girl to be her
own self and natural instead of always acting.
But am afraid I will never have a chance to hear
you play unless you come back to Chi and pay
us a visit as my "threat" to come to New York
was just a "threat" and I don't see any hope of
ever getting there unless some rich New Yorker
should fall in love with me and take me there to
live. Fine chance for poor little me, eh Mr.
Lewis?

Well, I guess I have "rattled on" long enough
and you will think I am writing a book unless I
quit and besides, Sis has asked me as a special
favor to make her a pie for dinner. Maybe you

Some Like Them Cold

don't know it, Mr. Man, but I am quite famous for my pie and pastry, but I don't suppose a "genius" is interested in common things like that.

Well, be sure and write soon and tell me what N.Y. is like and all about it and don't forget the little girlie who was "bad" and spoke to a strange man in the station and have been blushing over it ever since.

Your friend (?)
Mabelle Gillespie.

N. Y., Aug. 10.

Dear Girlie: I bet you will think I am a fresh guy commenceing that way but Miss Gillespie is too cold and a man can not do nothing cold in this kind of weather specially in this man's town which is the hottest place I ever been in and I guess maybe the reason why New Yorkers is so bad is because they think they are all ready in H—— and can not go no worse place no matter how they behave themselves. Honest girlie I certainly envy you being where there is a breeze off the old Lake and Chi may be dirty but I never heard of nobody dying because they was dirty but four people died here yesterday on acct. of the heat and I seen two different women flop right on Broadway and had to be taken away in the ambulance and it could not of been because they was dressed too warm because it would be impossible for the women here to leave off any more cloths.

Well have not had much luck yet in the battle of Broadway as all the heads of the big music publishers is out of town on their vacation and the big boys is the only ones I will do business with as it would be silly for a man with the stuff I have got to waste my time on somebody that is just on the staff and have not got the final say. But I did play a couple of my numbers for the people up to Levy's and Goebel's and they went crazy over them in both places. So it looks like all I have to do is wait for the big boys to get back and then play my numbers for them and I will be all set. What I want is to get taken on the staff of one of the big firms as that gives a man the inside and they will plug your numbers more if you are on the staff. In the mean wile have not got nothing to worry me but am just seeing the sights of the big town as have saved up enough money to play round for a wile and any way a man that can play piano like I can don't never have to worry about starveing. Can certainly make the old music box talk girlie and am always good for a $75 or $100 job.

Well have been here a week now and on the go every minute and I thought I would be lonesome down here but no chance of that as I have been treated fine by the people I have met and have

Some Like Them Cold

sure met a bunch of them. One of the boys living in the hotel is a vaudeville actor and he is a member of the Friars club and took me over there to dinner the other night and some way another the bunch got wise that I could play piano so of course I had to sit down and give them some of my numbers and everybody went crazy over them. One of the boys I met there was Paul Sears the song writer but he just writes the lyrics and has wrote a bunch of hits and when he heard some of my melodies he called me over to one side and said he would like to work with me on some numbers. How is that girlie as he is one of the biggest hit writers in N. Y.

N. Y. has got some mighty pretty girlies and I guess it would not be hard to get acquainted with them and in fact several of them has tried to make me since I been here but I always figure that a girl must be something wrong with her if she tries to make a man that she don't know nothing about so I pass them all up. But I did meet a couple of pips that a man here in the hotel went up on Riverside Drive to see them and insisted on me going along and they got on some way that I could make a piano talk so they was nothing but I must play for them so I sit down and played some of my own stuff and they went crazy over it.

One of the girls wanted I should come up and

see her again, and I said I might but I think I
better keep away as she acted like she wanted to
vamp me and I am not the kind that likes to
play round with a gal just for their company and
dance with them etc. but when I see the right
gal that will be a different thing and she won't
have to beg me to come and see her as I will
camp right on her trail till she says yes. And it
won't be none of these N. Y. fly by nights neither.
They are all right to look at but a man would be
a sucker to get serious with them as they might
take you up and next thing you know you would
have a wife on your hands that don't know a dish
rag from a waffle iron.

Well girlie will quit and call it a day as it is
too hot to write any more and I guess I will turn
on the cold water and lay in the tub a wile and
then turn in. Don't forget to write to

Your friend,
CHAS. F. LEWIS.

DEAR MR. MAN: Hope you won't think me a
"silly Billy" for starting my letter that way but
"Mr. Lewis" is so formal and "Charles" is too
much the other way and any way I would not dare
call a man by their first name after only knowing
them only two weeks. Though I may as well
confess that Charles is my favorite name for a
man and have always been crazy about it as it

Some Like Them Cold

was my father's name. Poor old dad, he died of
cancer three years ago, but left enough insurance
so that mother and we girls were well provided
for and do not have to do anything to support
ourselves though I have been earning my own
living for two years to make things easier for
mother and also because I simply can't bear to
be doing nothing as I feel like a "drone." So I
flew away from the "home nest" though mother
felt bad about it as I was her favorite and she
always said I was such a comfort to her as when
I was in the house she never had to worry about
how things would go.

But there I go gossiping about my domestic
affairs just like you would be interested in them
though I don't see how you could be though personly I always like to know all about my friends,
but I know men are different so will try and not
bore you any longer. Poor Man, I certainly feel
sorry for you if New York is as hot as all that.
I guess it has been very hot in Chi, too, at least
everybody has been complaining about how terrible it is. Suppose you will wonder why I say
"I guess" and you will think I ought to know if
it is hot. Well, sir, the reason I say "I guess" is
because I don't feel the heat like others do or at
least I don't let myself feel it. That sounds
crazy I know, but don't you think there is a good
deal in mental suggestion and not letting your-

How to Write Short Stories

self feel things? I believe that if a person simply won't allow themselves to be affected by disagreeable things, why such things won't bother them near as much. I know it works with me and that is the reason why I am never cross when things go wrong and "keep smiling" no matter what happens and as far as the heat is concerned, why I just don't let myself feel it and my friends say I don't even look hot no matter if the weather is boiling and Edith, my girl friend, often says that I am like a breeze and it cools her off just to have me come in the room. Poor Edie suffers terribly during the hot weather and says it almost makes her mad at me to see how cool and unruffled I look when everybody else is perspiring and have red faces etc.

I laughed when I read what you said about New York being so hot that people thought it was the "other place." I can appreciate a joke, Mr. Man, and that one did not go "over my head." Am still laughing at some of the things you said in the station though they probably struck me funnier than they would most girls as I always see the funny side and sometimes something is said and I laugh and the others wonder what I am laughing at as they cannot see anything in it themselves, but it is just the way I look at things so of course I cannot explain to them why I laughed and they think I am crazy. But I had

Some Like Them Cold

rather part with almost anything rather than my sense of humour as it helps me over a great many rough spots.

Sis has gone back home though I would of liked to of kept her here much longer, but she had to go though she said she would of liked nothing better than to stay with me and just listen to me "rattle on." She always says it is just like a show to hear me talk as I always put things in such a funny way and for weeks after she has been visiting me she thinks of some of the things I said and laughs over them. Since she left Edith and I have been pretty quiet though poor Edie wants to be on the "go" all the time and tries to make me go out with her every evening to the pictures and scolds me when I say I had rather stay home and read and calls me a "book worm." Well, it is true that I had rather stay home with a good book than go to some crazy old picture and the last two nights I have been reading myself to sleep with Robert W. Service's poems. Don't you love Service or don't you care for "highbrow" writings?

Personly there is nothing I love more than to just sit and read a good book or sit and listen to somebody play the piano, I mean if they can really play and I really believe I like popular music better than the classical though I suppose that is a terrible thing to confess, but I love all kinds of music but a specially the piano when it is played by somebody who can really play.

Am glad you have not "fallen" for the "ladies" who have tried to make your acquaintance in New York. You are right in thinking there must be something wrong with girls who try to "pick up" strange men as no girl with self respect would do such a thing and when I say that, Mr. Man, I know you will think it is a funny thing for me to say on account of the way our friendship started, but I mean it and I assure you that was the first time I ever done such a thing in my life and would never of thought of doing it had I not known you were the right kind of a man as I flatter myself that I am a good judge of character and can tell pretty well what a person is like by just looking at them and I assure you I had made up my mind what kind of a man you were before I allowed myself to answer your opening remark. Otherwise I am the last girl in the world that would allow myself to speak to a person without being introduced to them.

When you write again you must tell me all about the girl on Riverside Drive and what she looks like and if you went to see her again and all about her. Suppose you will think I am a little old "curiosity shop" for asking all those questions and will wonder why I want to know. Well, sir, I won't tell you why, so there, but I

Some Like Them Cold

insist on you answering all questions and will scold you if you don't. Maybe you will think that the reason why I am so curious is because I am "jealous" of the lady in question. Well, sir, I won't tell you whether I am or not, but will keep you "guessing." Now, don't you wish you knew?

Must close or you will think I am going to "rattle on" forever or maybe you have all ready become disgusted and torn my letter up. If so all I can say is poor little me—she was a nice little girl and meant well, but the man did not appreciate her.

There! Will stop or you will think I am crazy if you do not all ready.

Yours (?)

MABELLE.

N. Y., Aug. 20.

DEAR GIRLIE: Well girlie I suppose you thought I was never going to answer your letter but have been busier than a one armed paper hanger the last week as have been working on a number with Paul Sears who is one of the best lyric writers in N. Y. and has turned out as many hits as Berlin or Davis or any of them. And believe me girlie he has turned out another hit this time that is he and I have done it together. It is all done now and we are just waiting for the best chance to

63

How to Write Short Stories

place it but will not place it nowheres unless we get the right kind of a deal but maybe will publish it ourselves.

The song is bound to go over big as Sears has wrote a great lyric and I have give it a great tune or at least every body that has heard it goes crazy over it and it looks like it would go over bigger than any song since Mammy and would not be surprised to see it come out the hit of the year. If it is handled right we will make a bbl. of money and Sears says it is a cinch we will clean up as much as $25000 apiece which is pretty fair for one song but this one is not like the most of them but has got a great lyric and I have wrote a melody that will knock them out of their seats. I only wish you could hear it girlie and hear it the way I play it. I had to play it over and over about 50 times at the Friars last night.

I will copy down the lyric of the chorus so you can see what it is like and get the idea of the song though of course you can't tell much about it unless you hear it played and sang. The title of the song is When They're Like You and here is the chorus:

"Some like them hot, some like them cold.
Some like them when they're not too darn old.
Some like them fat, some like them lean.

64

Some Like Them Cold

Some like them only at sweet sixteen.
Some like them dark, some like them light.
Some like them in the park, late at night.
Some like them fickle, some like them true,
But the time I like them is when they're like you."

How is that for a lyric and I only wish I could play my melody for you as you would go nuts over it but will send you a copy as soon as the song is published and you can get some of your friends to play it over for you and I know you will like it though it is a different melody when I play it or when somebody else plays it.

Well girlie you will see how busy I have been and am libel to keep right on being busy as we are not going to let the grass grow under our feet but as soon as we have got this number placed we will get busy on another one as a couple like that will put me on Easy st. even if they don't go as big as we expect but even 25 grand is a big bunch of money and if a man could only turn out one hit a year and make that much out of it I would be on Easy st. and no more hammering on the old music box in some cabaret.

Who ever we take the song to we will make them come across with one grand for advance royaltys and that will keep me going till I can turn out another one. So the future looks bright and rosey to yours truly and I am certainly glad

How to Write Short Stories

I come to the big town though sorry I did not do it a whole lot quicker.

This is a great old town girlie and when you have lived here a wile you wonder how you ever stood for a burg like Chi which is just a hick town along side of this besides being dirty etc. and a man is a sucker to stay there all their life specially a man in my line of work as N. Y. is the Mecca for a man that has got the musical gift. I figure that all the time I spent in Chi I was just wasteing my time and never really started to live till I come down here and I have to laugh when I think of the boys out there that is trying to make a liveing in the song writeing game and most of them starve to death all their life and the first week I am down here I meet a man like Sears and the next thing you know we have turned out a song that will make us a fortune.

Well girlie you asked me to tell you about the girlie up on the Drive that tried to make me and asked me to come and see her again. Well I can assure you you have no reasons to be jealous in that quarter as I have not been back to see her as I figure it is wasteing my time to play round with a dame like she that wants to go out somewheres every night and if you married her she would want a house on 5th ave. with a dozen servants so I have passed her up as that is not my idea of home.

Some Like Them Cold

What I want when I get married is a real home where a man can stay home and work and maybe have a few of his friends in once in a wile and entertain them or go to a good musical show once in a wile and have a wife that is in sympathy with you and not nag at you all the wile but be a real help mate. The girlie up on the Drive would run me ragged and have me in the poor house inside of a year even if I was makeing 25 grand out of one song. Besides she wears a make up that you would have to blast to find out what her face looks like. So I have not been back there and don't intend to see her again so what is the use of me telling you about her. And the only other girlie I have met is a sister of Paul Sears who I met up to his house wile we was working on the song but she don't hardly count as she has not got no use for the boys but treats them like dirt and Paul says she is the coldest proposition he ever seen.

Well I don't know no more to write and besides have got a date to go out to Paul's place for dinner and play some of my stuff for him so as he can see if he wants to set words to some more of my melodies. Well don't do nothing I would not do and have as good a time as you can in old Chi and will let you know how we come along with the song.

CHAS. F. LEWIS.

How to Write Short Stories

DEAR MR. MAN: I am thrilled to death over the song and think the words awfully pretty and am crazy to hear the music which I know must be great. It must be wonderful to have the gift of writing songs and then hear people play and sing them and just think of making $25,000 in such a short time. My, how rich you will be and I certainly congratulate you though am afraid when you are rich and famous you will have no time for insignificant little me or will you be an exception and remember your "old" friends even when you are up in the world? I sincerely hope so.

Will look forward to receiving a copy of the song and will you be sure and put your name on it? I am all ready very conceited just to think that I know a man that writes songs and makes all that money.

Seriously I wish you success with your next song and I laughed when I read your remark about being busier than a one armed paper hanger. I don't see how you think up all those comparisons and crazy things to say. The next time one of the girls asks me to go out with them I am going to tell them I can't go because I am busier than a one armed paper hanger and then they will think I made it up and say: "The girl is clever."

Seriously I am glad you did not go back to see

Some Like Them Cold

the girl on the Drive and am also glad you don't
like girls who makes themselves up so much as
I think it is disgusting and would rather go round
looking like a ghost than put artificial color on
my face. Fortunately I have a complexion that
does not need "fixing" but even if my coloring
was not what it is I would never think of lower-
ing myself to "fix" it. But I must tell you a
joke that happened just the other day when
Edith and I were out at lunch and there was another girl in the restaurant whom Edie knew and
she introduced her to me and I noticed how this
girl kept staring at me and finally she begged my
pardon and asked if she could ask me a personal
question and I said yes and she asked me if my
complexion was really "mine." I assured her it
was and she said: "Well, I thought so because I
did not think anybody could put it on so artis-
tically. I certainly envy you." Edie and I both
laughed.

Well, if that girl envies me my complexion,
why I envy you living in New York. Chicago
is rather dirty though I don't let that part of it
bother me as I bathe and change my clothing so
often that the dirt does not have time to "settle."
Edie often says she cannot see how I always keep
so clean looking and says I always look like I had
just stepped out of a band box. She also calls
me a fish (jokingly) because I spend so much

How to Write Short Stories

time in the water. But seriously I do love to bathe and never feel so happy as when I have just "cleaned up" and put on fresh clothing.

Edie has just gone out to see a picture and was cross at me because I would not go with her. I told her I was going to write a letter and she wanted to know to whom and I told her and she said: "You write to him so often that a person would almost think you was in love with him." I just laughed and turned it off, but she does say the most embarrassing things and I would be angry if it was anybody but she that said them.

Seriously I had much rather sit here and write letters or read or just sit and dream than go out to some crazy old picture show except once in awhile I do like to go to the theater and see a good play and a specially a musical play if the music is catchy. But as a rule I am contented to just stay home and feel cozy and lots of evenings Edie and I sit here without saying hardly a word to each other though she would love to talk but she knows I had rather be quiet and she often says it is just like living with a deaf and dumb mute to live with me because I make so little noise round the apartment. I guess I was born to be a home body as I so seldom care to go "gadding."

Though I do love to have company once in awhile, just a few congenial friends whom I can talk to and feel at home with and play cards or

Some Like Them Cold

have some music. My friends love to drop in here, too, as they say Edie and I always give them such nice things to eat. Though poor Edie has not much to do with it, I am afraid, as she hates anything connected with cooking which is one of the things I love best of anything and I often say that when I begin keeping house in my own home I will insist on doing most of my own work as I would take so much more interest in it than a servant, though I would want somebody to help me a little if I could afford it as I often think a woman that does all her own work is liable to get so tired that she loses interest in the bigger things of life like books and music. Though after all what bigger thing is there than home making a specially for a woman?

I am sitting in the dearest old chair that I bought yesterday at a little store on the North Side. That is my one extravagance, buying furniture and things for the house, but I always say it is economy in the long run as I will always have them and have use for them and when I can pick them up at a bargain I would be silly not to. Though heaven knows I will never be "poor" in regards to furniture and rugs and things like that as mother's house in Toledo is full of lovely things which she says she is going to give to Sis and myself as soon as we have real homes of our own. She is going to give me the first choice as I am her favorite. She has the loveliest old things that

How to Write Short Stories

you could not buy now for love or money including lovely old rugs and a piano which Sis wanted to have a player attachment put on it but I said it would be an insult to the piano so we did not get one. I am funny about things like that, a specially old furniture and feel towards them like people whom I love.

Poor mother, I am afraid she won't live much longer to enjoy her lovely old things as she has been suffering for years from stomach trouble and the doctor says it has been worse lately instead of better and her heart is weak besides. I am going home to see her a few days this fall as it may be the last time. She is very cheerful and always says she is ready to go now as she has had enough joy out of life and all she would like would be to see her girls settled down in their own homes before she goes.

There I go, talking about my domestic affairs again and I will bet you are bored to death though personly I am never bored when my friends tell me about themselves. But I won't "rattle on" any longer, but will say good night and don't forget to write and tell me how you come out with the song and thanks for sending me the words to it. Will you write a song about me some time? I would be thrilled to death! But I am afraid I am not the kind of girl that inspires men to write songs about them, but am just a

Some Like Them Cold

quiet "mouse" that loves home and am not giddy enough to be the heroine of a song.

Well, Mr. Man, good night and don't wait so long before writing again to

Yours (?)
MABELLE.

N. Y., Sept. 8.

DEAR GIRLIE: Well girlie have not got your last letter with me so cannot answer what was in it as I have forgotten if there was anything I was supposed to answer and besides have only a little time to write as I have a date to go out on a party with the Sears. We are going to the Georgie White show and afterwards somewheres for supper. Sears is the boy who wrote the lyric to my song and it is him and his sister I am going on the party with. The sister is a cold fish that has no use for men but she is show crazy and insists on Paul takeing her to 3 or 4 of them a week.

Paul wants me to give up my room here and come and live with them as they have plenty of room and I am running a little low on money but don't know if I will do it or not as am afraid I would freeze to death in the same house with a girl like the sister as she is ice cold but she don't hang round the house much as she is always takeing trips or going to shows or somewheres.

So far we have not had no luck with the song.

How to Write Short Stories

All the publishers we have showed it to has went crazy over it but they won't make the right kind of a deal with us and if they don't loosen up and give us a decent royalty rate we are libel to put the song out ourselves and show them up. The man up to Goebel's told us the song was O. K. and he liked it but it was more of a production number than anything else and ought to go in a show like the Follies but they won't be in N. Y. much longer and what we ought to do is hold it till next spring.

Mean wile I am working on some new numbers and also have taken a position with the orchestra at the Wilton and am going to work there starting next week. They pay good money $60 and it will keep me going.

Well girlie that is about all the news. I believe you said your father was sick and hope he is better and also hope you are getting along O. K. and take care of yourself. When you have nothing else to do write to your friend,

CHAS. F. LEWIS.

Chicago, Ill., Sept. 11.

DEAR MR. LEWIS: Your short note reached me yesterday and must say I was puzzled when I read it. It sounded like you was mad at me though I cannot think of any reason why you should be. If there was something I said in my

Some Like Them Cold

last letter that offended you I wish you would
tell me what it was and I will ask your pardon
though I cannot remember anything I could of
said that you could take offense at. But if there
was something, why I assure you, Mr. Lewis, that
I did not mean anything by it. I certainly did
not intend to offend you in any way.

Perhaps it is nothing I wrote you, but you are
worried on account of the publishers not treating
you fair in regards to your song and that is why
your letter sounded so distant. If that is the
case I hope that by this time matters have recti-
fied themselves and the future looks brighter.
But any way, Mr. Lewis, don't allow yourself to
worry over business cares as they will all come
right in the end and I always think it is silly for
people to worry themselves sick over temporary
troubles, but the best way is to "keep smiling"
and look for the "silver lining" in the cloud.
That is the way I always do and no matter what
happens, I manage to smile and my girl friend,
Edie, calls me Sunny because I always look on
the bright side.

Remember also, Mr. Lewis, that $60 is a salary
that a great many men would like to be getting
and are living on less than that and supporting a
wife and family on it. I always say that a person can get along on whatever amount they make
if they manage things in the right way.

How to Write Short Stories

So if it is business troubles, Mr. Lewis, I say don't worry, but look on the bright side. But if it is something I wrote in my last letter that offended you I wish you would tell me what it was so I can apologize as I assure you I meant nothing and would not say anything to hurt you for the world.

Please let me hear from you soon as I will not feel comfortable until I know I am not to blame for the sudden change.

Sincerely,

MABELLE GILLESPIE.

N. Y., Sept. 24.

DEAR MISS GILLESPIE: Just a few lines to tell you the big news or at least it is big news to me. I am engaged to be married to Paul Sears' sister and we are going to be married early next month and live in Atlantic City where the orchestra I have been playing with has got an engagement in one of the big cabarets.

I know this will be a surprise to you as it was even a surprise to me as I did not think I would ever have the nerve to ask the girlie the big question as she was always so cold and acted like I was just in the way. But she said she supposed she would have to marry somebody some time and she did not dislike me as much as most of the other men her brother brought round and she

Some Like Them Cold

would marry me with the understanding that she would not have to be a slave and work round the house and also I would have to take her to a show or somewheres every night and if I could not take her myself she would "run wild" alone. Atlantic City will be O. K. for that as a lot of new shows opens down there and she will be able to see them before they get to the big town. As for her being a slave, I would hate to think of marrying a girl and then have them spend their lives in druggery round the house. We are going to live in a hotel till we find something better but will be in no hurry to start house keeping as we will have to buy all new furniture.

Betsy is some doll when she is all fixed up and believe me she knows how to fix herself up. I don't know what she uses but it is weather proof as I have been out in a rain storm with her and we both got drowned but her face stayed on. I would almost think it was real only she tells me different.

Well girlie I may write to you again once in a wile as Betsy says she don't give a dam if I write to all the girls in the world just so I don't make her read the answers but that is all I can think of to say now except good bye and good luck and may the right man come along soon and he will be a lucky man getting a girl that is such a good cook and got all that furniture etc.

How to Write Short Stories

But just let me give you a word of advice before
I close and that is don't never speak to strange
men who you don't know nothing about as they
may get you wrong and think you are trying to
make them. It just happened that I knew better
so you was lucky in my case but the luck might
not last.   Your friend,

Chas. F. Lewis.

Chicago, Ill., Sept. 27.

My Dear Mr. Lewis: Thanks for your advice
and also thank your fiance for her generosity in
allowing you to continue your correspondence with
her "rivals," but personly I have no desire to take
advantage of that generosity as I have something
better to do than read letters from a man like
you, a specially as I have a man friend who is
not so generous as Miss Sears and would strongly
object to my continuing a correspondence with
another man. It is at his request that I am writing this note to tell you not to expect to hear from
me again.

Allow me to congratulate you on your engagement to Miss Sears and I am sure she is to be
congratulated too, though if I met the lady I
would be tempted to ask her to tell me her secret,
namely how she is going to "run wild" on $60.

Sincerely,

Mabelle Gillespie.

ALIBI IKE

A typical tale of the backwoods of Indiana some seventy years ago, very interestingly depicted. The author acknowledges his indebtedness to Chief Justice Taft for some of the slang employed.

III

ALIBI IKE

I

His right name was Frank X. Farrell, and I guess the X stood for "Excuse me." Because he never pulled a play, good or bad, on or off the field, without apologizin' for it.

"Alibi Ike" was the name Carey wished on him the first day he reported down South. O' course we all cut out the "Alibi" part of it right away for the fear he would overhear it and bust somebody. But we called him "Ike" right to his face and the rest of it was understood by everybody on the club except Ike himself.

He ast me one time, he says:

"What do you all call me Ike for? I ain't no Yid."

"Carey give you the name," I says. "It's his nickname for everybody he takes a likin' to."

"He mustn't have only a few friends then," says Ike. "I never heard him say 'Ike' to nobody else."

But I was goin' to tell you about Carey namin' him. We'd been workin' out two weeks and the

81

How to Write Short Stories

pitchers was showin' somethin' when this bird joined us. His first day out he stood up there so good and took such a reef at the old pill that he had everyone lookin'. Then him and Carey was together in left field, catchin' fungoes, and it was after we was through for the day that Carey told me about him.

"What do you think of Alibi Ike?" ast Carey.

"Who's that?" I says.

"This here Farrell in the outfield," says Carey.

"He looks like he could hit," I says.

"Yes," says Carey, "but he can't hit near as good as he can apologize."

Then Carey went on to tell me what Ike had been pullin' out there. He'd dropped the first fly ball that was hit to him and told Carey his glove wasn't broke in good yet, and Carey says the glove could easy of been Kid Gleason's gran'-father. He made a whale of a catch out o' the next one and Carey says "Nice work!" or somethin' like that, but Ike says he could of caught the ball with his back turned only he slipped when he started after it and, besides that, the air currents fooled him.

"I thought you done well to get to the ball," says Carey.

"I ought to been settin' under it," says Ike.

"What did you hit last year?" Carey ast him.

Alibi Ike

"I had malaria most o' the season," says Ike. "I wound up with .356."

"Where would I have to go to get malaria?" says Carey, but Ike didn't wise up.

I and Carey and him set at the same table together for supper. It took him half an hour longer'n us to eat because he had to excuse himself every time he lifted his fork.

"Doctor told me I needed starch," he'd say, and then toss a shovelful o' potatoes into him. Or, "They ain't much meat on one o' these chops," he'd tell us, and grab another one. Or he'd say: "Nothin' like onions for a cold," and then he'd dip into the perfumery.

"Better try that apple sauce," says Carey. "It'll help your malaria."

"Whose malaria?" says Ike. He'd forgot already why he didn't only hit .356 last year.

I and Carey begin to lead him on.

"Whereabouts did you say your home was?" I ast him.

"I live with my folks," he says. "We live in Kansas City—not right down in the business part —outside a ways."

"How's that come?" says Carey. "I should think you'd get rooms in the post office."

But Ike was too busy curin' his cold to get that one.

"Are you married?" I ast him.

83

How to Write Short Stories

"No," he says. "I never run round much with girls, except to shows onct in a wile and parties and dances and roller skatin'."

"Never take 'em to the prize fights, eh?" says Carey.

"We don't have no real good bouts," says Ike. "Just bush stuff. And I never figured a boxin' match was a place for the ladies."

Well, after supper he pulled a cigar out and lit it. I was just goin' to ask him what he done it for, but he beat me to it.

"Kind o' rests a man to smoke after a good work-out," he says. "Kind o' settles a man's supper, too."

"Looks like a pretty good cigar," says Carey.

"Yes," says Ike. "A friend o' mine give it to me —a fella in Kansas City that runs a billiard room."

"Do you play billiards?" I ast him.

"I used to play a fair game," he says. "I'm all out o' practice now—can't hardly make a shot."

We coaxed him into a four-handed battle, him and Carey against Jack Mack and I. Say, he couldn't play billiards as good as Willie Hoppe; not quite. But to hear him tell it, he didn't make a good shot all evenin'. I'd leave him an awful-lookin' layout and he'd gather 'em up in one try and then run a couple o' hundred, and between every carom he'd say he'd put too much

Alibi Ike

stuff on the ball, or the English didn't take, or the table wasn't true, or his stick was crooked, or somethin'. And all the time he had the balls actin' like they was Dutch soldiers and him Kaiser William. We started out to play fifty points, but we had to make it a thousand so as I and Jack and Carey could try the table.

The four of us set round the lobby a wile after we was through playin', and when it got along toward bedtime Carey whispered to me and says:

"Ike'd like to go to bed, but he can't think up no excuse."

Carey hadn't hardly finished whisperin' when Ike got up and pulled it:

"Well, good night, boys," he says. "I ain't sleepy, but I got some gravel in my shoes and it's killin' my feet."

We knowed he hadn't never left the hotel since we'd came in from the grounds and changed our clo'es. So Carey says:

"I should think they'd take them gravel pits out o' the billiard room."

But Ike was already on his way to the elevator, limpin'.

"He's got the world beat," says Carey to Jack and I. "I've knew lots o' guys that had an alibi for every mistake they made; I've heard pitchers say that the ball slipped when somebody cracked one off'n 'em; I've heard infielders complain of a

sore arm after heavin' one into the stand, and
I've saw outfielders tooken sick with a dizzy spell
when they've misjudged a fly ball. But this
baby can't even go to bed without apologizin',
and I bet he excuses himself to the razor when he
gets ready to shave."

"And at that," says Jack, "he's goin' to make
us a good man."

"Yes," says Carey, "unless rheumatism keeps
his battin' average down to .400."

Well, sir, Ike kept whalin' away at the ball all
through the trip till everybody knowed he'd won
a job. Cap had him in there regular the last
few exhibition games and told the newspaper
boys a week before the season opened that he
was goin' to start him in Kane's place.

"You're there, kid," says Carey to Ike, the
night Cap made the 'nnouncement. "They ain't
many boys that wins a big league berth their
third year out."

"I'd of been up here a year ago," says Ike,
"only I was bent over all season with lumbago."

II

It rained down in Cincinnati one day and somebody organized a little game o' cards. They was
shy two men to make six and ast I and Carey to
play.

Alibi Ike

"I'm with you if you get Ike and make it seven-handed," says Carey.

So they got a hold of Ike and we went up to Smitty's room.

"I pretty near forgot how many you deal," says Ike. "It's been a long wile since I played."

I and Carey give each other the wink, and sure enough, he was just as ig'orant about poker as billiards. About the second hand, the pot was opened two or three ahead of him, and they was three in when it come his turn. It cost a buck, and he throwed in two.

"It's raised, boys," somebody says.

"Gosh, that's right, I did raise it," says Ike.

"Take out a buck if you didn't mean to tilt her," says Carey.

"No," says Ike, "I'll leave it go."

Well, it was raised back at him and then he made another mistake and raised again. They was only three left in when the draw come. Smitty'd opened with a pair o' kings and he didn't help 'em. Ike stood pat. The guy that'd raised him back was flushin' and he didn't fill. So Smitty checked and Ike bet and didn't get no call. He tossed his hand away, but I grabbed it and give it a look. He had king, queen, jack and two tens. Alibi Ike he must have seen me peekin', for he leaned over and whispered to me.

"I overlooked my hand," he says. "I thought all the wile it was a straight."

"Yes," I says, "that's why you raised twice by mistake."

They was another pot that he come into with tens and fours. It was tilted a couple o' times and two o' the strong fellas drawed ahead of Ike. They each drawed one. So Ike throwed away his little pair and come out with four tens. And they was four treys against him. Carey'd looked at Ike's discards and then he says:

"This lucky bum busted two pair."

"No, no, I didn't," says Ike.

"Yes, yes, you did," says Carey, and showed us the two fours.

"What do you know about that?" says Ike. "I'd of swore one was a five spot."

Well, we hadn't had no pay day yet, and after a wile everybody except Ike was goin' shy. I could see him gettin' restless and I was wonderin' how he'd make the get-away. He tried two or three times. "I got to buy some collars before supper," he says.

"No hurry," says Smitty. "The stores here keeps open all night in April."

After a minute he opened up again.

"My uncle out in Nebraska ain't expected to live," he says. "I ought to send a telegram."

"Would that save him?" says Carey.

Alibi Ike

"No, it sure wouldn't," says Ike, "but I ought to leave my old man know where I'm at."

"When did you hear about your uncle?" says Carey.

"Just this mornin'," says Ike.

"Who told you?" ast Carey.

"I got a wire from my old man," says Ike.

"Well," says Carey, "your old man knows you're still here yet this afternoon if you was here this mornin'. Trains leavin' Cincinnati in the middle o' the day don't carry no ball clubs."

"Yes," says Ike, "that's true. But he don't know where I'm goin' to be next week."

"Ain't he got no schedule?" ast Carey.

"I sent him one openin' day," says Ike, "but it takes mail a long time to get to Idaho."

"I thought your old man lived in Kansas City," says Carey.

"He does when he's home," says Ike.

"But now," says Carey, "I s'pose he's went to Idaho so as he can be near your sick uncle in Nebraska."

"He's visitin' my other uncle in Idaho."

"Then how does he keep posted about your sick uncle?" ast Carey.

"He don't," says Ike. "He don't even know my other uncle's sick. That's why I ought to wire and tell him."

"Good night!" says Carey.

How to Write Short Stories

"What town in Idaho is your old man at?" I says.

Ike thought it over.

"No town at all," he says. "But he's near a town."

"Near what town?" I says.

"Yuma," says Ike.

Well, by this time he'd lost two or three pots and he was desperate. We was playin' just as fast as we could, because we seen we couldn't hold him much longer. But he was tryin' so hard to frame an escape that he couldn't pay no attention to the cards, and it looked like we'd get his whole pile away from him if we could make him stick.

The telephone saved him. The minute it begun to ring, five of us jumped for it. But Ike was there first.

"Yes," he says, answerin' it. "This is him. I'll come right down."

And he slammed up the receiver and beat it out o' the door without even sayin' good-by.

"Smitty'd ought to locked the door," says Carey.

"What did he win?" ast Carey.

We figured it up—sixty-odd bucks.

"And the next time we ask him to play," says Carey, "his fingers will be so stiff he can't hold the cards."

Well, we set round a wile talkin' it over, and

Alibi Ike

pretty soon the telephone rung again. Smitty
answered it. It was a friend of his'n from Hamil-
ton and he wanted to know why Smitty didn't
hurry down. He was the one that had called before and Ike had told him he was Smitty.

"Ike'd ought to split with Smitty's friend," says
Carey.

"No," I says, "he'll need all he won. It costs
money to buy collars and to send telegrams from
Cincinnati to your old man in Texas and keep him
posted on the health o' your uncle in Cedar Rapids, D. C."

III

And you ought to heard him out there on that
field! They wasn't a day when he didn't pull six
or seven, and it didn't make no difference whether
he was goin' good or bad. If he popped up in the
pinch he should of made a base hit and the reason
he didn't was so-and-so. And if he cracked one for
three bases he ought to had a home run, only the
ball wasn't lively, or the wind brought it back, or
he tripped on a lump o' dirt, roundin' first base.

They was one afternoon in New York when he
beat all records. Big Marquard was workin'
against us and he was good.

In the first innin' Ike hit one clear over that
right field stand, but it was a few feet foul. Then
he got another foul and then the count come to

91

two and two. Then Rube slipped one acrost on him and he was called out.

"What do you know about that!" he says afterward on the bench. "I lost count. I thought it was three and one, and I took a strike."

"You took a strike all right," says Carey. "Even the umps knowed it was a strike."

"Yes," says Ike, "but you can bet I wouldn't of took it if I'd knew it was the third one. The score board had it wrong."

"That score board ain't for you to look at," says Cap. "It's for you to hit that old pill against."

"Well," says Ike, "I could of hit that one over the score board if I'd knew it was the third."

"Was it a good ball?" I says.

"Well, no, it wasn't," says Ike. "It was inside."

"How far inside?" says Carey.

"Oh, two or three inches or half a foot," says Ike.

"I guess you wouldn't of threatened the score board with it then," says Cap.

"I'd of pulled it down the right foul line if I hadn't thought he'd call it a ball," says Ike.

Well, in New York's part o' the innin' Doyle cracked one and Ike run back a mile and a half and caught it with one hand. We was all sayin' what a whale of a play it was, but he had to apologize just the same as for gettin' struck out.

Alibi Ike

"That stand's so high," he says, "that a man don't never see a ball till it's right on top o' you."

"Didn't you see that one?" ast Cap.

"Not at first," says Ike; "not till it raised up above the roof o' the stand."

"Then why did you start back as soon as the ball was hit?" says Cap.

"I knowed by the sound that he'd got a good hold of it," says Ike.

"Yes," says Cap, "but how'd you know what direction to run in?"

"Doyle usually hits 'em that way, the way I run," says Ike.

"Why don't you play blindfolded?" says Carey.

"Might as well, with that big high stand to bother a man," says Ike. "If I could of saw the ball all the time I'd of got it in my hip pocket."

Along in the fifth we was one run to the bad and Ike got on with one out. On the first ball throwed to Smitty, Ike went down. The ball was outside and Meyers throwed Ike out by ten feet.

You could see Ike's lips movin' all the way to the bench and when he got there he had his piece learned.

"Why didn't he swing?" he says.

"Why didn't you wait for his sign?" says Cap.

"He give me his sign," says Ike.

"What is his sign with you?" says Cap.

"Pickin' up some dirt with his right hand," says Ike.

"Well, I didn't see him do it," Cap says.

"He done it all right," says Ike.

Well, Smitty went out and they wasn't no more argument till they come in for the next innin'. Then Cap opened it up.

"You fellas better get your signs straight," he says.

"Do you mean me?" says Smitty.

"Yes," Cap says. "What's your sign with Ike?"

"Slidin my left hand up to the end o' the bat and back," says Smitty.

"Do you hear that, Ike?" ast Cap.

"What of it?" says Ike.

"You says his sign was pickin' up dirt and he says it's slidin his hand. Which is right?"

"I'm right," says Smitty. "But if you're arguin' about him goin' last innin', I didn't give him no sign."

"You pulled your cap down with your right hand, didn't you?" ast Ike.

"Well, s'pose I did," says Smitty. "That don't mean nothin'. I never told you to take that for a sign, did I?"

"I thought maybe you meant to tell me and forgot," says Ike.

They couldn't none of us answer that and they wouldn't of been no more said if Ike had of shut

Alibi Ike

up. But wile we was settin' there Carey got on
with two out and stole second clean.

"There!" says Ike. "That's what I was tryin'
to do and I'd of got away with it if Smitty'd
swang and bothered the Indian."

"Oh!" says Smitty. "You was tryin' to steal
then, was you? I thought you claimed I give you
the hit and run."

"I didn't claim no such a thing," says Ike. "I
thought maybe you might of gave me a sign, but I
was goin' anyway because I thought I had a good
start."

Cap prob'ly would of hit him with a bat, only
just about that time Doyle booted one on Hayes
and Carey come acrost with the run that tied.

Well, we go into the ninth finally, one and one,
and Marquard walks McDonald with nobody out.

"Lay it down," says Cap to Ike.

And Ike goes up there with orders to bunt and
cracks the first ball into that right-field stand! It
was fair this time, and we're two ahead, but I
didn't think about that at the time. I was too
busy watchin' Cap's face. First he turned pale
and then he got red as fire and then he got blue
and purple, and finally he just laid back and busted
out laughin'. So we wasn't afraid to laugh our-
selfs when we seen him doin' it, and when Ike
come in everybody on the bench was in hysterics.

But instead o' takin' advantage, Ike had to try

and excuse himself. His play was to shut up and he didn't know how to make it.

"Well," he says, "if I hadn't hit quite so quick at that one I bet it'd oï cleared the center-field fence."

Cap stopped laughin'.

"It'll cost you plain fifty," he says.

"What for?" says Ike.

"When I say 'bunt' I mean 'bunt,'" says Cap.

"You didn't say 'bunt,'" says Ike.

"I says 'Lay it down,' " says Cap. "If that don't mean 'bunt,' what does it mean?"

" 'Lay it down' means 'bunt' all right," says Ike, "but I understood you to say 'Lay on it.' "

"All right," says Cap, "and the little misunderstandin' will cost you fifty."

Ike didn't say nothin' for a few minutes. Then he had another bright idear.

"I was just kiddin' about misunderstandin' you," he says. "I knowed you wanted me to bunt."

"Well, then, why didn't you bunt?" ast Cap.

"I was goin' to on the next ball," says Ike. "But I thought if I took a good wallop I'd have 'em all fooled. So I walloped at the first one to fool 'em, and I didn't have no intention o' hittin' it."

"You tried to miss it, did you?" says Cap.

"Yes," says Ike.

Alibi Ike

"How'd you happen to hit it?" ast Cap.

"Well," Ike says, "I was lookin' for him to throw me a fast one and I was goin' to swing under it. But he come with a hook and I met it right square where I was swingin' to go under the fast one."

"Great!" says Cap. "Boys," he says, "Ike's learned how to hit Marquard's curve. Pretend a fast one's comin' and then try to miss it. It's a good thing to know and Ike'd ought to be willin' to pay for the lesson. So I'm goin' to make it a hundred instead o' fifty."

The game wound up 3 to 1. The fine didn't go, because Ike hit like a wild man all through that trip and we made pretty near a clean-up. The night we went to Philly I got him cornered in the car and I says to him:

"Forget them alibis for a wile and tell me somethin'. What'd you do that for, swing that time against Marquard when you was told to bunt?"

"I'll tell you," he says. "That ball he throwed me looked just like the one I struck out on in the first innin' and I wanted to show Cap what I could of done to that other one if I'd knew it was the third strike."

"But," I says, "the one you struck out on in the first innin' was a fast ball."

"So was the one I cracked in the ninth," says Ike.

How to Write Short Stories

IV

You've saw Cap's wife, o' course. Well, her sister's about twict as good-lookin' as her, and that's goin' some.

Cap took his missus down to St. Louis the second trip and the other one come down from St. Joe to visit her. Her name is Dolly, and some doll is right.

Well, Cap was goin' to take the two sisters to a show and he wanted a beau for Dolly. He left it to her and she picked Ike. He'd hit three on the nose that afternoon—off'n Sallee, too.

They fell for each other that first evenin'. Cap told us how it come off. She begin flatterin' Ike for the star game he'd played and o' course he begin excusin' himself for not doin' better. So she thought he was modest and it went strong with her. And she believed everything he said and that made her solid with him—that and her make-up. They was together every mornin' and evenin' for the five days we was there. In the afternoons Ike played the grandest ball you ever see, hittin' and runnin' the bases like a fool and catchin' everything that stayed in the park.

I told Cap, I says: "You'd ought to keep the doll with us and he'd make Cobb's figures look sick."

Alibi Ike

But Dolly had to go back to St. Joe and we come home for a long serious.

Well, for the next three weeks Ike had a letter to read every day and he'd set in the clubhouse readin' it till mornin' practice was half over. Cap didn't say nothin' to him, because he was goin' so good. But I and Carey wasted a lot of our time tryin' to get him to own up who the letters was from. Fine chanct!

"What are you readin'?" Carey'd say. "A bill?"

"No," Ike'd say, "not exactly a bill. It's a letter from a fella I used to go to school with."

"High school or college?" I'd ask him.

"College," he'd say.

"What college?" I'd say.

Then he'd stall a wile and then he'd say:

"I didn't go to the college myself, but my friend went there."

"How did it happen you didn't go?" Carey'd ask him.

"Well," he'd say, "they wasn't no colleges near where I lived."

"Didn't you live in Kansas City?" I'd say to him.

One time he'd say he did and another time he didn't. One time he says he lived in Michigan.

"Where at?" says Carey.

"Near Detroit," he says.

How to Write Short Stories

"Well," I says, "Detroit's near Ann Arbor and that's where they got the university."

"Yes," says Ike, "they got it there now, but they didn't have it there then."

"I come pretty near goin' to Syracuse," I says, "only they wasn't no railroads runnin' through there in them days."

"Where'd this friend o' yours go to college?" says Carey.

"I forget now," says Ike.

"Was it Carlisle?" ast Carey.

"No," says Ike, "his folks wasn't very well off."

"That's what barred me from Smith," I says.

"I was goin' to tackle Cornell's," says Carey, "but the doctor told me I'd have hay fever if I didn't stay up North."

"Your friend writes long letters," I says.

"Yes," says Ike; "he's tellin' me about a ball player."

"Where does he play?" ast Carey.

"Down in the Texas League—Fort Wayne," says Ike.

"It looks like a girl's writin'," Carey says.

"A girl wrote it," says Ike. "That's my friend's sister, writin' for him."

"Didn't they teach writin' at this here college where he went?" says Carey.

"Sure," Ike says, "they taught writin', but he got his hand cut off in a railroad wreck."

Alibi Ike

"How long ago?" I says.

"Right after he got out o' college," says Ike.

"Well," I says, "I should think he'd of learned to write with his left hand by this time."

"It's his left hand that was cut off," says Ike; "and he was left-handed."

"You get a letter every day," says Carey. "They're all the same writin'. Is he tellin' you about a different ball player every time he writes?"

"No," Ike says. "It's the same ball player. He just tells me what he does every day."

"From the size o' the letters, they don't play nothin' but double-headers down there," says Carey.

We figured that Ike spent most of his evenin's answerin' the letters from his "friend's sister," so we kept tryin' to date him up for shows and parties to see how he'd duck out of 'em. He was bugs over spaghetti, so we told him one day that they was goin' to be a big feed of it over to Joe's that night and he was invited.

"How long'll it last?" he says.

"Well," we says, "we're goin' right over there after the game and stay till they close up."

"I can't go," he says, "unless they leave me come home at eight bells."

"Nothin' doin'," says Carey. "Joe'd get sore."

"I can't go then," says Ike.

"Why not?" I ast him.

How to Write Short Stories

"Well," he says, "my landlady locks up the house at eight and I left my key home."

"You can come and stay with me," says Carey.

"No," he says, "I can't sleep in a strange bed."

"How do you get along when we're on the road?" says I.

"I don't never sleep the first night anywheres," he says. "After that I'm all right."

"You'll have time to chase home and get your key right after the game," I told him.

"The key ain't home," says Ike. "I lent it to one o' the other fellas and he's went out o' town and took it with him."

"Couldn't you borry another key off'n the landlady?" Carey ast him.

"No," he says, "that's the only one they is."

Well, the day before we started East again, Ike come into the clubhouse all smiles.

"Your birthday?" I ast him.

"No," he says.

"What do you feel so good about?" I says.

"Got a letter from my old man," he says. "My uncle's goin' to get well."

"Is that the one in Nebraska?" says I.

"Not right in Nebraska," says Ike. "Near there."

But afterwards we got the right dope from Cap. Dolly'd blew in from Missouri and was goin' to make the trip with her sister.

102

Alibi Ike

V

Well, I want to alibi Carey and I for what come off in Boston. If we'd of had any idear what we was doin', we'd never did it. They wasn't nobody outside o' maybe Ike and the dame that felt worse over it than I and Carey.

The first two days we didn't see nothin' of Ike and her except out to the park. The rest o' the time they was sight-seein' over to Cambridge and down to Revere and out to Brook-a-line and all the other places where the rubes go.

But when we come into the beanery after the third game Cap's wife called us over.

"If you want to see somethin' pretty," she says, "look at the third finger on Sis's left hand."

Well, o' course we knowed before we looked that it wasn't going' to be no hangnail. Nobody was su'prised when Dolly blew into the dinin' room with it—a rock that Ike'd bought off'n Diamond Joe the first trip to New York. Only o' course it'd been set into a lady's-size ring instead o' the automobile tire he'd been wearin'.

Cap and his missus and Ike and Dolly ett supper together, only Ike didn't eat nothin', but just set there blushin' and spillin' things on the tablecloth. I heard him excusin' himself for not havin' no appetite. He says he couldn't never eat when

103

he was clost to the ocean. He'd forgot about them sixty-five oysters he destroyed the first night o' the trip before.

He was goin' to take her to a show, so after supper he went upstairs to change his collar. She had to doll up, too, and o' course Ike was through long before her.

If you remember the hotel in Boston, they's a little parlor where the piano's at and then they's another little parlor openin' off o' that. Well, when Ike come down Smitty was playin' a few chords and I and Carey was harmonizin'. We seen Ike go up to the desk to leave his key and we called him in. He tried to duck away, but we wouldn't stand for it.

We ast him what he was all duded up for and he says he was goin' to the theayter.

"Goin' alone?" says Carey.

"No," he says, "a friend o' mine's goin' with me."

"What do you say if we go along?" says Carey.

"I ain't only got two tickets," he says.

"Well," says Carey, "we can go down there with you and buy our own seats; maybe we can all get together."

"No," says Ike. "They ain't no more seats. They're all sold out."

"We can buy some off'n the scalpers," says Carey.

Alibi Ike

"I wouldn't if I was you," says Ike. "They say the show's rotten."

"What are you goin' for, then?" I ast.

"I didn't hear about it bein' rotten till I got the tickets," he says.

"Well," I says, "if you don't want to go I'll buy the tickets from you."

"No," says Ike, "I wouldn't want to cheat you. I'm stung and I'll just have to stand for it."

"What are you goin' to do with the girl, leave her here at the hotel?" I says.

"What girl?" says Ike.

"The girl you ett supper with," I says.

"Oh," he says, "we just happened to go into the dinin' room together, that's all. Cap wanted I should set down with 'em."

"I noticed," says Carey, "that she happened to be wearin' that rock you bought off'n Diamond Joe."

"Yes," says Ike. "I lent it to her for a wile."

"Did you lend her the new ring that goes with it?" I says.

"She had that already," says Ike. "She lost the set out of it."

"I wouldn't trust no strange girl with a rock o' mine," says Carey.

"Oh, I guess she's all right," Ike says. "Besides, I was tired o' the stone. When a girl asks you for somethin', what are you goin' to do?"

How to Write Short Stories

He started out toward the desk, but we flagged him.

"Wait a minute!" Carey says. "I got a bet with Sam here, and it's up to you to settle it."

"Well," says Ike, "make it snappy. My friend'll be here any minute."

"I bet," says Carey, "that you and that girl was engaged to be married."

"Nothin' to it," says Ike.

"Now look here," says Carey, "this is goin' to cost me real money if I lose. Cut out the alibi stuff and give it to us straight. Cap's wife just as good as told us you was roped."

Ike blushed like a kid.

"Well, boys," he says, "I may as well own up. You win, Carey."

"Yatta boy!" says Carey. "Congratulations!"

"You got a swell girl, Ike," I says.

"She's a peach," says Smitty.

"Well, I guess she's O. K.," says Ike. "I don't know much about girls."

"Didn't you never run round with 'em?" I says.

"Oh, yes, plenty of 'em," says Ike. "But I never seen none I'd fall for."

"That is, till you seen this one," says Carey.

"Well," says Ike, "this one's O. K., but I wasn't thinkin' about gettin' married yet a wile."

"Who done the askin'—her?" says Carey.

Alibi Ike

"Oh, no," says Ike, "but sometimes a man don't know what he's gettin' into. Take a good-lookin' girl, and a man gen'ally almost always does about what she wants him to."

"They couldn't no girl lasso me unless I wanted to be lassoed," says Smitty.

"Oh, I don't know," says Ike. "When a fella gets to feelin' sorry for one of 'em it's all off."

Well, we left him go after shakin' hands all round. But he didn't take Dolly to no show that night. Some time wile we was talkin' she'd came into that other parlor and she'd stood there and heard us. I don't know how much she heard. But it was enough. Dolly and Cap's missus took the midnight train for New York. And from there Cap's wife sent her on her way back to Missouri.

She'd left the ring and a note for Ike with the clerk. But we didn't ask Ike if the note was from his friend in Fort Wayne, Texas.

VI

When we'd came to Boston Ike was hittin' plain .397. When we got back home he'd fell off to pretty near nothin'. He hadn't drove one out o' the infield in any o' them other Eastern parks, and he didn't even give no excuse for it.

To show you how bad he was, he struck out three times in Brooklyn one day and never opened his

How to Write Short Stories

trap when Cap ast him what was the matter.
Before, if he'd whiffed oncet in a game he'd of
wrote a book tellin' why.

Well, we dropped from first place to fifth in
four weeks and we was still goin' down. I and
Carey was about the only ones in the club that
spoke to each other, and all as we did was remind
ourself o' what a boner we'd pulled.

"It's goin' to beat us out o' the big money,"
says Carey.

"Yes," I says. "I don't want to knock my
own ball club, but it looks like a one-man team, and
when that one man's dauber's down we couldn't
trim our whiskers."

"We ought to knew better," says Carey.

"Yes," I says, "but why should a man pull an
alibi for bein' engaged to such a bearcat as she
was?"

"He shouldn't," says Carey. "But I and you
knowed he would or we'd never started talkin' to
him about it. He wasn't no more ashamed o' the
girl than I am of a regular base hit. But he just
can't come clean on no subjec'."

Cap had the whole story, and I and Carey was
as pop'lar with him as an umpire.

"What do you want me to do, Cap?" Carey'd
say to him before goin' up to hit.

"Use your own judgment," Cap'd tell him.
"We want to lose another game."

Alibi Ike

But finally, one night in Pittsburgh, Cap had a letter from his missus and he come to us with it.

"You fellas," he says, "is the ones that put us on the bum, and if you're sorry I think they's a chancet for you to make good. The old lady's out to St. Joe and she's been tryin' her hardest to fix things up. She's explained that Ike don't mean nothin' with his talk; I've wrote and explained that to Dolly, too. But the old lady says that Dolly says that she can't believe it. But Dolly's still stuck on this baby, and she's pinin' away just the same as Ike. And the old lady says she thinks if you two fellas would write to the girl and explain how you was always kiddin' with Ike and leadin' him on, and how the ball club was all shot to pieces since Ike quit hittin', and how he acted like he was goin' to kill himself, and this and that, she'd fall for it and maybe soften down. Dolly, the old lady says, would believe you before she'd believe I and the old lady, because she thinks it's her we're sorry for, and not him."

Well, I and Carey was only too glad to try and see what we could do. But it wasn't no snap. We wrote about eight letters before we got one that looked good. Then we give it to the stenographer and had it wrote out on a typewriter and both of us signed it.

It was Carey's idear that made the letter good. He stuck in somethin' about the world's serious

109

money that our wives wasn't goin' to spend unless she took pity on a "boy who was so shy and modest that he was afraid to come right out and say that he had asked such a beautiful and handsome girl to become his bride."

That's prob'ly what got her, or maybe she couldn't of held out much longer anyway. It was four days after we sent the letter that Cap heard from his missus again. We was in Cincinnati.

"We've won," he says to us. "The old lady says that Dolly says she'll give him another chancet. But the old lady says it won't do no good for Ike to write a letter. He'll have to go out there."

"Send him to-night," says Carey.

"I'll pay half his fare," I says.

"I'll pay the other half," says Carey.

"No," says Cap, "the club'll pay his expenses. I'll send him scoutin'."

"Are you goin' to send him to-night?"

"Sure," says Cap. "But I'm goin' to break the news to him right now. It's time we win a ball game."

So in the clubhouse, just before the game, Cap told him. And I certainly felt sorry for Rube Benton and Red Ames that afternoon! I and Carey was standin' in front o' the hotel that night when Ike come out with his suitcase.

"Sent home?" I says to him.

Alibi Ike

"No," he says, "I'm goin' scoutin'."

"Where to?" I says. "Fort Wayne?"

"No, not exactly," he says.

"Well," says Carey, "have a good time."

"I ain't lookin' for no good time," says Ike. "I says I was goin' scoutin'."

"Well, then," says Carey, "I hope you see somebody you like."

"And you better have a drink before you go," I says.

"Well," says Ike, "they claim it helps a cold."

THE GOLDEN HONEYMOON

A story with "sex appeal."

IV

THE GOLDEN HONEYMOON

Mother says that when I start talking I never know when to stop. But I tell her the only time I get a chance is when she ain't around, so I have to make the most of it. I guess the fact is neither one of us would be welcome in a Quaker meeting, but as I tell Mother, what did God give us tongues for if He didn't want we should use them? Only she says He didn't give them to us to say the same thing over and over again, like I do, and repeat myself. But I say:

"Well, Mother," I say, "when people is like you and I and been married fifty years, do you expect everything I say will be something you ain't heard me say before? But it may be new to others, as they ain't nobody else lived with me as long as you have."

So she says:

"You can bet they ain't, as they couldn't nobody else stand you that long."

"Well," I tell her, "you look pretty healthy."

"Maybe I do," she will say, "but I looked even healthier before I married you."

How to Write Short Stories

You can't get ahead of Mother.

Yes, sir, we was married just fifty years ago the
seventeenth day of last December and my daughter
and son-in-law was over from Trenton to help us
celebrate the Golden Wedding. My son-in-law is
John H. Kramer, the real estate man. He made
$12,000 one year and is pretty well thought of
around Trenton; a good, steady, hard worker. The
Rotarians was after him a long time to join, but he
kept telling them his home was his club. But
Edie finally made him join. That's my daughter.

Well, anyway, they come over to help us celebrate the Golden Wedding and it was pretty
crimpy weather and the furnace don't seem to
heat up no more like it used to and Mother made
the remark that she hoped this winter wouldn't
be as cold as the last, referring to the winter
previous. So Edie said if she was us, and nothing
to keep us home, she certainly wouldn't spend no
more winters up here and why didn't we just
shut off the water and close up the house and go
down to Tampa, Florida? You know we was
there four winters ago and staid five weeks, but it
cost us over three hundred and fifty dollars for
hotel bill alone. So Mother said we wasn't going
no place to be robbed. So my son-in-law spoke up
and said that Tampa wasn't the only place in the
South, and besides we didn't have to stop at no
high price hotel but could rent us a couple rooms

116

The Golden Honeymoon

and board out somewheres, and he had heard that
St. Petersburg, Florida, was *the* spot and if we said
the word he would write down there and make in-
quiries.

Well, to make a long story short, we decided to
do it and Edie said it would be our Golden Honeymoon and for a present my son-in-law paid the
difference between a section and a compartment
so as we could have a compartment and have
more privatecy. In a compartment you have an
upper and lower berth just like the regular sleeper,
but it is a shut in room by itself and got a wash
bowl. The car we went in was all compartments
and no regular berths at all. It was all compartments.

We went to Trenton the night before and staid
at my daughter and son-in-law and we left Trenton
the next afternoon at 3.23 P. M.

This was the twelfth day of January. Mother
set facing the front of the train, as it makes her
giddy to ride backwards. I set facing her, which
does not affect me. We reached North Philadelphia at 4.03 P. M. and we reached West Philadelphia at 4.14, but did not go into Broad Street.
We reached Baltimore at 6.30 and Washington,
D.C., at 7.25. Our train laid over in Washington
two hours till another train come along to pick us
up and I got out and strolled up the platform and
into the Union Station. When I come back, our

car had been switched on to another track, but I remembered the name of it, the La Belle, as I had once visited my aunt out in Oconomowoc, Wisconsin, where there was a lake of that name, so I had no difficulty in getting located. But Mother had nearly fretted herself sick for fear I would be left.

"Well," I said, "I would of followed you on the next train."

"You could of," said Mother, and she pointed out that she had the money.

"Well," I said, "we are in Washington and I could of borrowed from the United States Treasury. I would of pretended I was an Englishman."

Mother caught the point and laughed heartily.

Our train pulled out of Washington at 9.40 P. M. and Mother and I turned in early, I taking the upper. During the night we passed through the green fields of old Virginia, though it was too dark to tell if they was green or what color. When we got up in the morning, we was at Fayetteville, North Carolina. We had breakfast in the dining car and after breakfast I got in conversation with the man in the next compartment to ours. He was from Lebanon, New Hampshire, and a man about eighty years of age. His wife was with him, and two unmarried daughters and I made the remark that I should think the four of them would be crowded in one compartment, but he said they had

The Golden Honeymoon

made the trip every winter for fifteen years and knowed how to keep out of each other's way. He said they was bound for Tarpon Springs.

We reached Charleston, South Carolina, at 12.50 p. m. and arrived at Savannah, Georgia, at 4.20. We reached Jacksonville, Florida, at 8.45 p. m. and had an hour and a quarter to lay over there, but Mother made a fuss about me getting off the train, so we had the darky make up our berths and retired before we left Jacksonville. I didn't sleep good as the train done a lot of hemming and hawing, and Mother never sleeps good on a train as she says she is always worrying that I will fall out. She says she would rather have the upper herself, as then she would not have to worry about me, but I tell her I can't take the risk of having it get out that I allowed my wife to sleep in an upper berth. It would make talk.

We was up in the morning in time to see our friends from New Hampshire get off at Tarpon Springs, which we reached at 6.53 a. m.

Several of our fellow passengers got off at Clearwater and some at Belleair, where the train backs right up to the door of the mammoth hotel. Belleair is the winter headquarters for the golf dudes and everybody that got off there had their bag of sticks, as many as ten and twelve in a bag. Women and all. When I was a young man we called it shinny and only needed one club to play with and

119

about one game of it would of been a-plenty for some of these dudes, the way we played it.

The train pulled into St. Petersburg at 8.20 and when we got off the train you would think they was a riot, what with all the darkies barking for the different hotels.

I said to Mother, I said:

"It is a good thing we have got a place picked out to go to and don't have to choose a hotel, as it would be hard to choose amongst them if every one of them is the best."

She laughed.

We found a jitney and I give him the address of the room my son-in-law had got for us and soon we was there and introduced ourselves to the lady that owns the house, a young widow about forty-eight years of age. She showed us our room, which was light and airy with a comfortable bed and bureau and washstand. It was twelve dollars a week, but the location was good, only three blocks from Williams Park.

St. Pete is what folks calls the town, though they also call it the Sunshine City, as they claim they's no other place in the country where they's fewer days when Old Sol don't smile down on Mother Earth, and one of the newspapers gives away all their copies free every day when the sun don't shine. They claim to of only give them away some sixty-odd times in the last eleven years. An-

The Golden Honeymoon

other nickname they have got for the town is "the Poor Man's Palm Beach," but I guess they's men that comes there that could borrow as much from the bank as some of the Willie boys over to the other Palm Beach.

During our stay we paid a visit to the Lewis Tent City, which is the headquarters for the Tin Can Tourists. But maybe you ain't heard about them. Well, they are an organization that takes their vacation trips by auto and carries everything with them. That is, they bring along their tents to sleep in and cook in and they don't patronize no hotels or cafeterias, but they have got to be bona fide auto campers or they can't belong to the organization.

They tell me they's over 200,000 members to it and they call themselves the Tin Canners on account of most of their food being put up in tin cans. One couple we seen in the Tent City was a couple from Brady, Texas, named Mr. and Mrs. Pence, which the old man is over eighty years of age and they had came in their auto all the way from home, a distance of 1,641 miles. They took five weeks for the trip, Mr. Pence driving the entire distance.

The Tin Canners hails from every State in the Union and in the summer time they visit places like New England and the Great Lakes region, but in the winter the most of them comes to Florida and scatters all over the State. While we was down there, they was a national convention of them at Gainesville, Florida, and they elected a Fredonia, New York, man as their president. His title is Royal Tin Can Opener of the World. They have got a song wrote up which everybody has got to learn it before they are a member:

"The tin can forever! Hurrah, boys! Hurrah!
   Up with the tin can! Down with the foe!
  We will rally round the campfire, we'll rally once
     again,
   Shouting, 'We auto camp forever!'"

That is something like it. And the members has also got to have a tin can fastened on to the front of their machine.

I asked Mother how she would like to travel around that way and she said:

"Fine, but not with an old rattle brain like you driving."

"Well," I said, "I am eight years younger than this Mr. Pence who drove here from Texas."

"Yes," she said, "but he is old enough to not be skittish."

You can't get ahead of Mother.

Well, one of the first things we done in St. Petersburg was to go to the Chamber of Commerce and register our names and where we was from as they's great rivalry amongst the different States in re-

The Golden Honeymoon

gards to the number of their citizens visiting in town and of course our little State don't stand much of a show, but still every little bit helps, as the fella says. All and all, the man told us, they was eleven thousand names registered, Ohio leading with some fifteen hundred-odd and New York State next with twelve hundred. Then come Michigan, Pennsylvania and so on down, with one man each from Cuba and Nevada.

The first night we was there, they was a meeting of the New York-New Jersey Society at the Congregational Church and a man from Ogdensburg, New York State, made the talk. His subject was Rainbow Chasing. He is a Rotarian and a very convicting speaker, though I forget his name.

Our first business, of course, was to find a place to eat and after trying several places we run on to a cafeteria on Central Avenue that suited us up and down. We eat pretty near all our meals there and it averaged about two dollars per day for the two of us, but the food was well cooked and everything nice and clean. A man don't mind paying the price if things is clean and well cooked.

On the third day of February, which is Mother's birthday, we spread ourselves and eat supper at the Poinsettia Hotel and they charged us seventy-five cents for a sirloin steak that wasn't hardly big enough for one.

I said to Mother: "Well," I said, "I guess it's a

good thing every day ain't your birthday or we
would be in the poorhouse."

"No," says Mother, "because if every day was
my birthday, I would be old enough by this time
to of been in my grave long ago."

You can't get ahead of Mother.

In the hotel they had a card-room where they
was several men and ladies playing five hundred
and this new fangled whist bridge. We also seen a
place where they was dancing, so I asked Mother
would she like to trip the light fantastic toe and
she said no, she was too old to squirm like you have
got to do now days. We watched some of the
young folks at it awhile till Mother got disgusted
and said we would have to see a good movie to take
the taste out of our mouth. Mother is a great
movie heroyne and we go twice a week here at
home.

But I want to tell you about the Park. The
second day we was there we visited the Park, which
is a good deal like the one in Tampa, only bigger,
and they's more fun goes on here every day than
you could shake a stick at. In the middle they's a
big bandstand and chairs for the folks to set and
listen to the concerts, which they give you music
for all tastes, from Dixie up to classical pieces like
Hearts and Flowers.

Then all around they's places marked off for
different sports and games—chess and checkers

The Golden Honeymoon

and dominoes for folks that enjoys those kind of games, and roque and horse-shoes for the nimbler ones. I used to pitch a pretty fair shoe myself, but ain't done much of it in the last twenty years.

Well, anyway, we bought a membership ticket in the club which costs one dollar for the season, and they tell me that up to a couple years ago it was fifty cents, but they had to raise it to keep out the riffraff.

Well, Mother and I put in a great day watching the pitchers and she wanted I should get in the game, but I told her I was all out of practice and would make a fool of myself, though I seen several men pitching who I guess I could take their measure without no practice. However, they was some good pitchers, too, and one boy from Akron, Ohio, who could certainly throw a pretty shoe. They told me it looked like he would win the championship of the United States in the February tournament. We come away a few days before they held that and I never did hear if he win. I forget his name, but he was a clean cut young fella and he has got a brother in Cleveland that's a Rotarian.

Well, we just stood around and watched the different games for two or three days and finally I set down in a checker game with a man named Weaver from Danville, Illinois. He was a pretty fair checker player, but he wasn't no match for me, and I hope that don't sound like bragging. But I al-

ways could hold my own on a checker-board and the folks around here will tell you the same thing. I played with this Weaver pretty near all morning for two or three mornings and he beat me one game and the only other time it looked like he had a chance, the noon whistle blowed and we had to quit and go to dinner.

While I was playing checkers, Mother would set and listen to the band, as she loves music, classical or no matter what kind, but anyway she was setting there one day and between selections the woman next to her opened up a conversation. She was a woman about Mother's own age, seventy or seventy-one, and finally she asked Mother's name and Mother told her her name and where she was from and Mother asked her the same question, and who do you think the woman was?

Well, sir, it was the wife of Frank M. Hartsell, the man who was engaged to Mother till I stepped in and cut him out, fifty-two years ago!

Yes, sir!

You can imagine Mother's surprise! And Mrs. Hartsell was surprised, too, when Mother told her she had once been friends with her husband, though Mother didn't say how close friends they had been, or that Mother and I was the cause of Hartsell going out West. But that's what we was. Hartsell left his town a month after the engagement was broke off and ain't never been back since. He

The Golden Honeymoon

had went out to Michigan and become a veterinary, and that is where he had settled down, in Hillsdale, Michigan, and finally married his wife.

Well, Mother screwed up her courage to ask if Frank was still living and Mrs. Hartsell took her over to where they was pitching horse-shoes and there was old Frank, waiting his turn. And he knowed Mother as soon as he seen her, though it was over fifty years. He said he knowed her by her eyes.

"Why, it's Lucy Frost!" he says, and he throwed down his shoes and quit the game.

Then they come over and hunted me up and I will confess I wouldn't of knowed him. Him and I is the same age to the month, but he seems to show it more, some way. He is balder for one thing. And his beard is all white, where mine has still got a streak of brown in it. The very first thing I said to him, I said:

"Well, Frank, that beard of yours makes me feel like I was back north. It looks like a regular blizzard."

"Well," he said, "I guess yourn would be just as white if you had it dry cleaned."

But Mother wouldn't stand that.

"Is that so!" she said to Frank. "Well, Charley ain't had no tobacco in his mouth for over ten years!"

And I ain't!

How to Write Short Stories

Well, I excused myself from the checker game and it was pretty close to noon, so we decided to all have dinner together and they was nothing for it only we must try their cafeteria on Third Avenue. It was a little more expensive than ours and not near as good, I thought. I and Mother had about the same dinner we had been having every day and our bill was $1.10. Frank's check was $1.20 for he and his wife. The same meal wouldn't of cost them more than a dollar at our place.

After dinner we made them come up to our house and we all set in the parlor, which the young woman had give us the use of to entertain company. We begun talking over old times and Mother said she was a-scared Mrs. Hartsell would find it tiresome listening to we three talk over old times, but as it turned out they wasn't much chance for nobody else to talk with Mrs. Hartsell in the company. I have heard lots of women that could go it, but Hartsell's wife takes the cake of all the women I ever seen. She told us the family history of everybody in the State of Michigan and bragged for a half hour about her son, who she said is in the drug business in Grand Rapids, and a Rotarian.

When I and Hartsell could get a word in edgeways we joked one another back and forth and I chafed him about being a horse doctor.

The Golden Honeymoon

"Well, Frank," I said, "you look pretty prosperous, so I suppose they's been plenty of glanders around Hillsdale."

"Well," he said, "I've managed to make more than a fair living. But I've worked pretty hard."

"Yes," I said, "and I suppose you get called out all hours of the night to attend births and so on."

Mother made me shut up.

Well, I thought they wouldn't never go home and I and Mother was in misery trying to keep awake, as the both of us generally always takes a nap after dinner. Finally they went, after we had made an engagement to meet them in the Park the next morning, and Mrs. Hartsell also invited us to come to their place the next night and play five hundred. But she had forgot that they was a meeting of the Michigan Society that evening, so it was not till two evenings later that we had our first card game.

Hartsell and his wife lived in a house on Third Avenue North and had a private setting room besides their bedroom. Mrs. Hartsell couldn't quit talking about their private setting room like it was something wonderful. We played cards with them, with Mother and Hartsell partners against his wife and I. Mrs. Hartsell is a miserable card player and we certainly got the worst of it.

After the game she brought out a dish of oranges

How to Write Short Stories

and we had to pretend it was just what we wanted, though oranges down there is like a young man's whiskers; you enjoy them at first, but they get to be a pesky nuisance.

We played cards again the next night at our place with the same partners and I and Mrs. Hartsell was beat again. Mother and Hartsell was full of compliments for each other on what a good team they made, but the both of them knowed well enough where the secret of their success laid. I guess all and all we must of played ten different evenings and they was only one night when Mrs. Hartsell and I come out ahead. And that one night wasn't no fault of hern.

When we had been down there about two weeks, we spent one evening as their guest in the Congregational Church, at a social give by the Michigan Society. A talk was made by a man named Bitting of Detroit, Michigan, on How I was Cured of Story Telling. He is a big man in the Rotarians and give a witty talk.

A woman named Mrs. Oxford rendered some selections which Mrs. Hartsell said was grand opera music, but whatever they was my daughter Edie could of give her cards and spades and not made such a hullaballoo about it neither.

Then they was a ventriloquist from Grand Rapids and a young woman about forty-five years of age that mimicked different kinds of birds. I

130

The Golden Honeymoon

whispered to Mother that they all sounded like a chicken, but she nudged me to shut up.

After the show we stopped in a drug store and I set up the refreshments and it was pretty close to ten o'clock before we finally turned in. Mother and I would of preferred tending the movies, but Mother said we mustn't offend Mrs. Hartsell, though I asked her had we came to Florida to enjoy ourselves or to just not offend an old chatterbox from Michigan.

I felt sorry for Hartsell one morning. The women folks both had an engagement down to the chiropodist's and I run across Hartsell in the Park and he foolishly offered to play me checkers.

It was him that suggested it, not me, and I guess he repented himself before we had played one game. But he was too stubborn to give up and set there while I beat him game after game and the worst part of it was that a crowd of folks had got in the habit of watching me play and there they all was, looking on, and finally they seen what a fool Frank was making of himself, and they began to chafe him and pass remarks. Like one of them said:

"Who ever told you you was a checker player!" And:

"You might maybe be good for tiddle-de-winks, but not checkers!"

I almost felt like letting him beat me a couple

games. But the crowd would of knowed it was a put up job.

Well, the women folks joined us in the Park and I wasn't going to mention our little game, but Hartsell told about it himself and admitted he wasn't no match for me.

"Well," said Mrs. Hartsell, "checkers ain't much of a game anyway, is it?" She said: "It's more of a children's game, ain't it? At least, I know my boy's children used to play it a good deal."

"Yes, ma'am," I said. "It's a children's game the way your husband plays it, too."

Mother wanted to smooth things over, so she said:

"Maybe they's other games where Frank can beat you."

"Yes," said Mrs. Hartsell, "and I bet he could beat you pitching horse-shoes."

"Well," I said, "I would give him a chance to try, only I ain't pitched a shoe in over sixteen years."

"Well," said Hartsell, "I ain't played checkers in twenty years."

"You ain't never played it," I said.

"Anyway," says Frank, "Lucy and I is your master at five hundred."

Well, I could of told him why that was, but had decency enough to hold my tongue.

It had got so now that he wanted to play

The Golden Honeymoon

cards every night and when I or Mother wanted
to go to a movie, any one of us would have to
pretend we had a headache and then trust to
goodness that they wouldn't see us sneak into the
theater. I don't mind playing cards when my
partner keeps their mind on the game, but you
take a woman like Hartsell's wife and how can
they play cards when they have got to stop every
couple seconds and brag about their son in Grand
Rapids?

Well, the New York-New Jersey Society announced that they was goin to give a social evening too and I said to Mother, I said:

"Well, that is one evening when we will have an
excuse not to play five hundred."

"Yes," she said, "but we will have to ask Frank
and his wife to go to the social with us as they
asked us to go to the Michigan social."

"Well," I said, "I had rather stay home than
drag that chatterbox everywheres we go."

So Mother said:

"You are getting too cranky. Maybe she does
talk a little too much but she is good hearted.
And Frank is always good company."

So I said:

"I suppose if he is such good company you
wished you had of married him."

Mother laughed and said I sounded like I was
jealous. Jealous of a cow doctor!

Anyway we had to drag them along to the

social and I will say that we give them a much better entertainment than they had given us.

Judge Lane of Paterson made a fine talk on business conditions and a Mrs. Newell of Westfield imitated birds, only you could really tell what they was the way she done it. Two young women from Red Bank sung a choral selection and we clapped them back and they gave us Home to Our Mountains and Mother and Mrs. Hartsell both had tears in their eyes. And Hartsell, too.

Well, some way or another the chairman got wind that I was there and asked me to make a talk and I wasn't even going to get up, but Mother made me, so I got up and said:

"Ladies and gentlemen," I said. "I didn't expect to be called on for a speech on an occasion like this or no other occasion as I do not set myself up as a speech maker, so will have to do the best I can, which I often say is the best anybody can do."

Then I told them the story about Pat and the motorcycle, using the brogue, and it seemed to tickle them and I told them one or two other stories, but altogether I wasn't on my feet more than twenty or twenty-five minutes and you ought to of heard the clapping and hollering when I set down. Even Mrs. Hartsell admitted that I am quite a speechifier and said if I ever went to Grand Rapids, Michigan, her son would make me talk to the Rotarians.

The Golden Honeymoon

When it was over, Hartsell wanted we should go to their house and play cards, but his wife reminded him that it was after 9.30 P. M., rather a late hour to start a card game, but he had went crazy on the subject of cards, probably because he didn't have to play partners with his wife. Anyway, we got rid of them and went home to bed.

It was the next morning, when we met over to the Park, that Mrs. Hartsell made the remark that she wasn't getting no exercise so I suggested that why didn't she take part in the roque game.

She said she had not played a game of roque in twenty years, but if Mother would play she would play. Well, at first Mother wouldn't hear of it, but finally consented, more to please Mrs. Hartsell than anything else.

Well, they had a game with a Mrs. Ryan from Eagle, Nebraska, and a young Mrs. Morse from Rutland, Vermont, who Mother had met down to the chiropodist's. Well, Mother couldn't hit a flea and they all laughed at her and I couldn't help from laughing at her myself and finally she quit and said her back was too lame to stoop over. So they got another lady and kept on playing and soon Mrs. Hartsell was the one everybody was laughing at, as she had a long shot to hit the black ball, and as she made the effort her teeth fell out on to the court. I never seen a woman so flustered in my life. And I never heard

How to Write Short Stories

so much laughing, only Mrs. Hartsell didn't join in and she was madder than a hornet and wouldn't play no more, so the game broke up.

Mrs. Hartsell went home without speaking to nobody, but Hartsell stayed around and finally he said to me, he said:

"Well, I played you checkers the other day and you beat me bad and now what do you say if you and me play a game of horse-shoes?"

I told him I hadn't pitched a shoe in sixteen years, but Mother said:

"Go ahead and play. You used to be good at it and maybe it will come back to you."

Well, to make a long story short, I give in. I oughtn't to of never tried it, as I hadn't pitched a shoe in sixteen years, and I only done it to humor Hartsell.

Before we started, Mother patted me on the back and told me to do my best, so we started in and I seen right off that I was in for it, as I hadn't pitched a shoe in sixteen years and didn't have my distance. And besides, the plating had wore off the shoes so that they was points right where they stuck into my thumb and I hadn't throwed more than two or three times when my thumb was raw and it pretty near killed me to hang on to the shoe, let alone pitch it.

Well, Hartsell throws the awkwardest shoe I ever seen pitched and to see him pitch you

The Golden Honeymoon

wouldn't think he would ever come nowheres near, but he is also the luckiest pitcher I ever seen and he made some pitches where the shoe lit five and six feet short and then schoonered up and was a ringer. They's no use trying to beat that kind of luck.

They was a pretty fair size crowd watching us and four or five other ladies besides Mother, and it seems like, when Hartsell pitches, he has got to chew and it kept the ladies on the anxious seat as he don't seem to care which way he is facing when he leaves go.

You would think a man as old as him would of learnt more manners.

Well, to make a long story short, I was just beginning to get my distance when I had to give up on account of my thumb, which I showed it to Hartsell and he seen I couldn't go on, as it was raw and bleeding. Even if I could of stood it to go on myself, Mother wouldn't of allowed it after she seen my thumb. So anyway I quit and Hartsell said the score was nineteen to six, but I don't know what it was. Or don't care, neither.

Well, Mother and I went home and I said I hoped we was through with the Hartsells as I was sick and tired of them, but it seemed like she had promised we would go over to their house that evening for another game of their everlasting cards.

How to Write Short Stories

Well, my thumb was giving me considerable pain and I felt kind of out of sorts and I guess maybe I forgot myself, but anyway, when we was about through playing Hartsell made the remark that he wouldn't never lose a game of cards if he could always have Mother for a partner.

So I said:

"Well, you had a chance fifty years ago to always have her for a partner, but you wasn't man enough to keep her."

I was sorry the minute I had said it and Hartsell didn't know what to say and for once his wife couldn't say nothing. Mother tried to smooth things over by making the remark that I must of had something stronger than tea or I wouldn't talk so silly. But Mrs. Hartsell had froze up like an iceberg and hardly said good night to us and I bet her and Frank put in a pleasant hour after we was gone.

As we was leaving, Mother said to him: "Never mind Charley's nonsense, Frank. He is just mad because you beat him all hollow pitching horseshoes and playing cards."

She said that to make up for my slip, but at the same time she certainly riled me. I tried to keep ahold of myself, but as soon as we was out of the house she had to open up the subject and begun to scold me for the break I had made.

Well, I wasn't in no mood to be scolded. So I said:

The Golden Honeymoon

"I guess he is such a wonderful pitcher and card player that you wished you had married him."

"Well," she said, "at least he ain't a baby to give up pitching because his thumb has got a few scratches."

"And how about you," I said, "making a fool of yourself on the roque court and then pretending your back is lame and you can't play no more!"

"Yes," she said, "but when you hurt your thumb I didn't laugh at you, and why did you laugh at me when I sprained my back?"

"Who could help from laughing!" I said.

"Well," she said, "Frank Hartsell didn't laugh."

"Well," I said, "why didn't you marry him?"

"Well," said Mother, "I almost wished I had!"

"And I wished so, too!" I said.

"I'll remember that!" said Mother, and that's the last word she said to me for two days.

We seen the Hartsells the next day in the Park and I was willing to apologize, but they just nodded to us. And a couple days later we heard they had left for Orlando, where they have got relatives.

I wished they had went there in the first place.

Mother and I made it up setting on a bench.

"Listen, Charley," she said. "This is our Golden Honeymoon and we don't want the whole thing spoilt with a silly old quarrel."

How to Write Short Stories

"Well," I said, "did you mean that about wishing you had married Hartsell?"

"Of course not," she said, "that is, if you didn't mean that you wished I had, too."

So I said:

"I was just tired and all wrought up. I thank God you chose me instead of him as they's no other woman in the world who I could of lived with all these years."

"How about Mrs. Hartsell?" says Mother.

"Good gracious!" I said. "Imagine being married to a woman that plays five hundred like she does and drops her teeth on the roque court!"

"Well," said Mother, "it wouldn't be no worse than being married to a man that expectorates towards ladies and is such a fool in a checker game."

So I put my arm around her shoulder and she stroked my hand and I guess we got kind of spoony.

They was two days left of our stay in St. Petersburg and the next to the last day Mother introduced me to a Mrs. Kendall from Kingston, Rhode Island, who she had met at the chiropodist's.

Mrs. Kendall made us acquainted with her husband, who is in the grocery business. They have got two sons and five grandchildren and one great-grandchild. One of their sons lives in Providence and is way up in the Elks as well as a Rotarian.

The Golden Honeymoon

We found them very congenial people and we played cards with them the last two nights we was there. They was both experts and I only wished we had met them sooner instead of running into the Hartsells. But the Kendalls will be there again next winter and we will see more of them, that is, if we decide to make the trip again.

We left the Sunshine City on the eleventh day of February, at 11 A. M. This give us a day trip through Florida and we seen all the country we had passed through at night on the way down.

We reached Jacksonville at 7 P. M. and pulled out of there at 8.10 P. M. We reached Fayetteville, North Carolina, at nine o'clock the following morning, and reached Washington, D. C., at 6.30 P. M., laying over there half an hour.

We reached Trenton at 11.01 P. M. and had wired ahead to my daughter and son-in-law and they met us at the train and we went to their house and they put us up for the night. John would of made us stay up all night, telling about our trip, but Edie said we must be tired and made us go to bed. That's my daughter.

The next day we took our train for home and arrived safe and sound, having been gone just one month and a day.

Here comes Mother, so I guess I better shut up.

CHAMPION

An example of the mystery story. The mystery is how it came to get printed.

V

CHAMPION

Midge Kelly scored his first knockout when he was seventeen. The knockee was his brother Connie, three years his junior and a cripple. The purse was a half dollar given to the younger Kelly by a lady whose electric had just missed bumping his soul from his frail little body.

Connie did not know Midge was in the house, else he never would have risked laying the prize on the arm of the least comfortable chair in the room, the better to observe its shining beauty. As Midge entered from the kitchen, the crippled boy covered the coin with his hand, but the movement lacked the speed requisite to escape his brother's quick eye.

"Watcha got there?" demanded Midge.

"Nothin'," said Connie.

"You're a one legged liar!" said Midge.

He strode over to his brother's chair and grasped the hand that concealed the coin.

"Let loose!" he ordered.

Connie began to cry.

"Let loose and shut up your noise," said the elder, and jerked his brother's hand from the chair arm.

145

How to Write Short Stories

The coin fell onto the bare floor. Midge pounced on it. His weak mouth widened in a triumphant smile.

"Nothin', huh?" he said. "All right, if it's nothin' you don't want it."

"Give that back," sobbed the younger.

"I'll give you a red nose, you little sneak! Where'd you steal it?"

"I didn't steal it. It's mine. A lady give it to me after she pretty near hit me with a car."

"It's a crime she missed you," said Midge.

Midge started for the front door. The cripple picked up his crutch, rose from his chair with difficulty, and, still sobbing, came toward Midge. The latter heard him and stopped.

"You better stay where you're at," he said.

"I want my money," cried the boy.

"I know what you want," said Midge.

Doubling up the fist that held the half dollar, he landed with all his strength on his brother's mouth. Connie fell to the floor with a thud, the crutch tumbling on top of him. Midge stood beside the prostrate form.

"Is that enough?" he said. "Or do you want this, too?"

And he kicked him in the crippled leg.

"I guess that'll hold you," he said.

There was no response from the boy on the floor. Midge looked at him a moment, then at the coin in his hand, and then went out into the street, whistling.

An hour later, when Mrs. Kelly came home from her day's work at Faulkner's Steam Laundry, she found Connie on the floor, moaning. Dropping on her knees beside him, she called him by name a score of times. Then she got up and, pale as a ghost, dashed from the house. Dr. Ryan left the Kelly abode about dusk and walked toward Halsted Street. Mrs. Dorgan spied him as he passed her gate.

"Who's sick, Doctor?" she called.

"Poor little Connie," he replied. "He had a bad fall."

"How did it happen?"

"I can't say for sure, Margaret, but I'd almost bet he was knocked down."

"Knocked down!" exclaimed Mrs. Dorgan. "Why, who——?"

"Have you seen the other one lately?"

"Michael? No, not since mornin'. You can't be thinkin'——"

"I wouldn't put it past him, Margaret," said the doctor gravely. "The lad's mouth is swollen and cut, and his poor, skinny little leg is bruised. He surely didn't do it to himself and I think Helen suspects the other one."

"Lord save us!" said Mrs. Dorgan. "I'll run over and see if I can help."

147

How to Write Short Stories

"That's a good woman," said Doctor Ryan, and went on down the street.

Near midnight, when Midge came home, his mother was sitting at Connie's bedside. She did not look up.

"Well," said Midge, "what's the matter?"

She remained silent. Midge repeated his question.

"Michael, you know what's the matter," she said at length.

"I don't know nothin'," said Midge.

"Don't lie to me, Michael. What did you do to your brother?"

"Nothin'."

"You hit him."

"Well, then, I hit him. What of it? It ain't the first time."

Her lips pressed tightly together, her face like chalk, Ellen Kelly rose from her chair and made straight for him. Midge backed against the door.

"Lay off'n me, Ma. I don't want to fight no woman."

Still she came on breathing heavily.

"Stop where you're at, Ma," he warned.

There was a brief struggle and Midge's mother lay on the floor before him.

"You ain't hurt, Ma. You're lucky I didn't land good. And I told you to lay off'n me."

148

Champion

"God forgive you, Michael!"

Midge found Hap Collins in the showdown game at the Royal.

"Come on out a minute," he said.

Hap followed him out on the walk.

"I'm leavin' town for a w'ile," said Midge.

"What for?"

"Well, we had a little run-in up to the house. The kid stole a half buck off'n me, and when I went after it he cracked me with his crutch. So I nailed him. And the old lady came at me with a chair and I took it off'n her and she fell down."

"How is Connie hurt?"

"Not bad."

"What are you runnin' away for?"

"Who the hell said I was runnin' away? I'm sick and tired o' gettin' picked on; that's all. So I'm leavin' for a w'ile and I want a piece o' money."

"I ain't only got six bits," said Happy.

"You're in bad shape, ain't you? Well, come through with it."

Happy came through.

"You oughtn't to hit the kid," he said.

"I ain't astin' you who can I hit," snarled Midge. "You try to put somethin' over on me and you'll get the same dose. I'm goin' now."

"Go as far as you like," said Happy, but not until he was sure that Kelly was out of hearing.

149

How to Write Short Stories

Early the following morning, Midge boarded a train for Milwaukee. He had no ticket, but no one knew the difference. The conductor remained in the caboose.

On a night six months later, Midge hurried out of the "stage door" of the Star Boxing Club and made for Duane's saloon, two blocks away. In his pocket were twelve dollars, his reward for having battered up one Demon Dempsey through the six rounds of the first preliminary.

It was Midge's first professional engagement in the manly art. Also it was the first time in weeks that he had earned twelve dollars.

On the way to Duane's he had to pass Niemann's. He pulled his cap over his eyes and increased his pace until he had gone by. Inside Niemann's stood a trusting bartender, who for ten days had staked Midge to drinks and allowed him to ravage the lunch on a promise to come in and settle the moment he was paid for the "prelim."

Midge strode into Duane's and aroused the napping bartender by slapping a silver dollar on the festive board.

"Gimme a shot," said Midge.

The shooting continued until the wind-up at the Star was over and part of the fight crowd joined Midge in front of Duane's bar. A youth in the early twenties, standing next to young Kelly,

Champion

finally summoned sufficient courage to address him.

"Wasn't you in the first bout?" he ventured.

"Yeh," Midge replied.

"My name's Hersch," said the other.

Midge received the startling information in silence.

"I don't want to butt in," continued Mr. Hersch, "but I'd like to buy you a drink."

"All right," said Midge, "but don't overstrain yourself."

Mr. Hersch laughed uproariously and beckoned to the bartender.

"You certainly gave that wop a trimmin' tonight," said the buyer of the drink, when they had been served. "I thought you'd kill him."

"I would if I hadn't let up," Midge replied. "I'll kill 'em all."

"You got the wallop all right," the other said admiringly.

"Have I got the wallop?" said Midge. "Say, I can kick like a mule. Did you notice them muscles in my shoulders?"

"Notice 'em? I couldn't help from noticin' 'em," said Hersch. "I says to the fella settin' alongside o' me, I says: 'Look at them shoulders! No wonder he can hit,' I says to him."

"Just let me land and it's good-by, baby," said Midge. "I'll kill 'em all."

How to Write Short Stories

The oral manslaughter continued until Duane's closed for the night. At parting, Midge and his new friend shook hands and arranged for a meeting the following evening.

For nearly a week the two were together almost constantly. It was Hersch's pleasant rôle to listen to Midge's modest revelations concerning himself, and to buy every time Midge's glass was empty. But there came an evening when Hersch regretfully announced that he must go home to supper.

"I got a date for eight bells," he confided. "I could stick till then, only I must clean up and put on the Sunday clo'es, 'cause she's the prettiest little thing in Milwaukee."

"Can't you fix it for two?" asked Midge.

"I don't know who to get," Hersch replied. "Wait, though. I got a sister and if she ain't busy, it'll be O. K. She's no bum for looks herself."

So it came about that Midge and Emma Hersch and Emma's brother and the prettiest little thing in Milwaukee foregathered at Wall's and danced half the night away. And Midge and Emma danced every dance together, for though every little onestep seemed to induce a new thirst of its own, Lou Hersch stayed too sober to dance with his own sister.

The next day, penniless at last in spite of his

Champion

phenomenal ability to make someone else settle, Midge Kelly sought out Doc Hammond, matchmaker for the Star, and asked to be booked for the next show.

"I could put you on with Tracy for the next bout," said Doc.

"What's they in it?" asked Midge.

"Twenty if you cop," Doc told him.

"Have a heart," protested Midge. "Didn't I look good the other night?"

"You looked all right. But you aren't Freddie Welsh yet by a consid'able margin."

"I ain't scared of Freddie Welsh or none of 'em," said Midge.

"Well, we don't pay our boxers by the size of their chests," Doc said. "I'm offerin' you this Tracy bout. Take it or leave it."

"All right; I'm on," said Midge, and he passed a pleasant afternoon at Duane's on the strength of his booking.

Young Tracy's manager came to Midge the night before the show.

"How do you feel about this go?" he asked.

"Me?" said Midge "I feel all right. What do you mean, how do I feel?"

"I mean," said Tracy's manager, "that we're mighty anxious to win, 'cause the boy's got a chanct in Philly if he cops this one."

How to Write Short Stories

"What's your proposition?" asked Midge.

"Fifty bucks," said Tracy's manager.

"What do you think I am, a crook? Me lay down for fifty bucks. Not me!"

"Seventy-five, then," said Tracy's manager.

The market closed on eighty and the details were agreed on in short order. And the next night Midge was stopped in the second round by a terrific slap on the forearm.

This time Midge passed up both Niemann's and Duane's, having a sizable account at each place, and sought his refreshment at Stein's farther down the street.

When the profits of his deal with Tracy were gone, he learned, by first-hand information from Doc Hammond and the matchmakers at the other "clubs," that he was no longer desired for even the cheapest of preliminaries. There was no danger of his starving or dying of thirst while Emma and Lou Hersch lived. But he made up his mind, four months after his defeat by Young Tracy, that Milwaukee was not the ideal place for him to live.

"I can lick the best of 'em," he reasoned, "but there ain't no more chanct for me here. I can maybe go east and get on somewheres. And besides——"

But just after Midge had purchased a ticket to Chicago with the money he had "borrowed" from

Champion

Emma Hersch "to buy shoes," a heavy hand was laid on his shoulders and he turned to face two strangers.

"Where are you goin', Kelly?" inquired the owner of the heavy hand.

"Nowheres," said Midge. "What the hell do you care?"

The other stranger spoke:

"Kelly, I'm employed by Emma Hersch's mother to see that you do right by her. And we want you to stay here till you've done it."

"You won't get nothin' but the worst of it, monkeying with me," said Midge.

Nevertheless, he did not depart for Chicago that night. Two days later, Emma Hersch became Mrs. Kelly, and the gift of the groom, when once they were alone, was a crushing blow on the bride's pale cheek.

Next morning, Midge left Milwaukee as he had entered it—by fast freight.

"They's no use kiddin' ourself any more," said Tommy Haley. "He might get down to thirty-seven in a pinch, but if he done below that a mouse could stop him. He's a welter; that's what he is and he knows it as well as I do. He's growed like a weed in the last six mont's. I told him, I says, 'If you don't quit growin' they won't be nobody for you to box, only Willard and them.'

How to Write Short Stories

He says, 'Well, I wouldn't run away from Willard if I weighed twenty pounds more.'"

"He must hate himself," said Tommy's brother.

"I never seen a good one that didn't," said Tommy. "And Midge is a good one; don't make no mistake about that. I wisht we could of got Welsh before the kid growed so big. But it's too late now. I won't make no holler, though, if we can match him up with the Dutchman."

"Who do you mean?"

"Young Goetz, the welter champ. We mightn't not get so much dough for the bout itself, but it'd roll in afterward. What a drawin' card we'd be, 'cause the people pays their money to see the fella with the wallop, and that's Midge. And we'd keep the title just as long as Midge could make the weight."

"Can't you land no match with Goetz?"

"Sure, 'cause he needs the money. But I've went careful with the kid so far and look at the results I got! So what's the use of takin' a chanct? The kid's comin' every minute and Goetz is goin' back faster'n big Johnson did. I think we could lick him now; I'd bet my life on it. But six mont's from now they won't be no risk. He'll of licked hisself before that time. Then all as we'll have to do is sign up with him and wait for the referee to stop it. But Midge is so crazy to get at him now that I can't hardly hold him back."

Champion

The brothers Haley were lunching in a Boston hotel. Dan had come down from Holyoke to visit with Tommy and to watch the latter's protégé go twelve rounds, or less, with Bud Cross. The bout promised little in the way of a contest, for Midge had twice stopped the Baltimore youth and Bud's reputation for gameness was all that had earned him the date. The fans were willing to pay the price to see Midge's hay-making left, but they wanted to see it used on an opponent who would not jump out of the ring the first time he felt its crushing force. But Cross was such an opponent, and his willingness to stop boxing-gloves with his eyes, ears, nose and throat had long enabled him to escape the horrors of honest labor. A game boy was Bud, and he showed it in his battered, swollen, discolored face.

"I should think," said Dan Haley, "that the kid'd do whatever you tell him after all you done for him."

"Well," said Tommy, "he's took my dope pretty straight so far, but he's so sure of hisself that he can't see no reason for waitin'. He'll do what I say, though; he'd be a sucker not to."

"You got a contrac' with him?"

"No, I don't need no contrac'. He knows it was me that drug him out o' the gutter and he ain't goin' to turn me down now, when he's got the dough and bound to get more. Where'd he of been at if I hadn't listened to him when he

How to Write Short Stories

first come to me? That's pretty near two years ago now, but it seems like last week. I was settin' in the s'loon acrost from the Pleasant Club in Philly, waitin' for McCann to count the dough and come over, when this little bum blowed in and tried to stand the house off for a drink. They told him nothin' doin' and to beat it out o' there, and then he seen me and come over to where I was settin' and ast me wasn't I a boxin' man and I told him who I was. Then he ast me for money to buy a shot and I told him to set down and I'd buy it for him.

"Then we got talkin' things over and he told me his name and told me about fightn' a couple o' prelims out to Milwaukee. So I says, 'Well, boy, I don't know how good or how rotten you are, but you won't never get nowheres trainin' on that stuff.' So he says he'd cut it out if he could get on in a bout and I says I would give him a chanct if he played square with me and didn't touch no more to drink. So we shook hands and I took him up to the hotel with me and give him a bath and the next day I bought him some clo'es. And I staked him to eats and sleeps for over six weeks. He had a hard time breakin' away from the polish, but finally I thought he was fit and I give him his chanct. He went on with Smiley Sayer and stopped him so quick that Smiley thought sure he was poisoned.

"Well, you know what he's did since. The

Champion

only beatin' in his record was by Tracy in Milwaukee before I got hold of him, and he's licked Tracy three times in the last year.

"I've gave him all the best of it in a money way and he's got seven thousand bucks in cold storage. How's that for a kid that was in the gutter two years ago? And he'd have still more yet if he wasn't so nuts over clo'es and got to stop at the good hotels and so forth."

"Where's his home at?"

"Well, he ain't really got no home. He came from Chicago and his mother canned him outro' the house for bein' no good. She give him a raw deal, I guess, and he says he won't have nothin' to do with her unlest she comes to him first. She's got a pile o' money, he says, so he ain't worryin' about her."

The gentleman under discussion entered the café and swaggered to Tommy's table, while the whole room turned to look.

Midge was the picture of health despite a slightly colored eye and an ear that seemed to have no opening. But perhaps it was not his healthiness that drew all eyes. His diamond horse-shoe tie pin, his purple cross-striped shirt, his orange shoes and his light blue suit fairly screamed for attention.

"Where you been?" he asked Tommy. "I been lookin' all over for you."

"Set down," said his manager.

How to Write Short Stories

"No time," said Midge. "I'm goin' down to the w'arf and see 'em unload the fish."

"Shake hands with my brother Dan," said Tommy.

Midge shook with the Holyoke Haley.

"If you're Tommy's brother, you're O. K. with me," said Midge, and the brothers beamed with pleasure.

Dan moistened his lips and murmured an embarrassed reply, but it was lost on the young gladiator.

"Leave me take twenty," Midge was saying. "I prob'ly won't need it, but I don't like to be caught short."

Tommy parted with a twenty dollar bill and recorded the transaction in a small black book the insurance company had given him for Christmas.

"But," he said, "it won't cost you no twenty to look at them fish. Want me to go along?"

"No," said Midge hastily. "You and your brother here prob'ly got a lot to say to each other."

"Well," said Tommy, "don't take no bad money and don't get lost. And you better be back at four o'clock and lay down a w'ile."

"I don't need no rest to beat this guy," said Midge. "He'll do enough layin' down for the both of us."

Champion

And laughing even more than the jest called
for, he strode out through the fire of admiring
and startled glances.

The corner of Boylston and Tremont was the
nearest Midge got to the wharf, but the lady awaiting him was doubtless a more dazzling sight than
the catch of the luckiest Massachusetts fisherman.
She could talk, too—probably better than the
fish.

"O you Kid!" she said, flashing a few silver
teeth among the gold. "O you fighting man!"

Midge smiled up at her.

"We'll go somewheres and get a drink," he
said. "One won't hurt."

In New Orleans, five months after he had re-
arranged the map of Bud Cross for the third time,
Midge finished training for his championship
bout with the Dutchman.

Back in his hotel after the final workout, Midge
stopped to chat with some of the boys from up
north, who had made the long trip to see a champion dethroned, for the result of this bout was so
nearly a foregone conclusion that even the experts
had guessed it.

Tommy Haley secured the key and the mail
and ascended to the Kelly suite. He was bathing
when Midge came in, half hour later.

"Any mail?" asked Midge.

How to Write Short Stories

"There on the bed," replied Tommy from the tub.

Midge picked up the stack of letters and post-cards and glanced them over. From the pile he sorted out three letters and laid them on the table. The rest he tossed into the waste-basket. Then he picked up the three and sat for a few moments holding them, while his eyes gazed off into space. At length he looked again at the three unopened letters in his hand; then he put one in his pocket and tossed the other two at the basket. They missed their target and fell on the floor.

"Hell!" said Midge, and stooping over picked them up.

He opened one postmarked Milwaukee and read:

DEAR HUSBAND:

I have wrote to you so manny times and got no anser and I dont know if you ever got them, so I am writeing again in the hopes you will get this letter and anser. I dont like to bother you with my trubles and I would not only for the baby and I am not asking you should write to me but only send a little money and I am not asking for my-self but the baby has not been well a day sence last Aug. and the dr. told me she cant live much longer unless I give her better food and thats im-

162

Champion

possible the way things are. Lou has not been working for a year and what I make dont hardley pay for the rent. I am not asking for you to give me any money, but only you should send what I loaned when convenient and I think it amts. to about $36.00. Please try and send that amt. and it will help me, but if you cant send the whole amt. try and send me something.

Your wife,

EMMA.

Midge tore the letter into a hundred pieces and scattered them over the floor.

"Money, money, money!" he said. "They must think I'm made o' money. I s'pose the old woman's after it too."

He opened his mother's letter:

dear Michael Connie wonted me to rite and say you must beet the dutchman and he is sur you will and wonted me to say we wont you to rite and tell us about it, but I gess you havent no time to rite or we herd from you long beffore this but I wish you would rite jest a line or 2 boy becaus it wuld be better for Connie then a barl of medisin. It wuld help me to keep things going if you send me money now and then when you can spair it but if you cant send no money try and

fine time to rite a letter onley a few lines and it
will please Connie. jest think boy he hasent got
out of bed in over 3 yrs. Connie says good luck.

Your Mother,

ELLEN F. KELLY.

"I thought so," said Midge. "They're all
alike."

The third letter was from New York. It read:

HON:—This is the last letter you will get from
me before your champ, but I will send you a telegram Saturday, but I can't say as much in a telegram as in a letter and I am writeing this to let
you know I am thinking of you and praying for
good luck.

Lick him good hon and don't wait no longer
than you have to and don't forget to wire me as
soon as its over. Give him that little old left of
yours on the nose hon and don't be afraid of spoil-
ing his good looks because he couldn't be no
homlier than he is. But don't let him spoil my
baby's pretty face. You won't will you hon.

Well hon I would give anything to be there
and see it, but I guess you love Haley better than
me or you wouldn't let him keep me away. But
when your champ hon we can do as we please and
tell Haley to go to the devil.

Well hon I will send you a telegram Saturday

Champion

and I almost forgot to tell you I will need some
more money, a couple hundred say and you will
have to wire it to me as soon as you get this.
You will won't you hon.

I will send you a telegram Saturday and remember hon I am pulling for you.

Well good-by sweetheart and good luck.

GRACE.

"They're all alike," said Midge. "Money,
money, money."

Tommy Haley, shining from his ablutions, came
in from the adjoining room.

"Thought you'd be layin' down," he said.

"I'm goin' to," said Midge, unbuttoning his
orange shoes.

"I'll call you at six and you can eat up here
without no bugs to pester you. I got to go down
and give them birds their tickets."

"Did you hear from Goldberg?" asked Midge.

"Didn't I tell you? Sure; fifteen weeks at five
hundred, if we win. And we can get a guarantee
o' twelve thousand, with privileges either in New
York or Milwaukee."

"Who with?"

"Anybody that'll stand up in front of you. You
don't care who it is, do you?"

"Not me. I'll make 'em all look like a monkey."

How to Write Short Stories

"Well you better lay down aw'ile."

"Oh, say, wire two hundred to Grace for me, will you? Right away; the New York address."

"Two hundred! You just sent her three hundred last Sunday."

"Well, what the hell do you care?"

"All right, all right. Don't get sore about it. Anything else?"

"That's all," said Midge, and dropped onto the bed.

"And I want the deed done before I come back," said Grace as she rose from the table. "You won't fall down on me, will you, hon?"

"Leave it to me," said Midge. "And don't spend no more than you have to."

Grace smiled a farewell and left the café. Midge continued to sip his coffee and read his paper.

They were in Chicago and they were in the middle of Midge's first week in vaudeville. He had come straight north to reap the rewards of his glorious victory over the broken down Dutchman. A fortnight had been spent in learning his act, which consisted of a gymnastic exhibition and a ten minutes' monologue on the various excellences of Midge Kelly. And now he was twice daily turning 'em away from the Madison Theater.

His breakfast over and his paper read, Midge

Champion

sauntered into the lobby and asked for his key. He then beckoned to a bell-boy, who had been hoping for that very honor.

"Find Haley, Tommy Haley," said Midge. "Tell him to come up to my room."

"Yes, sir, Mr. Kelly," said the boy, and proceeded to break all his former records for diligence.

Midge was looking out of his seventh-story window when Tommy answered the summons.

"What'll it be?" inquired his manager.

There was a pause before Midge replied.

"Haley," he said, "twenty-five per cent's a whole lot o' money."

"I guess I got it comin', ain't I?" said Tommy.

"I don't see how you figger it. I don't see where you're worth it to me."

"Well," said Tommy, "I didn't expect nothin' like this. I thought you was satisfied with the bargain. I don't want to beat nobody out o' nothin', but I don't see where you could have got anybody else that would of did all I done for you."

"Sure, that's all right," said the champion. "You done a lot for me in Philly. And you got good money for it, didn't you?"

"I ain't makin' no holler. Still and all, the big money's still ahead of us yet. And if it hadn't of been for me, you wouldn't of never got within grabbin' distance."

167

How to Write Short Stories

"Oh, I guess I could of went along all right," said Midge. "Who was it that hung that left on the Dutchman's jaw, me or you?"

"Yes, but you wouldn't been in the ring with the Dutchman if it wasn't for how I handled you."

"Well, this won't get us nowheres. The idear is that you ain't worth no twenty-five per cent now and it don't make no diff'rence what come off a year or two ago."

"Don't it?" said Tommy. "I'd say it made a whole lot of difference."

"Well, I say it don't and I guess that settles it."

"Look here, Midge," Tommy said, "I thought I was fair with you, but if you don't think so, I'm willin' to hear what you think is fair. I don't want nobody callin' me a Sherlock. Let's go down to business and sign up a contrac'. What's your figger?"

"I ain't namin' no figger," Midge replied. "I'm sayin' that twenty-five's too much. Now what are you willin' to take?"

"How about twenty?"

"Twenty's too much," said Kelly.

"What ain't too much?" asked Tommy.

"Well, Haley, I might as well give it to you straight. They ain't nothin' that ain't too much."

"You mean you don't want me at no figger?"

Champion

"That's the idear."

There was a minute's silence. Then Tommy Haley walked toward the door.

"Midge," he said, in a choking voice, "you're makin' a big mistake, boy. You can't throw down your best friends and get away with it. That damn woman will ruin you."

Midge sprang from his seat.

"You shut your mouth!" he stormed. "Get out o' here before they have to carry you out. You been spongin' off o' me long enough. Say one more word about the girl or about anything else and you'll get what the Dutchman got. Now get out!"

And Tommy Haley, having a very vivid memory of the Dutchman's face as he fell, got out.

Grace came in later, dropped her numerous bundles on the lounge and perched herself on the arm of Midge's chair.

"Well?" she said.

"Well," said Midge, "I got rid of him."

"Good boy!" said Grace. "And now I think you might give me that twenty-five per cent."

"Besides the seventy-five you're already gettin'?" said Midge.

"Don't be no grouch, hon. You don't look pretty when you're grouchy."

"It ain't my business to look pretty," Midge replied.

"Wait till you see how I look with the stuff I bought this mornin'!"

Midge glanced at the bundles on the lounge.

"There's Haley's twenty-five per cent," he said, "and then some."

The champion did not remain long without a manager. Haley's successor was none other than Jerome Harris, who saw in Midge a better meal ticket than his popular-priced musical show had been.

The contract, giving Mr. Harris twenty-five per cent of Midge's earnings, was signed in Detroit the week after Tommy Haley had heard his dismissal read. It had taken Midge just six days to learn that a popular actor cannot get on without the ministrations of a man who thinks, talks and means business. At first Grace objected to the new member of the firm, but when Mr. Harris had demanded and secured from the vaudeville people a one-hundred dollar increase in Midge's weekly stipend, she was convinced that the champion had acted for the best.

"You and my missus will have some great old times," Harris told Grace. "I'd of wired her to join us here, only I seen the Kid's bookin' takes us to Milwaukee next week, and that's where she is."

But when they were introduced in the Milwaukee hotel, Grace admitted to herself that her feeling for Mrs. Harris could hardly be called love at first sight. Midge, on the contrary, gave his new manager's wife the many times over and seemed loath to end the feast of his eyes.

"Some doll," he said to Grace when they were alone.

"Doll is right," the lady replied, "and sawdust where her brains ought to be."

"I'm li'ble to steal that baby," said Midge, and he smiled as he noted the effect of his words on his audience's face.

On Tuesday of the Milwaukee week the champion successfully defended his title in a bout that the newspapers never reported. Midge was alone in his room that morning when a visitor entered without knocking. The visitor was Lou Hersch.

Midge turned white at sight of him.

"What do you want?" he demanded.

"I guess you know," said Lou Hersch. "Your wife's starvin' to death and your baby's starvin' to death and I'm starvin' to death. And you're dirty with money."

"Listen," said Midge, "if it wasn't for you, I wouldn't never saw your sister. And, if you ain't man enough to hold a job, what's that to me? The best thing you can do is keep away from me."

"You give me a piece o' money and I'll go."

How to Write Short Stories

Midge's reply to the ultimatum was a straight right to his brother-in-law's narrow chest.

"Take that home to your sister."

And after Lou Hersch had picked himself up and slunk away, Midge thought: "It's lucky I didn't give him my left or I'd of croaked him. And if I'd hit him in the stomach, I'd of broke his spine."

There was a party after each evening performance during the Milwaukee engagement. The wine flowed freely and Midge had more of it than Tommy Haley ever would have permitted him. Mr. Harris offered no objection, which was possibly just as well for his own physical comfort.

In the dancing between drinks, Midge had his new manager's wife for a partner as often as Grace. The latter's face as she floundered round in the arms of the portly Harris, belied her frequent protestations that she was having the time of her life.

Several times that week, Midge thought Grace was on the point of starting the quarrel he hoped to have. But it was not until Friday night that she accommodated. He and Mrs. Harris had disappeared after the matinee and when Grace saw him again at the close of the night show, she came to the point at once.

172

Champion

"What are you tryin' to pull off?" she demanded.

"It's none o' your business, is it?" said Midge.

"You bet it's my business; mine and Harris's. You cut it short or you'll find out."

"Listen," said Midge, "have you got a mortgage on me or somethin'? You talk like we was married."

"We're goin' to be, too. And to-morrow's as good a time as any."

"Just about," Midge said. "You got as much chanct o' marryin' me to-morrow as the next day or next year and that ain't no chanct at all."

"We'll find out," said Grace.

"You're the one that's got somethin' to find out."

"What do you mean?"

"I mean I'm married already."

"You lie!"

"You think so, do you? Well, s'pose you go to this here address and get acquainted with my missus."

Midge scrawled a number on a piece of paper and handed it to her. She stared at it unseeingly.

"Well," said Midge, "I ain't kiddin' you. You go there and ask for Mrs. Michael Kelly, and if you don't find her, I'll marry you to-morrow before breakfast."

Still Grace stared at the scrap of paper. To Midge it seemed an age before she spoke again.

"You lied to me all this w'ile."

"You never ast me was I married. What's more, what the hell diff'rence did it make to you? You got a split, didn't you? Better'n fifty-fifty."

He started away.

"Where you goin'?"

"I'm goin' to meet Harris and his wife."

"I'm goin' with you. You're not goin' to shake me now."

"Yes, I am, too," said Midge quietly. "When I leave town to-morrow night, you're going to stay here. And if I see where you're goin' to make a fuss, I'll put you in a hospital where they'll keep you quiet. You can get your stuff to-morrow mornin' and I'll slip you a hundred bucks. And then I don't want to see no more o' you. And don't try and tag along now or I'll have to add another K. O. to the old record."

When Grace returned to the hotel that night, she discovered that Midge and the Harrises had moved to another. And when Midge left town the following night, he was again without a manager, and Mr. Harris was without a wife.

Three days prior to Midge Kelly's ten-round bout with Young Milton in New York City, the sporting editor of *The News* assigned Joe Morgan

Champion

to write two or three thousand words about the champion to run with a picture lay-out for Sunday.

Joe Morgan dropped in at Midge's training quarters Friday afternoon. Midge, he learned, was doing road work, but Midge's manager, Wallie Adams, stood ready and willing to supply reams of dope about the greatest fighter of the age.

"Let's hear what you've got," said Joe, "and then I'll try to fix up something."

So Wallie stepped on the accelerator of his imagination and shot away.

"Just a kid; that's all he is; a regular boy. Get what I mean? Don't know the meanin' o' bad habits. Never tasted liquor in his life and would prob'bly get sick if he smelled it. Clean livin' put him up where he's at. Get what I mean? And modest and unassumin' as a school girl. He's so quiet you wouldn't never know he was round. And he'd go to jail before he'd talk about himself.

"No job at all to get him in shape, 'cause he's always that way. The only trouble we have with him is gettin' him to light into these poor bums they match him up with. He's scared he'll hurt somebody. Get what I mean? He's tickled to death over this match with Milton, 'cause everybody says Milton can stand the gaff. Midge'll maybe be able to cut loose a little this time. But

175

the last two bouts he had, the guys hadn't no
business in the ring with him, and he was holdin'
back all the w'ile for the fear he'd kill somebody.
Get what I mean?"

"Is he married?" inquired Joe.

"Say, you'd think he was married to hear him
rave about them kiddies he's got. His fam'ly's
up in Canada to their summer home and Midge
is wild to get up there with 'em. He thinks more
o' that wife and them kiddies than all the money
in the world. Get what I mean?"

"How many children has he?"

"I don't know, four or five, I guess. All boys
and every one of 'em a dead ringer for their dad."

"Is his father living?"

"No, the old man died when he was a kid. But
he's got a grand old mother and a kid brother out
in Chi. They're the first ones he thinks about
after a match, them and his wife and kiddies.
And he don't forget to send the old woman a
thousand bucks after every bout. He's goin to
buy her a new home as soon as they pay him off for
this match."

"How about his brother? Is he going to tackle
the game?"

"Sure, and Midge says he'll be a champion
before he's twenty years old. They're a fightin'
fam'ly and all of 'em honest and straight as a die.
Get what I mean? A fella that I can't tell you

Champion

his name come to Midge in Milwaukee onct and
wanted him to throw a fight and Midge give him
such a trimmin' in the street that he couldn't
go on that night. That's the kind he is. Get
what I mean?"

Joe Morgan hung around the camp until Midge
and his trainers returned.

"One o' the boys from *The News*," said Wallie
by way of introduction. "I been givin' him your
fam'ly hist'ry."

"Did he give you good dope?" he inquired.

"He's some historian," said Joe.

"Don't call me no names," said Wallie smiling.
"Call us up if they's anything more you want.
And keep your eyes on us Monday night. Get
what I mean?"

The story in Sunday's *News* was read by thou-
sands of lovers of the manly art. It was well written and full of human interest. Its slight inac-
curacies went unchallenged, though three readers,
besides Wallie Adams and Midge Kelly, saw and
recognized them. The three were Grace, Tommy
Haley and Jerome Harris and the comments they
made were not for publication.

Neither the Mrs. Kelly in Chicago nor the Mrs.
Kelly in Milwaukee knew that there was such a
paper as the New York *News*. And even if they
had known of it and that it contained two columns
of reading matter about Midge, neither mother

How to Write Short Stories

nor wife could have bought it. For *The News* on Sunday is a nickel a copy.

Joe Morgan could have written more accurately, no doubt, if instead of Wallie Adams, he had interviewed Ellen Kelly and Connie Kelly and Emma Kelly and Lou Hersch and Grace and Jerome Harris and Tommy Haley and Hap Collins and two or three Milwaukee bartenders.

But a story built on their evidence would never have passed the sporting editor.

"Suppose you can prove it," that gentleman would have said, "It wouldn't get us anything but abuse to print it. The people don't want to see him knocked. He's champion."

MY ROOMY

A house party in a fashionable Third Avenue laundry and the predicament of a hero who has posed as a famous elevator starter form the background of this delightful tale of life in the Kiwanis Club.

VI

MY ROOMY

I

No—I ain't signed for next year; but there won't be no trouble about that. The dough part of it is all fixed up. John and me talked it over and I'll sign as soon as they send me a contract. All I told him was that he'd have to let me pick my own roommate after this and not sic no wild man on to me.

You know I didn't hit much the last two months o' the season. Some o' the boys, I notice, wrote some stuff about me gettin' old and losin' my battin' eye. That's all bunk! The reason I didn't hit was because I wasn't gettin' enough sleep. And the reason for that was Mr. Elliott.

He wasn't with us after the last part o' May, but I roomed with him long enough to get the insomny. I was the only guy in the club game enough to stand for him; but I was sorry afterward that I done it, because it sure did put a crimp in my little old average.

And do you know where he is now? I got a letter today and I'll read it to you. No—I guess

How to Write Short Stories

I better tell you somethin' about him first. You
fellers never got acquainted with him and you
ought to hear the dope to understand the letter.
I'll make it as short as I can.

He didn't play in no league last year. He was
with some semi-pros over in Michigan and somebody writes John about him. So John sends Needham over to look at him. Tom stayed there
Saturday and Sunday, and seen him work twice.
He was playin' the outfield, but as luck would
have it they wasn't a fly ball hit in his direction
in both games. A base hit was made out his way
and he booted it, and that's the only report Tom
could get on his fieldin'. But he wallops two over
the wall in one day and they catch two line drives
off him. The next day he gets four blows and two
o' them is triples.

So Tom comes back and tells John the guy is
a whale of a hitter and fast as Cobb, but he don't
know nothin' about his fieldin'. Then John signs
him to a contract—twelve hundred or somethin'
like that. We'd been in Tampa a week before he
showed up. Then he comes to the hotel and just
sits round all day, without tellin' nobody who he
was. Finally the bellhops was going to chase him
out and he says he's one o' the ballplayers. Then
the clerk gets John to go over and talk to him.
He tells John his name and says he hasn't had
nothin' to eat for three days, because he was

My Roomy

broke. John told me afterward that he'd drew
about three hundred in advance—last winter some-
time. Well, they took him in the dinin' room and
they tell me he inhaled about four meals at once.
That night they roomed him with Heine.

Next mornin' Heine and me walks out to the
grounds together and Heine tells me about him.
He says:

"Don't never call me a bug again. They got
me roomin' with the champion o' the world."

"Who is he?" I says.

"I don't know and I don't want to know,"
says Heine; "but if they stick him in there with
me again I'll jump to the Federals. To start with,
he ain't got no baggage. I ast him where his trunk
was and he says he didn't have none. Then I
ast him if he didn't have no suitcase, and he says:
'No. What do you care?' I was goin' to lend
him some pajamas, but he put on the shirt o' the
uniform John give him last night and slept in
that. He was asleep when I got up this mornin'.
I seen his collar layin' on the dresser and it looked
like he had wore it in Pittsburgh every day for a
year. So I throwed it out the window and he
comes down to breakfast with no collar. I ast
him what size collar he wore and he says he didn't
want none, because he wasn't goin' out nowheres.
After breakfast he beat it up to the room again
and put on his uniform. When I got up there he

183

How to Write Short Stories

was lookin' in the glass at himself, and he done it all the time I was dressin'."

When we got out to the park I got my first look at him. Pretty good-lookin' guy, too, in his unie —big shoulders and well put together; built somethin' like Heine himself. He was talkin' to John when I come up.

"What position do you play?" John was askin' him.

"I play anywheres," says Elliott.

"You're the kind I'm lookin' for," says John. Then he says: "You was an outfielder up there in Michigan, wasn't you?"

"I don't care where I play," says Elliott.

John sends him to the outfield and forgets all about him for a while. Pretty soon Miller comes in and says:

"I ain't goin' to shag for no bush outfielder!"

John ast him what was the matter, and Miller tells him that Elliott ain't doin' nothin' but just standin' out there; that he ain't makin' no attemp' to catch the fungoes, and that he won't even chase 'em. Then John starts watchin' him, and it was just like Miller said. Larry hit one pretty near in his lap and he stepped out o' the way. John calls him in and ast him:

"Why don't you go after them fly balls?"

"Because I don't want 'em," says Elliott.

John gets sarcastic and says:

My Roomy

"What do you want? Of course we'll see that you get anythin' you want!"

"Give me a ticket back home," says Elliott.

"Don't you want to stick with the club?" says John, and the busher tells him, no, he certainly did not. Then John tells him he'll have to pay his own fare home and Elliott don't get sore at all. He just says:

"Well, I'll have to stick, then—because I'm broke."

We was havin' battin' practice and John tells him to go up and hit a few. And you ought to of seen him bust 'em!

Lavender was in there workin' and he'd been pitchin' a little all winter, so he was in pretty good shape. He lobbed one up to Elliott, and he hit it 'way up in some trees outside the fence—about a mile, I guess. Then John tells Jimmy to put somethin' on the ball. Jim comes through with one of his fast ones and the kid slams it agin the right-field wall on a line.

"Give him your spitter!" yells John, and Jim handed him one. He pulled it over first base so fast that Bert, who was standin' down there, couldn't hardly duck in time. If it'd hit him it'd killed him.

Well, he kep' on hittin' everythin' Jim give him—and Jim had somethin' too. Finally John gets Pierce warmed up and sends him out to pitch,

185

tellin' him to hand Elliott a flock o' curve balls. He wanted to see if lefthanders was goin' to bother him. But he slammed 'em right along, and I don't b'lieve he hit more'n two the whole mornin' that wouldn't of been base hits in a game.

They sent him out to the outfield again in the afternoon, and after a lot o' coaxin' Leach got him to go after fly balls; but that's all he did do —just go after 'em. One hit him on the bean and another on the shoulder. He run back after the short ones and 'way in after the ones that went over his head. He catched just one—a line drive that he couldn't get out o' the way of; and then he acted like it hurt his hands.

I come back to the hotel with John. He ast me what I thought of Elliott.

"Well," I says, "he'd be the greatest ballplayer in the world if he could just play ball. He sure can bust 'em."

John says he was afraid he couldn't never make an outfielder out o' him. He says:

"I'll try him on the infield to-morrow. They must be some place he can play. I never seen a lefthand hitter that looked so good agin lefthand pitchin'—and he's got a great arm; but he acts like he'd never saw a fly ball."

Well, he was just as bad on the infield. They put him at short and he was like a sieve. You could of drove a hearse between him and second base

My Roomy

without him gettin' near it. He'd stoop over for a ground ball about the time it was bouncin' up agin the fence; and when he'd try to cover the bag on a peg he'd trip over it.

They tried him at first base and sometimes he'd run 'way over in the coachers' box and sometimes out in right field lookin' for the bag. Once Heine shot one acrost at him on a line and he never touched it with his hands. It went bam! right in the pit of his stomach—and the lunch he'd ate didn't do him no good.

Finally John just give up and says he'd have to keep him on the bench and let him earn his pay by bustin' 'em a couple o' times a week or so. We all agreed with John that this bird would be a whale of a pinch hitter—and we was right too. He was hittin' 'way over five hundred when the blowoff come, along about the last o' May.

II

Before the trainin' trip was over, Elliott had roomed with pretty near everybody in the club. Heine raised an awful holler after the second night down there and John put the bug in with Needham. Tom stood him for three nights. Then he doubled up with Archer, and Schulte, and Miller, and Leach, and Saier—and the whole bunch in turn, averagin' about two nights with each one before they put up a kick. Then John tried him with some o' the youngsters, but they wouldn't stand for him no more'n the others. They all said he was crazy and they was afraid he'd get violent some night and stick a knife in 'em.

He always insisted on havin' the water run in the bathtub all night, because he said it reminded him of the sound of the dam near his home. The fellers might get up four or five times a night and shut off the faucet, but he'd get right up after 'em and turn it on again. Carter, a big bush pitcher from Georgia, started a fight with him about it one night, and Elliott pretty near killed him. So the rest o' the bunch, when they'd saw Carter's map next mornin', didn't have the nerve to do nothin' when it come their turn.

Another o' his habits was the thing that scared 'em, though. He'd brought a razor with him—in his pocket, I guess—and he used to do his shavin' in the middle o' the night. Instead o' doin' it in the bathroom he'd lather his face and then come out and stand in front o' the lookin'-glass on the dresser. Of course he'd have all the lights turned on, and that was bad enough when a feller wanted to sleep; but the worst of it was that he'd stop shavin' every little while and turn round and stare at the guy who was makin' a failure o' tryin' to sleep. Then he'd wave his razor round in the air and laugh, and begin shavin' agin. You can imagine how comf'table his roomies felt!

My Roomy

John had bought him a suitcase and some clothes and things, and charged 'em up to him. He'd drew so much dough in advance that he didn't have nothin' comin' till about June. He never thanked John and he'd wear one shirt and one collar till some one throwed 'em away.

Well, we finally gets to Indianapolis, and we was goin' from there to Cincy to open. The last day in Indianapolis John come and ast me how I'd like to change roomies. I says I was perfectly satisfied with Larry. Then John says:

"I wisht you'd try Elliott. The other boys all kicks on him, but he seems to hang round you a lot and I b'lieve you could get along all right."

"Why don't you room him alone?" I ast.

"The boss or the hotels won't stand for us roomin' alone," says John. "You go ahead and try it, and see how you make out. If he's too much for you let me know; but he likes you and I think he'll be diff'rent with a guy who can talk to him like you can."

So I says I'd tackle it, because I didn't want to throw John down. When we got to Cincy they stuck Elliott and me in one room, and we was together till he quit us.

III

I went to the room early that night, because we was goin' to open next day and I wanted to feel

189

like somethin'. First thing I done when I got undressed was turn on both faucets in the bathtub. They was makin' an awful racket when Elliott finally come in about midnight. I was layin' awake and I opened right up on him. I says:

"Don't shut off that water, because I like to hear it run."

Then I turned over and pretended to be asleep. The bug got his clothes off, and then what did he do but go in the bathroom and shut off the water! Then he come back in the room and says:

"I guess no one's goin' to tell me what to do in here."

But I kep' right on pretendin' to sleep and didn't pay no attention. When he'd got into his bed I jumped out o' mine and turned on all the lights and begun stroppin' my razor. He says:

"What's comin' off?"

"Some o' my whiskers," I says. "I always shave along about this time."

"No, you don't!" he says. "I was in your room one mornin' down in Louisville and I seen you shavin' then."

"Well," I says, "the boys tell me you shave in the middle o' the night; and I thought if I done all the things you do mebbe I'd get so's I could hit like you."

"You must be superstitious!" he says. And I told him I was. "I'm a good hitter," he says,

My Roomy

"and I'd be a good hitter if I never shaved at all. That don't make no diff'rence."

"Yes, it does," I says. "You prob'ly hit good because you shave at night; but you'd be a better fielder if you shaved in the mornin'."

You see, I was tryin' to be just as crazy as him—though that wasn't hardly possible.

"If that's right," says he, "I'll do my shavin' in the mornin'—because I seen in the papers where the boys says that if I could play the outfield like I can hit I'd be as good as Cobb. They tell.me Cobb gets twenty thousand a year."

"No," I says; "he don't get that much—but he gets about ten times as much as you do."

"Well," he says, "I'm goin' to be as good as him, because I need the money."

"What do you want with money?" I says.

He just laughed and didn't say nothin'; but from that time on the water didn't run in the bathtub nights and he done his shavin' after breakfast. I didn't notice, though, that he looked any better in fieldin' practice.

IV

It rained one day in Cincy and they trimmed us two out o' the other three; but it wasn't Elliott's fault.

They had Larry beat four to one in the ninth innin' o' the first game. Archer gets on with two out, and John sends my roomy up to hit—though Benton, a lefthander, is workin' for them. The first thing Benton serves up there Elliott cracks it a mile over Hobby's head. It would of been good for three easy—only Archer—playin' safe, o' course—pulls up at third base. Tommy couldn't do nothin' and we was licked.

The next day he hits one out o' the park off the Indian; but we was 'way behind and they was nobody on at the time. We copped the last one without usin' no pinch hitters.

I didn't have no trouble with him nights durin' the whole series. He come to bed pretty late while we was there and I told him he'd better not let John catch him at it.

"What would he do?" he says.

"Fine you fifty," I says.

"He can't fine me a dime," he says, "because I ain't got it."

Then I told him he'd be fined all he had comin' if he didn't get in the hotel before midnight; but he just laughed and says he didn't think John had a kick comin' so long as he kep' bustin' the ball.

"Some day you'll go up there and you won't bust it," I says.

"That'll be an accident," he says.

That stopped me and I didn't say nothin'. What could you say to a guy who hated himself like that?

My Roomy

The "accident" happened in St. Louis the first day. We needed two runs in the eighth and Saier and Brid was on, with two out. John tells Elliott to go up in Pierce's place. The bug goes up and Griner gives him two bad balls—'way outside. I thought they was goin' to walk him—and it looked like good judgment, because they'd heard what he done in Cincy. But no! Griner comes back with a fast one right over and Elliott pulls it down the right foul line, about two foot foul. He hit it so hard you'd of thought they'd sure walk him then; but Griner gives him another fast one. He slammed it again just as hard, but foul. Then Griner gives him one 'way outside and it's two and three. John says, on the bench:

"If they don't walk him now he'll bust that fence down."

I thought the same and I was sure Griner wouldn't give him nothin' to hit; but he come with a curve and Rigler calls Elliott out. From where we sat the last one looked low, and I thought Elliott'd make a kick. He come back to the bench smilin'.

John starts for his position, but stopped and ast the bug what was the matter with that one. Any busher I ever knowed would of said, "It was too low," or "It was outside," or "It was inside." Elliott says:

"Nothin' at all. It was right over the middle."

193

How to Write Short Stories

"Why didn't you bust it, then?" says John.

"I was afraid I'd kill somebody," says Elliott, and laughed like a big boob.

John was pretty near chokin'.

"What are you laughin' at?" he says.

"I was thinkin' of a nickel show I seen in Cincinnati," says the bug.

"Well," says John, so mad he couldn't hardly see, "that show and that laugh'll cost you fifty."

We got beat, and I wouldn't of blamed John if he'd fined him his whole season's pay.

Up 'n the room that night I told him he'd better cut out that laughin' stuff when we was gettin' trimmed or he never would have no pay day. Then he got confidential.

"Pay day wouldn't do me no good," he says. "When I'm all squared up with the club and begin to have a pay day I'll only get a hundred bucks at a time, and I'll owe that to some o' you fellers. I wisht we could win the pennant and get in on that World's Series dough. Then I'd get a bunch at once."

"What would you do with a bunch o' dough?" I ast him.

"Don't tell nobody, sport," he says; "but if I ever get five hundred at once I'm goin' to get married."

"Oh!" I says. "And who's the lucky girl?"

My Roomy

"She's a girl up in Muskegon," says Elliott; "and you're right when you call her lucky."

"You don't like yourself much, do you?" I says.

"I got reason to like myself," says he. "You'd like yourself, too, if you could hit 'em like me."

"Well," I says, "you didn't show me no hittin' to-day."

"I couldn't hit because I was laughin' too hard," says Elliott.

"What was it you was laughin' at?" I says.

"I was laughin' at that pitcher," he says. "He thought he had somethin' and he didn't have nothin'."

"He had enough to whiff you with," I says.

"He didn't have nothin'!" says he again. "I was afraid if I busted one off him they'd can him, and then I couldn't never hit agin him no more."

Naturally I didn't have no comeback to that. I just sort o' gasped and got ready to go to sleep; but he wasn't through.

"I wisht you could see this bird!" he says.

"What bird?" I says.

"This dame that's nuts about me," he says.

"Good-looker?" I ast.

"No," he says; "she ain't no bear for looks. They ain't nothin' about her for a guy to rave over till you hear her sing. She sure can holler some."

"What kind o' voice has she got?" I ast.

How to Write Short Stories

"A bear," says he.

"No," I says; "I mean is she a barytone or an air?"

"I don't know," he says; "but she's got the loudest voice I ever hear on a woman. She's pretty near got me beat."

"Can you sing?" I says; and I was sorry right afterward that I ast him that question.

I guess it must of been bad enough to have the water runnin' night after night and to have him wavin' that razor round; but that couldn't of been nothin' to his singin'. Just as soon as I'd pulled that boner he says, "Listen to me!" and starts in on 'Silver Threads Among the Gold.' Mind you, it was after midnight and they was guests all round us tryin' to sleep!

They used to be noise enough in our club when we had Hofman and Sheckard and Richie harmonizin'; but this bug's voice was louder'n all o' theirn combined. We once had a pitcher named Martin Walsh—brother o' Big Ed's—and I thought he could drown out the Subway; but this guy made a boiler factory sound like Dummy Taylor. If the whole hotel wasn't awake when he'd howled the first line it's a pipe they was when he cut loose, which he done when he come to "Always young and fair to me." Them words could of been heard easy in East St. Louis.

He didn't get no encore from me, but he goes

My Roomy

right through it again—or starts to. I knowed somethin' was goin' to happen before he finished—and somethin' did. The night clerk and the house detective come bangin' at the door. I let 'em in and they had plenty to say. If we made another sound the whole club'd be canned out o' the hotel. I tried to salve 'em, and I says:

"He won't sing no more."

But Elliott swelled up like a poisoned pup.

"Won't I?" he says. "I'll sing all I want to."

"You won't sing in here," says the clerk.

"They ain't room for my voice in here anyways," he says. "I'll go outdoors and sing."

And he puts his clothes on and ducks out. I didn't make no attemp' to stop him. I heard him bellowin' 'Silver Threads' down the corridor and down the stairs, with the clerk and the dick chasin' him all the way and tellin' him to shut up.

Well, the guests make a holler the next mornin'; and the hotel people tells Charlie Williams that he'll either have to let Elliott stay somewheres else or the whole club'll have to move. Charlie tells John, and John was thinkin' o' settlin' the question by releasin' Elliott.

I guess he'd about made up his mind to do it; but that afternoon they had us three to one in the ninth, and we got the bases full, with two down and Larry's turn to hit. Elliott had been sittin' on the bench sayin' nothin'.

How to Write Short Stories

"Do you think you can hit one today?" says John.

"I can hit one any day," says Elliott.

"Go up and hit that lefthander, then," says John, "and remember there's nothin' to laugh at."

Sallee was workin'—and workin' good; but that didn't bother the bug. He cut into one, and it went between Oakes and Whitted like a shot. He come into third standin' up and we was a run to the good. Sallee was so sore he kind o' forgot himself and took pretty near his full wind-up pitchin' to Tommy. And what did Elliott do but steal home and get away with it clean!

Well, you couldn't can him after that, could you? Charlie gets him a room somewheres and I was relieved of his company that night. The next evenin' we beat it for Chi to play about two weeks at home. He didn't tell nobody where he roomed there and I didn't see nothin' of him, 'cep' out to the park. I ast him what he did with himself nights and he says:

"Same as I do on the road—borrow some dough some place and go to the nickel shows."

"You must be stuck on 'em," I says.

"Yes," he says; "I like the ones where they kill people—because I want to learn how to do it. I may have that job some day."

"Don't pick on me," I says.

My Roomy

"Oh," says the bug, "you never can tell who I'll pick on."

It seemed as if he just couldn't learn nothin' about fieldin', and finally John told him to keep out o' the practice.

"A ball might hit him in the temple and croak him," says John.

But he busted up a couple o' games for us at home, beatin' Pittsburgh once and Cincy once.

V

They give me a great big room at the hotel in Pittsburgh; so the fellers picked it out for the poker game. We was playin' along about ten o'clock one night when in come Elliott—the earliest he'd showed up since we'd been roomin' together. They was only five of us playin' and Tom ast him to sit in.

"I'm busted," he says.

"Can you play poker?" I ast him.

"They's nothin' I can't do!" he says. "Slip me a couple o' bucks and I'll show you."

So I slipped him a couple o' bucks and honestly hoped he'd win, because I knowed he never had no dough. Well, Tom dealt him a hand and he picks it up and says:

"I only got five cards."

"How many do you want?" I says.

How to Write Short Stories

"Oh," he says, "if that's all I get I'll try to make 'em do."

The pot was cracked and raised, and he stood the raise. I says to myself: "There goes my two bucks!" But no—he comes out with three queens and won the dough. It was only about seven bucks; but you'd of thought it was a million to see him grab it. He laughed like a kid.

"Guess I can't play this game!" he says; and he had me fooled for a minute—I thought he must of been kiddin' when he complained of only havin' five cards.

He copped another pot right afterward and was sittin' there with about eleven bucks in front of him when Jim opens a roodle pot for a buck. I stays and so does Elliott. Him and Jim both drawed one card and I took three. I had kings or queens—I forget which. I didn't help 'em none; so when Jim bets a buck I throws my hand away.

"How much can I bet?" says the bug.

"You can raise Jim a buck if you want to," I says.

So he bets two dollars. Jim comes back at him. He comes right back at Jim. Jim raises him again and he tilts Jim right back. Well, when he'd boosted Jim with the last buck he had, Jim says:

"I'm ready to call. I guess you got me beat. What have you got?"

My Roomy

"I know what I've got, all right," says Elliott. "I've got a straight." And he throws his hand down. Sure enough, it was a straight, eight high. Jim pretty near fainted and so did I.

The bug had started pullin' in the dough when Jim stops him.

"Here! Wait a minute!" says Jim. "I thought you had somethin'. I filled up." Then Jim lays down his nine full.

"You beat me, I guess," says Elliott, and he looked like he'd lost his last friend.

"Beat you?" says Jim. "Of course I beat you! What did you think I had?"

"Well," says the bug, "I thought you might have a small flush or somethin'."

When I regained consciousness he was beggin' for two more bucks.

"What for?" I says. "To play poker with? You're barred from the game for life!"

"Well," he says, "if I can't play no more I want to go to sleep, and you fellers will have to get out o' this room."

Did you ever hear o' nerve like that? This was the first night he'd came in before twelve and he orders the bunch out so's he can sleep! We politely suggested to him to go to Brooklyn.

Without sayin' a word he starts in on his 'Silver Threads'; and it wasn't two minutes till the game was busted up and the bunch—all but me—was

201

out o' there. I'd of beat it too, only he stopped
yellin' as soon as they'd went.

"You're some buster!" I says. "You bust up
ball games in the afternoon and poker games at
night."

"Yes," he says; "that's my business—bustin'
things."

And before I knowed what he was about he
picked up the pitcher of ice-water that was on the
floor and throwed it out the window—through
the glass and all.

Right then I give him a plain talkin' to. I tells
him how near he come to gettin' canned down in
St. Louis because he raised so much Cain singin'
in the hotel.

"But I had to keep my voice in shape," he
says. "If I ever get dough enough to get married
the girl and me'll go out singin' together."

"Out where?" I ast.

"Out on the vaudeville circuit," says Elliott.

"Well," I says, "if her voice is like yours you'll
be wastin' money if you travel round. Just stay
up in Muskegon and we'll hear you, all right!"

I told him he wouldn't never get no dough if
he didn't behave himself. That, even if we got
in the World's Series, he wouldn't be with us—
unless he cut out the foolishness.

"We ain't goin' to get in no World's Series,"
he says, "and I won't never get a bunch o' money

My Roomy

at once; so it looks like I couldn't get married this fall."

Then I told him we played a city series every fall. He'd never thought o' that and it tickled him to death. I told him the losers always got about five hundred apiece and that we were about due to win it and get about eight hundred. "But," I says, "we still got a good chance for the old pennant; and if I was you I wouldn't give up hope o' that yet—not where John can hear you, anyway."

"No," he says, "we won't win no pennant, because he won't let me play reg'lar; but I don't care so long as we're sure o' that city-series dough."

"You ain't sure of it if you don't behave," I says.

"Well," says he, very serious, "I guess I'll behave." And he did—till we made our first Eastern trip.

VI

We went to Boston first, and that crazy bunch goes out and piles up a three-run lead on us in seven innin's the first day. It was the pitcher's turn to lead off in the eighth, so up goes Elliott to bat for him. He kisses the first thing they hands him for three bases; and we says, on the bench: "Now we'll get 'em!"—because, you know, a three-run lead wasn't nothin' in Boston.

How to Write Short Stories

"Stay right on that bag!" John hollers to El-liott.

Mebbe if John hadn't said nothin' to him everythin' would of been all right; but when Per-due starts to pitch the first ball to Tommy, Elliott starts to steal home. He's out as far as from here to Seattle.

If I'd been carryin' a gun I'd of shot him right through the heart. As it was, I thought John'd kill him with a bat, because he was standin' there with a couple of 'em, waitin' for his turn; but I guess John was too stunned to move. He didn't even seem to see Elliott when he went to the bench. After I'd cooled off a little I says:

"Beat it and get into your clothes before John comes in. Then go to the hotel and keep out o' sight."

When I got up in the room afterward, there was Elliott, lookin' as innocent and happy as though he'd won fifty bucks with a pair o' treys.

"I thought you might of killed yourself," I says.

"What for?" he says.

"For that swell play you made," says I.

"What was the matter with the play?" ast Elliott, surprised. "It was all right when I done it in St. Louis."

"Yes," I says; "but they was two out in St. Louis and we wasn't no three runs behind."

My Roomy

"Well," he says, "if it was all right in St. Louis I don't see why it was wrong here."

"It's a diff'rent climate here," I says, too disgusted to argue with him.

"I wonder if they'd let me sing in this climate?" says Elliott.

"No," I says. "Don't sing in this hotel, because we don't want to get fired out o' here—the eats is too good."

"All right," he says. "I won't sing." But when I starts down to supper he says: "I'm li'ble to do somethin' worse'n sing."

He didn't show up in the dinin' room and John went to the boxin' show after supper; so it looked like him and Elliott wouldn't run into each other till the murder had left John's heart. I was glad o' that—because a Mass'chusetts jury might not consider it justifiable hommercide if one guy croaked another for givin' the Boston club a game.

I went down to the corner and had a couple o' beers; and then I come straight back, intendin' to hit the hay. The elevator boy had went for a drink or somethin', and they was two old ladies already waitin' in the car when I stepped in. Right along after me comes Elliott.

"Where's the boy that's supposed to run this car?" he says. I told him the boy'd be right back; but he says: "I can't wait. I'm much too sleepy."

How to Write Short Stories

And before I could stop him he'd slammed the door and him and I and the poor old ladies was shootin' up.

"Let us off at the third floor, please!" says one o' the ladies, her voice kind o' shakin'.

"Sorry, madam," says the bug; "but this is a express and we don't stop at no third floor."

I grabbed his arm and tried to get him away from the machinery; but he was as strong as a ox and he throwed me agin the side o' the car like I was a baby. We went to the top faster'n I ever rode in an elevator before. And then we shot down to the bottom, hittin' the bumper down there so hard I thought we'd be smashed to splinters.

The ladies was too scared to make a sound durin' the first trip; but while we was goin' up and down the second time—even faster'n the first—they begun to scream. I was hollerin' my head off at him to quit and he was makin' more noise than the three of us—pretendin' he was the locomotive and the whole crew o' the train.

Don't never ask me how many times we went up and down! The women fainted on the third trip and I guess I was about as near it as I'll ever get. The elevator boy and the bellhops and the waiters and the night clerk and everybody was jumpin' round the lobby screamin'; but no one seemed to know how to stop us.

My Roomy

Finally—on about the tenth trip, I guess—he slowed down and stopped at the fifth floor, where we was roomin'. He opened the door and beat it for the room, while I, though I was tremblin' like a leaf, run the car down to the bottom.

The night clerk knowed me pretty well and knowed I wouldn't do nothin' like that; so him and I didn't argue, but just got to work together to bring the old women to. While we was doin' that Elliott must of run down the stairs and slipped out o' the hotel, because when they sent the officers up to the room after him he'd blowed.

They was goin' to fire the club out; but Charlie had a good stand-in with Amos, the proprietor, and he fixed it up to let us stay—providin' Elliott kep' away. The bug didn't show up at the ball park next day and we didn't see no more of him till we got on the rattler for New York. Charlie and John both bawled him, but they give him a berth—an upper—and we pulled into the Grand Central Station without him havin' made no effort to wreck the train.

VII

I'd studied the thing pretty careful, but hadn't come to no conclusion. I was sure he wasn't no stew, because none o' the boys had ever saw him even take a glass o' beer, and I couldn't never detect the odor o' booze on him. And if he'd been a dope I'd of knew about it—roomin' with him.

There wouldn't of been no mystery about it if he'd been a lefthand pitcher—but he wasn't. He wasn't nothin' but a whale of a hitter and he throwed with his right arm. He hit lefthanded, o' course; but so did Saier and Brid and Schulte and me, and John himself; and none of us was violent. I guessed he must of been just a plain nut and li'ble to break out any time.

They was a letter waitin' for him at New York, and I took it, intendin' to give it to him at the park, because I didn't think they'd let him room at the hotel; but after breakfast he come up to the room, with his suitcase. It seems he'd promised John and Charlie to be good, and made it so strong they b'lieved him.

I give him his letter, which was addressed in a girl's writin' and come from Muskegon.

"From the girl?" I says.

"Yes," he says; and, without openin' it, he tore it up and throwed it out the window.

"Had a quarrel?" I ast.

"No, no," he says; "but she can't tell me nothin' I don't know already. Girls always writes the same junk. I got one from her in Pittsburgh, but I didn't read it."

"I guess you ain't so stuck on her," I says.

My Roomy

He swells up and says:

"Of course I'm stuck on her! If I wasn't, do you think I'd be goin' round with this bunch and gettin' insulted all the time? I'm stickin' here because o' that series dough, so's I can get hooked."

"Do you think you'd settle down if you was married?" I ast him.

"Settle down?" he says. "Sure, I'd settle down. I'd be so happy that I wouldn't have to look for no excitement."

Nothin' special happened that night 'cep' that he come in the room about one o'clock and woke me up by pickin' up the foot o' the bed and droppin' it on the floor, sudden-like.

"Give me a key to the room," he says.

"You must of had a key," I says, "or you couldn't of got in."

"That's right!" he says, and beat it to bed.

One o' the reporters must of told Elliott that John had ast for waivers on him and New York had refused to waive, because next mornin' he come to me with that dope.

"New York's goin' to win this pennant!" he says.

"Well," I says, "they will if some one else don't. But what of it?"

"I'm goin' to play with New York," he says, "so's I can get the World's Series dough."

How to Write Short Stories

"How you goin' to get away from this club?"
I ast.

"Just watch me!" he says. "I'll be with New York before this series is over."

Well, the way he goes after the job was original, anyway. Rube'd had one of his good days the day before and we'd got a trimmin'; but this second day the score was tied up at two runs apiece in the tenth, and Big Jeff'd been wabblin' for two or three innin's.

Well, he walks Saier and me, with one out, and Mac sends for Matty, who was warmed up and ready. John sticks Elliott in in Brid's place and the bug pulls one into the right-field stand.

It's a cinch McGraw thinks well of him then, and might of went after him if he hadn't went crazy the next afternoon. We're tied up in the ninth and Matty's workin'. John sends Elliott up with the bases choked; but he doesn't go right up to the plate. He walks over to their bench and calls McGraw out. Mac tells us about it afterward.

"I can bust up this game right here!" says Elliott.

"Go ahead," says Mac; "but be careful he don't whiff you."

Then the bug pulls it.

"If I whiff," he says, "will you get me on your club?"

My Roomy

"Sure!" says Mac, just as anybody would.

By this time Bill Koem was hollerin' about the delay; so up goes Elliott and gives the worst burlesque on tryin' to hit that you ever see. Matty throws one a mile outside and high, and the bug swings like it was right over the heart. Then Matty throws one at him and he ducks out o' the way—but swings just the same. Matty must of been wise by this time, for he pitches one so far outside that the Chief almost has to go to the coachers' box after it. Elliott takes his third healthy and runs through the field down to the clubhouse.

We got beat in the eleventh; and when we went in to dress he has his street clothes on. Soon as he seen John comin' he says: "I got to see McGraw!" And he beat it.

John was goin' to the fights that night; but before he leaves the hotel he had waivers on Elliott from everybody and had sold him to Atlanta.

"And," says John, "I don't care if they pay for him or not."

My roomy blows in about nine and got the letter from John out of his box. He was goin' to tear it up, but I told him they was news in it. He opens it and reads where he's sold. I was still sore at him; so I says:

"Thought you was goin' to get on the New York club?"

"No," he says. "I got turned down cold. McGraw says he wouldn't have me in his club. He says he'd had Charlie Faust—and that was enough for him."

He had a kind o' crazy look in his eyes; so when he starts up to the room I follows him.

"What are you goin' to do now?" I says.

"I'm goin' to sell this ticket to Atlanta," he says, "and go back to Muskegon, where I belong."

"I'll help you pack," I says.

"No," says the bug. "I come into this league with this suit o'clothes and a collar. They can have the rest of it." Then he sits down on the bed and begins to cry like a baby. "No series dough for me," he blubbers, "and no weddin' bells! My girl'll die when she hears about it!"

Of course that made me feel kind o' rotten, and I says:

"Brace up, boy! The best thing you can do is go to Atlanta and try hard. You'll be up here again next year."

"You can't tell me where to go!" he says, and he wasn't cryin' no more. "I'll go where I please —and I'm li'ble to take you with me."

I didn't want no argument, so I kep' still. Pretty soon he goes up to the lookin'-glass and stares at himself for five minutes. Then, all of a sudden, he hauls off and takes a wallop at his reflection in the glass. Naturally he smashed the glass all to pieces and he cut his hand somethin' awful.

Without lookin' at it he come over to me and says: "Well, good-by, sport!"—and holds out his other hand to shake. When I starts to shake with him he smears his bloody hand all over my map. Then he laughed like a wild man and run out o' the room and out o' the hotel.

VIII

Well, boys, my sleep was broke up for the rest o' the season. It might of been because I was used to sleepin' in all kinds o' racket and excitement, and couldn't stand for the quiet after he'd went—or it might of been because I kep' thinkin' about him and feelin' sorry for him.

I of'en wondered if he'd settle down and be somethin' if he could get married; and finally I got to b'lievin' he would. So when we was dividin' the city series dough I was thinkin' of him and the girl. Our share o' the money—the losers', as usual—was twelve thousand seven hundred sixty bucks or somethin' like that. They was twenty-one of us and that meant six hundred seven bucks apiece. We was just goin' to cut it up that way when I says:

"Why not give a divvy to poor old Elliott?"

213

How to Write Short Stories

About fifteen of 'em at once told me that I was crazy. You see, when he got canned he owed everybody in the club. I guess he'd stuck me for the most—about seventy bucks—but I didn't care nothin' about that. I knowed he hadn't never reported to Atlanta, and I thought he was prob'ly busted and a bunch o' money might make things all right for him and the other songbird.

I made quite a speech to the fellers, tellin' 'em how he'd cried when he left us and how his heart'd been set on gettin' married on the series dough. I made it so strong that they finally fell for it. Our shares was cut to five hundred eighty apiece, and John sent him a check for a full share.

For a while I was kind o' worried about what I'd did. I didn't know if I was doin' right by the girl to give him the chance to marry her.

He'd told me she was stuck on him, and that's the only excuse I had for tryin' to fix it up between 'em; but, b'lieve me, if she was my sister or a friend o' mine I'd just as soon of had her manage the Cincinnati Club as marry that bird. I thought to myself:

"If she's all right she'll take acid in a month—and it'll be my fault; but if she's really stuck on him they must be somethin' wrong with her too, so what's the diff'rence?"

Then along comes this letter that I told you about. It's from some friend of hisn up there—

214

My Roomy

and they's a note from him. I'll read 'em to you and then I got to beat it for the station:

DEAR SIR: They have got poor Elliott locked up and they are goin' to take him to the asylum at Kalamazoo. He thanks you for the check, and we will use the money to see that he is made comf'table.

When the poor boy come back here he found that his girl was married to Joe Bishop, who runs a soda fountain. She had wrote to him about it, but he did not read her letters. The news drove him crazy—poor boy—and he went to the place where they was livin' with a baseball bat and very near killed 'em both. Then he marched down the street singin' 'Silver Threads Among the Gold' at the top of his voice. They was goin' to send him to prison for assault with intent to kill, but the jury decided he was crazy.

He wants to thank you again for the money.

Yours truly,

JIM——

I can't make out his last name—but it don't make no diff'rence. Now I'll read you his note:

OLD ROOMY: I was at bat twice and made two hits; but I guess I did not meet 'em square. They tell me they are both alive yet, which I did

215

not mean 'em to be. I hope they got good curve-
ball pitchers where I am goin'. I sure can bust
them curves—can't I, sport?

> Yours,
>
> B. ELLIOTT.

P. S.—The B stands for Buster.

That's all of it, fellers; and you can see I had
some excuse for not hittin'. You can also see why
I ain't never goin' to room with no bug again—
not for John or nobody else!

A CADDY'S DIARY

Critics have charged that this story is a direct steal from some of Barrie's earlier tales of adventures on the golf course. The author denies this, but admits his indebtedness to Gertrude Atherton for some of the scenes in the barber shop. Curiosity has often been expressed as to the identity of the man from whom the leading character is drawn, and guesses have ranged all the way from Al Jennings to Saavedra Miguel de Cervantes. The author takes this opportunity to announce that the original of the caddy is Wilkie Collins, and the story is based on the latter's actual experiences while he was night order clerk at the Pennsylvania Hotel.

VII

A CADDY'S DIARY

Wed. Apr. 12.

I am 16 of age and am a caddy at the Pleasant View Golf Club but only temporary as I expect to soon land a job some wheres as asst pro as my game is good enough now to be a pro but to young looking. My pal Joe Bean also says I have not got enough swell head to make a good pro but suppose that will come in time, Joe is a wise cracker.

But first will put down how I come to be writeing this diary, we have got a member name Mr Colby who writes articles in the newspapers and I hope for his sakes that he is a better writer then he plays golf but any way I cadded for him a good many times last yr and today he was out for the first time this yr and I cadded for him and we got talking about this in that and something was mentioned in regards to the golf articles by Alex Laird that comes out every Sun in the paper Mr Colby writes his articles for so I asked Mr Colby did he know how much Laird got paid for the articles and he said he did not know but supposed

219

that Laird had to split 50-50 with who ever wrote the articles for him. So I said don't he write the articles himself and Mr Colby said why no he guessed not. Laird may be a master mind in regards to golf he said, but that is no sign he can write about it as very few men can write decent let alone a pro. Writeing is a nag.

How do you learn it I asked him.

Well he said read what other people writes and study them and write things yourself, and maybe you will get on to the nag and maybe you wont.

Well Mr Colby I said do you think I could get on to it?

Why he said smileing I did not know that was your ambition to be a writer.

Not exactly was my reply, but I am going to be a golf pro myself and maybe some day I will get good enough so as the papers will want I should write them articles and if I can learn to write them myself why I will not have to hire another writer and split with them.

Well said Mr Colby smileing you have certainly got the right temperament for a pro, they are all big hearted fellows.

But listen Mr Colby I said if I want to learn it would not do me no good to copy down what other writers have wrote, what I would have to do would be write things out of my own head.

That is true said Mr Colby.

A Caddy's Diary

Well I said what could I write about?

Well said Mr Colby why don't you keep a diary and every night after your supper set down and write what happened that day and write who you cadded for and what they done only leave me out of it. And you can write down what people say and what you think and etc., it will be the best kind of practice for you, and once in a wile you can bring me your writeings and I will tell you the truth if they are good or rotten.

So that is how I come to be writeing this diary is so as I can get some practice writeing and maybe if I keep at it long enough I can get on to the nag.

Friday, Apr. 14.

We been haveing Apr. showers for a couple days and nobody out on the course so they has been nothing happen that I could write down in my diary but dont want to leave it go to long or will never learn the trick so will try and write a few lines about a caddys life and some of our members and etc.

Well I and Joe Bean is the 2 oldest caddys in the club and I been cadding now for 5 yrs and quit school 3 yrs ago tho my mother did not like it for me to quit but my father said he can read and write and figure so what is the use in keeping him there any longer as greek and latin dont get you no credit at the grocer, so they lied about my age to

221

the trunce officer and I been cadding every yr
from March till Nov and the rest of the winter I
work around Heismans store in the village.

Dureing the time I am cadding I genally always
manage to play at lease 9 holes a day myself on
wk days and some times 18 and am never more
then 2 or 3 over par figures on our course but it
is a cinch.

I played the engineers course 1 day last summer
in 75 which is some golf and some of our members who has been playing 20 yrs would give their
right eye to play as good as myself.

I use to play around with our pro Jack Andrews
till I got so as I could beat him pretty near every
time we played and now he wont play with me no
more, he is not a very good player for a pro but
they claim he is a good teacher. Personly I think
golf teachers is a joke tho I am glad people is
suckers enough to fall for it as I expect to make my
liveing that way. We have got a member Mr
Dunham who must of took 500 lessons in the past
3 yrs and when he starts to shoot he trys to remember all the junk Andrews has learned him
and he gets dizzy and they is no telling where the
ball will go and about the safest place to stand
when he is shooting is between he and the hole.

I dont beleive the club pays Andrews much
salery but of course he makes pretty fair money
giveing lessons but his best graft is a 3 some which

A Caddy's Diary

he plays 2 and 3 times a wk with Mr Perdue and
Mr Lewis and he gives Mr Lewis a stroke a hole
and they genally break some wheres near even but
Mr Perdue made a 83 one time so he thinks that
is his game so he insists on playing Jack even,
well they always play for $5.00 a hole and Andrews
makes $20.00 to $30.00 per round and if he wanted
to cut loose and play his best he could make $50.00
to $60.00 per round but a couple of wallops like
that and Mr Perdue might get cured so Jack
figures a small stedy income is safer.

I have got a pal name Joe Bean and we pal
around together as he is about my age and he
says some comical things and some times will
wisper some thing comical to me wile we are
cadding and it is all I can do to help from laughing
out loud, that is one of the first things a caddy
has got to learn is never laugh out loud only when
a member makes a joke. How ever on the days
when theys ladies on the course I dont get a
chance to caddy with Joe because for some reason
another the woman folks dont like Joe to caddy
for them wile on the other hand they are always
after me tho I am no Othello for looks or do I seek
their flavors, in fact it is just the opp and I try
to keep in the back ground when the fair sex ap-
pears on the seen as cadding for ladies means you
will get just so much money and no more as theys
no chance of them loosning up. As Joe says the

rule against tipping is the only rule the woman folks keeps.

Theys one lady how ever who I like to caddy for as she looks like Lillian Gish and it is a pleasure to just look at her and I would caddy for her for nothing tho it is hard to keep your eye on the ball when you are cadding for this lady, her name is Mrs Doane.

Sat. Apr. 15.

This was a long day and am pretty well wore out but must not get behind in my writeing practice. I and Joe carried all day for Mr Thomas and Mr Blake. Mr Thomas is the vice president of one of the big banks down town and he always slips you a $1.00 extra per round but beleive me you earn it cadding for Mr Thomas, there is just 16 clubs in his bag includeing 5 wood clubs tho he has not used the wood in 3 yrs but says he has got to have them along in case his irons goes wrong on him. I dont know how bad his irons will have to get before he will think they have went wrong on him but personly if I made some of the tee shots he made today I would certainly considder some kind of a change of weppons.

Mr Thomas is one of the kind of players that when it has took him more than 6 shots to get on the green he will turn to you and say how many have I had caddy and then you are suppose to pretend like you was thinking a minute and then

A Caddy's Diary

say 4, then he will say to the man he is playing with well I did not know if I had shot 4 or 5 but the caddy says it is 4. You see in this way it is not him that is cheating but the caddy but he makes it up to the caddy afterwards with a $1.00 tip.

Mr Blake gives Mr Thomas a stroke a hole and they play a $10.00 nassua and niether one of them wins much money from the other one but even if they did why $10.00 is chickens food to men like they. But the way they crab and squak about different things you would think their last $1.00 was at stake. Mr Thomas started out this A. M. with a 8 and a 7 and of course that spoilt the day for him and me to. Theys lots of men that if they dont make a good score on the first 2 holes they will founder all the rest of the way around and raze H with their caddy and if I was laying out a golf course I would make the first 2 holes so darn easy that you could not help from getting a 4 or better on them and in that way everybody would start off good natured and it would be a few holes at lease before they begun to turn sour.

Mr Thomas was beat both in the A. M. and P. M. in spite of my help as Mr Blake is a pretty fair counter himself and I heard him say he got a 88 in the P. M. which is about a 94 but any way it was good enough to win. Mr Blakes regular game is about a 90 takeing his own figures and he is one of these cocky guys that takes his own

225

How to Write Short Stories

game serious and snears at men that cant break
100 and if you was to ask him if he had ever been
over 100 himself he would say not since the first
yr he begun to play. Well I have watched a
lot of those guys like he and I will tell you how
they keep from going over 100 namely by doing
just what he done this A. M. when he come to the
13th hole. Well he missed his tee shot and dubbed
along and finely he got in a trap on his 4th shot
and I seen him take 6 wallops in the trap and when
he had took the 6th one his ball was worse off then
when he started so he picked it up and marked a
X down on his score card. Well if he had of
played out the hole why the best he could of got
was a 11 by holeing his next niblick shot but he
would of probly got about a 20 which would of
made him around 108 as he admitted takeing a
88 for the other 17 holes. But I bet if you was to
ask him what score he had made he would say O
I was terrible and I picked up on one hole but if I
had of played them all out I guess I would of had
about a 92.

These is the kind of men that laughs themselfs
horse when they hear of some dub takeing 10
strokes for a hole but if they was made to play
out every hole and mark down their real score
their card would be decorated with many a big
casino.

Well as I say I had a hard day and was pretty

A Caddy's Diary

sore along towards the finish but still I had to laugh at Joe Bean on the 15th hole which is a par 3 and you can get there with a fair drive and personly I am genally hole high with a midiron, but Mr Thomas topped his tee shot and dubbed a couple with his mashie and was still quiet a ways off the green and he stood studing the situation a minute and said to Mr Blake well I wonder what I better take here. So Joe Bean was standing by me and he said under his breath take my advice and quit you old rascal.

Mon. Apr. 17.

Yesterday was Sun and I was to wore out last night to write as I cadded 45 holes. I cadded for Mr Colby in the A. M. and Mr Langley in the P. M. Mr Thomas thinks golf is wrong on the sabath tho as Joe Bean says it is wrong any day the way he plays it.

This A. M. they was nobody on the course and I played 18 holes by myself and had a 5 for a 76 on the 18th hole but the wind got a hold of my drive and it went out of bounds. This P. M. they was 3 of us had a game of rummy started but Miss Rennie and Mrs Thomas come out to play and asked for me to caddy for them, they are both terrible.

Mrs Thomas is Mr Thomas wife and she is big and fat and shakes like jell and she always says she plays golf just to make her skinny and she dont care how rotten she plays as long as she is getting the exercise, well maybe so but when we find her ball in a bad lie she aint never sure it is hers till she picks it up and smells it and when she puts it back beleive me she don't cram it down no gopher hole.

Miss Rennie is a good looker and young and they say she is engaged to Chas Crane, he is one of our members and is the best player in the club and dont cheat hardly at all and he has got a job in the bank where Mr Thomas is the vice president. Well I have cadded for Miss Rennie when she was playing with Mr Crane and I have cadded for her when she was playing alone or with another lady and I often think if Mr Crane could hear her talk when he was not around he would not be so stuck on her. You would be surprised at some of the words that falls from those fare lips.

Well the 2 ladies played for 2 bits a hole and Miss Rennie was haveing a terrible time wile Mrs Thomas was shot with luck on the greens and sunk 3 or 4 putts that was murder. Well Miss Rennie used some expressions which was best not repeated but towards the last the luck changed around and it was Miss Rennie that was sinking the long ones and when they got to the 18th tee Mrs Thomas was only 1 up.

Well we had started pretty late and when we

A Caddy's Diary

left the 17th green Miss Rennie made the remark
that we would have to hurry to get the last hole
played, well it was her honor and she got the best
drive she made all day about 120 yds down the
fair way. Well Mrs Thomas got nervous and
looked up and missed her ball a ft and then done
the same thing right over and when she finely hit
it she only knocked it about 20 yds and this made
her lay 3. Well her 4th went wild and lit over in
the rough in the apple trees. It was a cinch Miss
Rennie would win the hole unless she dropped dead.

Well we all went over to hunt for Mrs Thomas
ball but we would of been lucky to find it even in
day light but now you could not hardly see under
the trees, so Miss Rennie said drop another ball
and we will not count no penalty. Well it is some
job any time to make a woman give up hunting
for a lost ball and all the more so when it is going
to cost her 2 bits to play the hole out so there we
stayed for at lease 10 minutes till it was so dark
we could not see each other let alone a lost ball
and finely Mrs Thomas said well it looks like we
could not finish, how do we stand? Just like
she did not know how they stood.

You had me one down up to this hole said Miss
Rennie.

Well that is finishing pretty close said Mrs
Thomas.

I will have to give Miss Rennie credit that what

ever word she thought of for this occassion she did not say it out loud but when she was paying me she said I might of give you a quarter tip only I have to give Mrs Thomas a quarter she dont deserve so you dont get it.

Fat chance I would of had any way.

Well we been haveing some more bad weather but today the weather was all right but that was the only thing that was all right. This P. M. I cadded double for Mr Thomas and Chas Crane the club champion who is stuck on Miss Rennie. It was a 4 some with he and Mr Thomas against Mr Blake and Jack Andrews the pro, they was only playing best ball so it was really just a match between Mr Crane and Jack Andrews and Mr Crane win by 1 up. Joe Bean cadded for Jack and Mr Blake. Mr Thomas was terrible and I put in a swell P. M. lugging that heavy bag of his besides Mr Cranes bag.

Mr Thomas did not go off of the course as much as usual but he kept hitting behind the ball and he run me ragged replaceing his divots but still I had to laugh when we was playing the 4th hole which you have to drive over a ravine and every time Mr Thomas misses his tee shot on this hole why he makes a squak about the ravine and says it ought not to be there and etc.

A Caddy's Diary

Today he had a terrible time getting over it and afterwards he said to Jack Andrews this is a joke hole and ought to be changed. So Joe Bean wispered to me that if Mr Thomas kept on playing like he was the whole course would be changed.

Then a little wile later when we come to the long 9th hole Mr Thomas got a fair tee shot but then he whiffed twice missing the ball by a ft and the 3d time he hit it but it only went a little ways and Joe Bean said that is 3 trys and no gain, he will have to punt.

But I must write down about my tough luck, well we finely got through the 18 holes and Mr Thomas reached down in his pocket for the money to pay me and he genally pays for Mr Crane to when they play together as Mr Crane is just a employ in the bank and dont have much money but this time all Mr Thomas had was a $20.00 bill so he said to Mr Crane I guess you will have to pay the boy Charley so Charley dug down and got the money to pay me and he paid just what it was and not a dime over, where if Mr Thomas had of had the change I would of got a $1.00 extra at lease and maybe I was not sore and Joe Bean to because of course Andrews never gives you nothing and Mr Blake dont tip his caddy unless he wins.

They are a fine bunch of tight wads said Joe and I said well Crane is all right only he just has not got no money.

How to Write Short Stories

He aint all right no more than the rest of them said Joe.

Well at lease he dont cheat on his score I said.

And you know why that is said Joe, neither does Jack Andrews cheat on his score but that is because they play to good. Players like Crane and Andrews that goes around in 80 or better cant cheat on their score because they make the most of the holes in around 4 strokes and the 4 strokes includes their tee shot and a couple of putts which everybody is right there to watch them when they make them and count them right along with them. So if they make a 4 and claim a 3 why people would just laugh in their face and say how did the ball get from the fair way on to the green, did it fly? But the boys that takes 7 and 8 strokes to a hole can shave their score and you know they are shaveing it but you have to let them get away with it because you cant prove nothing. But that is one of the penaltys for being a good player, you cant cheat.

To hear Joe tell it pretty near everybody are born crooks, well maybe he is right.

Wed. Apr. 26.

Today Mrs Doane was out for the first time this yr and asked for me to caddy for her and you bet I was on the job. Well how are you Dick she said, she always calls me by name. She asked me

232

A Caddy's Diary

what had I been doing all winter and was I glad
to see her and etc.

She said she had been down south all winter and
played golf pretty near every day and would I
watch her and notice how much she had improved.

Well to tell the truth she was no better then
last yr and wont never be no better and I guess
she is just to pretty to be a golf player but of course
when she asked me did I think her game was improved I had to reply yes indeed as I would not
hurt her feelings and she laughed like my reply
pleased her. She played with Mr and Mrs Carter
and I carried the 2 ladies bags wile Joe Bean
cadded for Mr Carter. Mrs Carter is a ugly dame
with things on her face and it must make Mr
Carter feel sore when he looks at Mrs Doane to
think he married Mrs Carter but I suppose they
could not all marry the same one and besides
Mrs Doane would not be a sucker enough to marry
a man like he who drinks all the time and is pretty
near always stood, tho Mr Doane who she did
marry aint such a H of a man himself tho dirty
with money.

They all gave me the laugh on the 3d hole
when Mrs Doane was makeing her 2d shot and
the ball was in the fair way but laid kind of bad
and she just ticked it and then she asked me if
winter rules was in force and I said yes so we teed
her ball up so as she could get a good shot at it and

233

they gave me the laugh for saying winter rules was in force.

You have got the caddys bribed Mr Carter said to her.

But she just smiled and put her hand on my sholder and said Dick is my pal. That is enough of a bribe to just have her touch you and I would caddy all day for her and never ask for a cent only to have her smile at me and call me her pal.

Sat. Apr. 29.

Today they had the first club tournament of the yr and they have a monthly tournament every month and today was the first one, it is a handicap tournament and everybody plays in it and they have prizes for low net score and low gross score and etc. I cadded for Mr Thomas today and will tell what happened.

They played a 4 some and besides Mr Thomas we had Mr Blake and Mr Carter and Mr Dunham. Mr Dunham is the worst man player in the club and the other men would not play with him a specialy on a Saturday only him and Mr Blake is partners together in business. Mr Dunham has got the highest handicap in the club which is 50 but it would have to be 150 for him to win a prize. Mr Blake and Mr Carter has got a handicap of about 15 a piece I think and Mr Thomas is 30, the first prize for the low net score for the day was

A Caddy's Diary

a dozen golf balls and the second low score a ½ dozen golf balls and etc.

Well we had a great battle and Mr Colby ought to been along to write it up or some good writer. Mr Carter and Mr Dunham played partners against Mr Thomas and Mr Blake which ment that Mr Carter was playing Thomas and Blakes best ball, well Mr Dunham took the honor and the first ball he hit went strate off to the right and over the fence outside of the grounds, well he done the same thing 3 times. Well when he finely did hit one in the course why Mr Carter said why not let us not count them 3 first shots of Mr Dunham as they was just practice. Like H we wont count them said Mr Thomas we must count every shot and keep our scores correct for the tournament.

All right said Mr Carter.

Well we got down to the green and Mr Dunham had about 11 and Mr Carter sunk a long putt for a par 5, Mr Blake all ready had 5 strokes and so did Mr Thomas and when Mr Carter sunk his putt why Mr Thomas picked his ball up and said Carter wins the hole and I and Blake will take 6s. Like H you will said Mr Carter, this is a tournament and we must play every hole out and keep our scores correct. So Mr Dunham putted and went down in 13 and Mr Blake got a 6 and Mr Thomas missed 2 easy putts and took a 8 and maybe he was not boiling.

How to Write Short Stories

Well it was still their honor and Mr Dunham had one of his dizzy spells on the 2d tee and he missed the ball twice before he hit it and then Mr Carter drove the green which is only a midiron shot and then Mr Thomas stepped up and missed the ball just like Mr Dunham. He was wild and yelled at Mr. Dunham no man could play golf playing with a man like you, you would spoil anybodys game.

Your game was all ready spoiled said Mr Dunham, it turned sour on the 1st green.

You would turn anybody sour said Mr Thomas.

Well Mr Thomas finely took a 8 for the hole which is a par 3 and it certainly looked bad for him winning a prize when he started out with 2 8s, and he and Mr Dunham had another terrible time on No 3 and wile they was messing things up a 2 some come up behind us and hollered fore and we left them go through tho it was Mr Clayton and Mr Joyce and as Joe Bean said they was probly dissapointed when we left them go through as they are the kind that feels like the day is lost if they cant write to some committee and preffer charges.

Well Mr Thomas got a 7 on the 3d and he said well it is no wonder I am off of my game today as I was up ½ the night with my teeth.

Well said Mr Carter if I had your money why on the night before a big tournament like this

A Caddy's Diary

I would hire somebody else to set up with my teeth.

Well I wished I could remember all that was said and done but any way Mr Thomas kept getting sore and sore and we got to the 7th tee and he had not made a decent tee shot all day so Mr Blake said to him why dont you try the wood as you cant do no worse?

By Geo I beleive I will said Mr Thomas and took his driver out of the bag which he had not used it for 3 yrs.

Well he swang and zowie away went the ball pretty near 8 inchs distants wile the head of the club broke off clean and saled 50 yds down the course. Well I have got a hold on myself so as I dont never laugh out loud and I beleive the other men was scarred to laugh or he would of killed them so we all stood there in silents waiting for what would happen.

Well without saying a word he come to where I was standing and took his other 4 wood clubs out of the bag and took them to a tree which stands a little ways from the tee box and one by one he swang them with all his strength against the trunk of the tree and smashed them to H and gone, all right gentlemen that is over he said.

Well to cut it short Mr Thomas score for the first 9 was a even 60 and then we started out on the 2d 9 and you would not think it was the same man playing, on the first 3 holes he made 2 4s and a 5 and beat Mr Carter even and followed up with a 6 and a 5 and that is how he kept going up to the 17th hole.

What has got in to you Thomas said Mr Carter.

Nothing said Mr Thomas only I broke my hoodoo when I broke them 5 wood clubs.

Yes I said to myself and if you had broke them 5 wood clubs 3 yrs ago I would not of broke my back lugging them around.

Well we come to the 18th tee and Mr Thomas had a 39 which give him a 99 for 17 holes, well everybody drove off and as we was following along why Mr Klabor come walking down the course from the club house on his way to the 17th green to join some friends and Mr Thomas asked him what had he made and he said he had turned in a 93 but his handicap is only 12 so that give him a 81.

That wont get me no wheres he said as Charley Crane made a 75.

Well said Mr Thomas I can tie Crane for low net if I get a 6 on this hole.

Well it come his turn to make his 2d and zowie he hit the ball pretty good but they was a hook on it and away she went in to the woods on the left, the ball laid in behind a tree so as they was only one thing to do and that was waste a shot getting it back on the fair so that is what Mr Thomas done and it took him 2 more to reach the green.

A Caddy's Diary

How many have you had Thomas said Mr
Carter when we was all on the green.

Let me see said Mr Thomas and then turned
to me, how many have I had caddy?

I dont know I said.

Well it is either 4 or 5 said Mr Thomas.

I think it is 5 said Mr Carter.

I think it is 4 said Mr Thomas and turned to
me again and said how many have I had caddy?

So I said 4.

Well said Mr Thomas personly I was not sure
myself but my caddy says 4 and I guess he is
right.

Well the other men looked at each other and
I and Joe Bean looked at each other but Mr
Thomas went ahead and putted and was down
in 2 putts.

Well he said I certainly come to life on them
last 9 holes.

So he turned in his score as 105 and with his
handicap of 30 why that give him a net of 75 which
was the same as Mr Crane so instead of Mr Crane
getting 1 dozen golf balls and Mr Thomas getting
$\frac{1}{2}$ a dozen golf balls why they will split the 1st
and 2d prize makeing 9 golf balls a piece.

Tues. May 2.

This was the first ladies day of the season and
even Joe Bean had to carry for the fair sex. We
cadded for a 4 some which was Miss Rennie and

239

How to Write Short Stories

Mrs Thomas against Mrs Doane and Mrs Carter. I guess if they had of kept their score right the total for the 4 of them would of ran well over a 1000.

Our course has a great many trees and they seemed to have a traction for our 4 ladies today and we was in amongst the trees more then we was on the fair way.

Well said Joe Bean theys one thing about cadding for these dames, it keeps you out of the hot sun.

And another time he said he felt like a boy scout studing wood craft.

These dames is always up against a stump he said.

And another time he said that it was not fair to charge these dames regular ladies dues in the club as they hardly ever used the course.

Well it seems like they was a party in the village last night and of course the ladies was talking about it and Mrs Doane said what a lovely dress Miss Rennie wore to the party and Miss Rennie said she did not care for the dress herself.

Well said Mrs Doane if you want to get rid of it just hand it over to me.

I wont give it to you said Miss Rennie but I will sell it to you at $\frac{1}{2}$ what it cost me and it was a bargain at that as it only cost me a $100.00 and I will sell it to you for $50.00.

240

A Caddy's Diary

I have not got $50.00 just now to spend said Mrs Doane and besides I dont know would it fit me.

Sure it would fit you said Miss Rennie, you and I are exactly the same size and figure, I tell you what I will do with you I will play you golf for it and if you beat me you can have the gown for nothing and if I beat you why you will give me $50.00 for it.

All right but if I loose you may have to wait for your money said Mrs Doane.

So this was on the 4th hole and they started from there to play for the dress and they was both terrible and worse then usual on acct of being nervous as this was the biggest stakes they had either of them ever played for tho the Doanes has got a bbl of money and $50.00 is chickens food.

Well we was on the 16th hole and Mrs Doane was 1 up and Miss Rennie sliced her tee shot off in the rough and Mrs Doane landed in some rough over on the left so they was clear across the course from each other. Well I and Mrs Doane went over to her ball and as luck would have it it had come to rest in a kind of a groove where a good player could not hardly make a good shot of it let alone Mrs Doane. Well Mrs. Thomas was out in the middle of the course for once in her life and the other 2 ladies was over on the right side and Joe Bean with them so they was nobody near Mrs Doane and I.

How to Write Short Stories

Do I have to play it from there she said. I guess you do was my reply.

Why Dick have you went back on me she said and give me one of her looks.

Well I looked to see if the others was looking and then I kind of give the ball a shove with my toe and it come out of the groove and laid where she could get a swipe at it.

This was the 16th hole and Mrs Doane win it by 11 strokes to 10 and that made her 2 up and 2 to go. Miss Rennie win the 17th but they both took a 10 for the 18th and that give Mrs Doane the match.

Well I wont never have a chance to see her in Miss Rennies dress but if I did I aint sure that I would like it on her.

Fri. May 5.

Well I never thought we would have so much excitement in the club and so much to write down in my diary but I guess I better get busy writeing it down as here it is Friday and it was Wed. A. M. when the excitement broke loose and I was getting ready to play around when Harry Lear the caddy master come running out with the paper in his hand and showed it to me on the first page.

It told how Chas Crane our club champion had went south with $8000 which he had stole out of Mr Thomas bank and a swell looking dame that was a stenographer in the bank had clloped with

A Caddy's Diary

him and they had her picture in the paper and I will say she is a pip but who would of thought a nice quiet young man like Mr Crane was going to prove himself a gay Romeo and a specialy as he was engaged to Miss Rennie tho she now says she broke their engagement a month ago but any way the whole affair has certainly give everybody something to talk about and one of the caddys Lou Crowell busted Fat Brunner in the nose because Fat claimed to of been the last one that cadded for Crane. Lou was really the last one and cadded for him last Sunday which was the last time Crane was at the club.

Well everybody was thinking how sore Mr Thomas would be and they would better not mention the affair around him and etc. but who should show up to play yesterday but Mr Thomas himself and he played with Mr Blake and all they talked about the whole P. M. was Crane and what he had pulled.

Well Thomas said Mr Blake I am curious to know if the thing come as a suprise to you or if you ever had a hunch that he was libel to do a thing like this.

Well Blake said Mr Thomas I will admit that the whole thing come as a complete suprise to me as Crane was all most like my son you might say and I was going to see that he got along all right and that is what makes me sore is not only that

How to Write Short Stories

he has proved himself dishonest but that he could
be such a sucker as to give up a bright future for
a sum of money like $8000 and a doll face girl
that cant be no good or she would not of let him
do it.   When you think how young he was and
the carreer he might of had why it certainly seems
like he sold his soul pretty cheap.

That is what Mr Thomas had to say or at lease
part of it as I cant remember a ½ of all he said
but any way this P. M. I cadded for Mrs Thomas
and Mrs Doane and that is all they talked about
to, and Mrs Thomas talked along the same lines
like her husband and said she had always thought
Crane was to smart a young man to pull a thing
like that and ruin his whole future.

He was getting $4000 a yr said Mrs Thomas
and everybody liked him and said he was bound
to get ahead so that is what makes it such a silly
thing for him to of done, sell his soul for $8000 and
a pretty face.

Yes indeed said Mrs Doane.

Well all the time I was listening to Mr Thomas
and Mr Blake and Mrs Thomas and Mrs Doane
why I was thinking about something which I
wanted to say to them but it would of ment me
looseing my job so I kept it to myself but I sprung
it on my pal Joe Bean on the way home tonight.

Joe I said what do these people mean when
they talk about Crane selling his soul?

A Caddy's Diary

Why you know what they mean said Joe, they mean that a person that does something dishonest for a bunch of money or a gal or any kind of a reward why the person that does it is selling his soul.

All right I said and it dont make no differents does it if the reward is big or little?

Why no said Joe only the bigger it is the less of a sucker the person is that goes after it.

Well I said here is Mr Thomas who is vice president of a big bank and worth a bbl of money and it is just a few days ago when he lied about his golf score in order so as he would win 9 golf balls instead of a ½ a dozen.

Sure said Joe.

And how about his wife Mrs Thomas I said, who plays for 2 bits a hole and when her ball dont lie good why she picks it up and pretends to look at it to see if it is hers and then puts it back in a good lie where she can sock it.

And how about my friend Mrs Doane that made me move her ball out of a rut to help her beat Miss Rennie out of a party dress.

Well said Joe what of it?

Well I said it seems to me like these people have got a lot of nerve to pan Mr Crane and call him a sucker for doing what he done, it seems to me like $8000 and a swell dame is a pretty fair reward compared with what some of these other people sells their soul for, and I would like to tell them about it.

Well said Joe go ahead and tell them but maybe they will tell you something right back.

What will they tell me?

Well said Joe they might tell you this, that when Mr Thomas asks you how many shots he has had and you say 4 when you know he has had 5, why you are selling your soul for a $1.00 tip. And when you move Mrs Doanes ball out of a rut and give it a good lie, what are you selling your soul for? Just a smile.

O keep your mouth shut I said to him.

I am going to said Joe and would advice you to do the same.

A FRAME–UP

*A stirring romance of the Hundred Years' War,
detailing the adventures in France and Castile
of a pair of well-bred weasels. The story is an
example of what can be done with a stub pen.*

VIII

A FRAME–UP

I

I suppose you could call it a frame. But it wasn't like no frame that was ever pulled before. They's been plenty where one guy was paid to lay down. This is the first I heard of where a guy had to be bribed to win. And it's the first where a bird was bribed and didn't know it.

You know they've postponed the match with Britton. Nate said at first that his boy wasn't ready yet, but the papers all kidded him. Because anybody that seen Burke in the Kemp fight knows he's ready. So Nate had to change his story and say Burke had hurt one of his hands on Kemp's egg, and he wasn't going to take no chance boxing again till he was O. K., which mightn't be for a couple of months. Say, Kemp's head may be hard, but it ain't hard enough to hurt one of them hands of Burkey's. He could play catch with Big Bertha.

No, they's another reason why Nate ast for a postponement of the Britton date. It's got to be another frame-up that may take a long w'ile to fix, and he ain't got no plans made yet. And till

249

he's all set, he'd be a dumbbell to send Burke against a man as good as Jack Britton.

The papers has printed a lot of stuff about Burke —how he ain't only been boxing a little over a year, and won't be twenty-one till next July, and five or six bouts is all he's been in, and now look at him, offered a match for the welterweight championship and $10,000 win, lose or draw! But if they knew Burke like some of us knows him, they could write a book. Because he certainly is Duke of the Cuckoos and the world's greatest sap. How they got him ready for the Kemp bout is a story in itself, but it won't come out till he's through with the game. So what I tell you is between you and I.

It was one afternoon about a year ago. Bill Brennan was in Kid Howard's gymnasium in Chi, working out, and they was a gang looking on. Howard seen one boy in the crowd that you couldn't help from noticing. He was made up for one of the hicks in "'Way Down East." He'd bought his collar in Akron and his coat sleeves died just south of his elbow. From his pants to his vest was a toll call. He hadn't never shaved and his w'iskers was just the right number and len'th to string a violin. Thinks Howard to himself: "If you seen a stage rube dressed like that, you'd say it was overdone."

Well, it got late and the gang thinned out till

A Frame-up

finally they wasn't nobody left but Howard and this sap. So Howard ast him if he wanted to see somebody.

"Yes," said the kid. "I want to see a man that can learn me to fight."

So Howard ast him if he meant box.

"Box or fight, I don't care which, just so's I can learn the rules," said the hick.

"Did you ever box?" says Howard.

"No," says the kid, "but I can learn quick and I'm willing to pay for it. I got plenty of money. I got pretty close to $700."

Howard ast him what was his name and where he come from and his business.

"My name's Burke and I work on my old man's farm," he says. "It's acrost the Lake, outside of Benton Harbor. We raise peaches."

"Has your old man got money?" ast Howard.

"Plenty," says the kid.

"Well," said Howard, "if you work on a farm, you're getting plenty of exercise. And if your old man's rich, you ain't after the sugar. So what's the idear of going into this game?"

"I don't want to go in no game," he says. "I just want to learn good enough so's I can win this one match and then I'm through."

"What one match?" says Howard.

"With Charley Porter," says Burke.

Well, of course you've heard of Charley Porter.

How to Write Short Stories

He's a Benton Harbor boy too. He'd fought
Lewis twice and Britton once and he'd give them
both a sweet battle. He was considered about
fourth or fifth best amongst the welters. So it
struck Howard funny that this green rube, that
hadn't never boxed, should think he could take
a few lessons and then be good enough to beat a
boy like Porter.

"You're an ambitious kid," he says to him,
"but if I was you I'd take my seven hundred
men and invest it some other way. Porter's had
forty fights, and that's what counts. You could
take all the lessons in the world, and he'd make a
monkey out of you. Unless you're a boy wonder
or something. But even if you are, you couldn't
get no match with Porter till you'd proved it.
And that means you'd have to beat some other
good boys first."

So Burke said: "All I come to Chicago for is to
take some boxing lessons. They told me you
was the man to come and see. If I'm willing to
pay the money, it shouldn't ought to make no
difference to you if I get a match with Porter or
not. Or if I lick him or not."

"That's right," said Howard. "Only I ain't
no burglar or no con man. I'm in this business
for money, but I don't want to take nobody's
money without they get what they think they're
paying for. And if you had seven million smackers

A Frame-up

I couldn't guarantee to make you a good boxer, not good enough to land you a match with Porter."

"I ain't asking you to land no match," says Burke. "I'll tend to that part. He'll fight me as soon as I think I'm ready. If he don't, I'll run him out of Michigan. He wouldn't dast stay round there if everybody was saying I had him scared. And that's what they'd say if he wouldn't fight me."

"Why would they?" says Howard. "He's in the game for money, too, and he couldn't get no money for a bout with a guy like you that nobody ever heard of. They wouldn't no club match you up."

"I won't have no trouble getting matched up," says Burke. "Fitzsimmons will put us on right there in Benton Harbor. The town's nuts over Porter and they'll pay to see him any time. And whatever purse they offer is all his. I'll fight him for nothing."

"Oh!" says Howard. "That makes it different! You're sore at him!"

"No," says the hick, "I'm not sore at him."

"You just don't like him," says Howard.

"I don't know if I like him or not," said Burke. "I don't even know him."

"But for some reason you want to give him a trimming," says Howard. "Well, listen, boy: I

How to Write Short Stories

understand they's no capital punishment in your State, so it looks to me like you'd run less risk of getting killed if you'd sneak in Porter's house some night w'ile he's asleep and kiss him on the brow with a meat ax."

Burke didn't crack a smile.

"That wouldn't get me nowheres," he said. "They's a reason I got to box him. If you can learn me, all right. If not, I'll go somewheres else."

So Howard made a date for him to come back the next day.

II

Well, when the kid stripped for action, Howard's eyes popped out. With them comic clothes on, he'd looked awkward; he was a picture with them off. Howard says he felt like inviting the best sculptures in Chi to come and take a look.

"I was going to box with him myself," says Howard, "but not after I seen them shoulder muscles. I figured I didn't have enough insurance to justify me putting on the gloves with this bird. So I made Joe Rivers take him."

Well, they could see in a minute that the rube was a born boxer. He was fast as a streak and in one lesson he learnt more than most boys picks up in a month. They just showed him how to stand and the rest seemed to come natural. In a little w'ile Joe, with all his experience, was having trouble to land, whereas Burkey was hitting Joe as often as he felt like. Only he didn't put no zip in his punches. He pulled them all.

"Cut loose once!" says Howard. "Let's see if you can knock him down!"

"Oh, no," said Burkey. "This ain't in earnest."

Rivers looked just as well satisfied, but Howard says:

"You got to be in earnest, even when you're just working out. They's lots of boys as strong as you that don't know how to get their stren'th into their punch. That's a thing that's got to be learnt, and I can't learn you if I can't see you wallop."

"No," says Burke. "I ain't going to hurt nobody for nothing."

And all Howard's coaxing done no good. He wouldn't cut loose.

But at the end of the six weeks he stuck round Howard's he was one of the sweetest boxers you ever seen and Howard thought so well of him that he tried to sign him up.

"Let me handle you, Burkey," he says. "I'll get you on in Milwaukee and I'll take you down east and make you some money. If you're handled right, they's no reason why you shouldn't be welterweight champion some day."

"I don't want to be welterweight champion,"

said Burke. "I just want to be champion of
Charley Porter. And when I've beat him, I'm
through."

"All right," says Howard. "You know what
you want. But let me tell you one thing—you
won't beat Porter or no one else if you just pet
them. You've got to hit!"

The kid smiled.

"I'll hit when it's time," he says.

So that was the last Howard heard of him till
pretty near a month later, when he picked up a
paper and read where Young Burke, a farmer boy
living outside of Benton Harbor, had stopped
Charley Porter, an aspirant for the welterweight
title, in one round.

III

About a month more went by before Burke
showed up in Chi again and called on Nate. As
soon as he mentioned his name and where he
was from, Nate was interested. Because Howard
had told him about his experience with the kid.
But Burkey wasn't made up no more like Howard
had described him. He was wearing the best suit
of clothes twenty dollars could buy.

"I went to see Howard," he says, "but he's
out of town. So I come to you. I want to go in
the fight game."

A Frame-up

"I understood from Howard," says Nate, "that you was going to quit after that one bout."

"I thought I was," says Burkey. "But it's different now. You see, I and my old man has busted up. So I got to make a living."

"What was the bust-up over?" ast Nate. "Didn't he like you boxing?"

"He didn't care nothing about that," says the kid. "But they was a gal he wanted I should marry. And I give her the air. So he done the same to me."

"Why did you quit the gal?" ast Nate.

"I figured I could do better," he says. "She's just a gal round home there, and why should I marry her? I can pretty near pick who I want to marry."

"Everybody can pick who they want to marry," said Nate.

"Yes, but who I pick, I can pretty near have," says the kid. "I thought I was stuck on this gal, but I found I wasn't. I hadn't seen hardly any other gals, and she was always round. So I thought she was about the only gal in the world. I know better now. But I did like her and my old man liked her and kept after me to ask her. So I ast her and she told me she was stuck on somebody else. So I ast her who was it and she said Charley Porter. She didn't know him, but she'd seen him on the street a lot of times, and he'd smiled at her. She thought he was handsome and made a hero out of him. He was the best fighter in the world, to her mind. So I said I could beat him and she laughed at me. She says, 'You might beat him plowing.' So I said, 'I can beat him boxing.' So she says, 'All right. You do it and I'll like you better than him.' So I come up here and took a few lessons and knocked him cock-eyed.

"When she seen me afterwards, she throwed her arms round my neck and said I was the best man in the world, and we got engaged. But during the time I was up here in Chi learning to box, I learnt to dance too. And I bought me these good clothes. So after I trimmed Porter I got to going over to St. Joe, to the pavilion, nights, and I seen all the gals was nuts over me. So I said to myself, 'What's the idear of tying up to this rube gal when you can marry somebody that is somebody—maybe one of these rich Chicago society dames.' So I give this hick the air and my old man throwed me out of the house."

Well, Nate's handled a lot of boxers and never seen one yet that despised himself, but after he'd listened to this bird a w'ile, he begin to think that all the rest of them was lilies of the valley.

"Which Chicago society gal have you picked out?" he says, to lead him on.

"I don't know yet," says Burkey. "Some of

A Frame-up

them at the dances in St. Joe looked good, but I want to see them all before I tie myself up."

If you ever been to St. Joe, you know the Chicago society gals that attends them dances. If you want to see one of them in the middle of the week, go up to the Draperies and ask for Min.

"You got the right dope," Nate says. "You'd be a sucker to make a choice till you'd looked over the whole field. And in the meanw'ile, I'll try and get you fixed up with a couple of matches so as you can grab some spending money."

But Burke was still thinking of the dames.

"I read a great story the other day," he says. "It was a young fella that was a boxer and one night he was walking along the street and he heard a gal scream. She was up on the porch of a big house and they was a dude there, trying to make love to her. So she didn't like him and that's why she screamed. So this young fella went in and grabbed the dude and knocked him for a long trip. So the gal got stuck on this young fella, the boxer, and married him and she turned out to be a millionaire."

"A great story!" said Nate. "I certainly wished I could of read it. But suppose he'd married her and then found out that her old man made automobiles and owed everybody. A young fella can't be too careful who he lets marry him. And if I was you I'd go slow. In the first place,

most of the gals with the real class and the big
money lives in New York. So why not wait till
you've win a couple of bouts in Milwaukee or
somewheres so's I can get you dated up in the
Big Town? Then you can walk up and down
Eighth Avenue and help yourself to the cream."

This was to stall him along so's he'd forget the
skirts for a w'ile and tend to business.

Nate made him work out every day and box
with some of the boys. But he was just as shy of
a punch as when Howard had him.

"Cut loose and slug!" Nate told him.

"What for?" he says.

"To show me if you've got a haymaker," says
Nate.

"Ask Porter if I have," said the kid.

Finally Nate got him matched with Red Harris
in a semi-wind-up at Milwaukee. Harris can
wallop, but he's slow. Well, Burkey made him
look like he was handcuffed. Red never laid a
glove on him the whole bout, w'ile Nate's boy
played him like a piano. But it was soft music
and when it was over neither of them had a mark.
The crowd liked Burke at first on account of his
speed. But they razzed him the last few rounds
because it looked like he wasn't trying. The
papers couldn't do nothing but give him the best
of it, but said he wouldn't never get nowheres
till he learned to punch. Nate had begged him

A Frame-up

all through to tear in and end it, but he might as well of tried to argue with Central.

Well, Fitzsimmons was putting on a show over to Benton Harbor and he wired Nate and ast him if he'd bring Burke there for a wind-up with a Grand Rapids boy named Hap Stein. This kid had met some of the best boys round Michigan and beat them all, and, of course, Burke'd draw good in his home town, especially after what he done to Porter.

So Nate took Burkey over there and Fitz ast Nate how the kid was coming and Nate told him:

"One of the sweetest boxers I ever seen, but he ain't showed enough of a wallop to annoy a soap bubble."

"It's a funny thing," said Fitz, "because he hit Porter just once and broke his jaw. And Charley's jaw ain't glass, neither. I know a punch when I see one and I doubt if Dempsey could hit harder than this bird plugged this baby."

"Well," says Nate, "I wished we had the prescription. He made a monkey out of Harris at Milwaukee, but he wouldn't even slap him hard. And the boys he works out with, I've had them rough him so's he'd get mad, but it didn't do no good."

"I don't suppose so," says Fitz, "because he wasn't sore at Porter. Charley didn't even know him."

How to Write Short Stories

"But he had a reason to show Porter up," said Nate, and he told Fitz about the rube gal.

"That's news to me," said Fitz. "Maybe he'll only fight when they's a dame for a prize. Why don't you hire some chorus doll to vamp him and have her tell him she's his as soon as he's knocked all the other welters for a corpse?"

"You don't know this bird!" said Nate. "Chorus gals would be beneath his notice. He wants a millionaire society belle and I'd have a fat chance of getting one of them to play the part."

Well, the bout with Stein was a farce. Burkey was so fast that Hap thought they'd ganged on him, but nothing Nate could say or do had any effect. He couldn't make the kid cut loose and punch.

IV

When they'd been back in Chi a couple of months and Burke had had one more fight in Milwaukee—he made a monkey out of Jimmy Mason—well, he begin fretting and wanted to know how soon Nate was going to take him east.

"As soon as I can get you matched," said Nate. "But if I do date you up down there, you'll have to cut out the cuddling and really fight or they won't want you a second time."

A Frame-up

"Maybe I'll be different down there," said Burkey.

So along late in the fall Nate got him matched with Battling Igoe, in Boston.

"Now here's your chance," Nate told him. "I got Rickard's promise that if you trim Igoe he'll put you on in New York with Willie Kemp. And the man that beats Willie Kemp will get a whack at Britton and the big money."

All Burke said was:

"How's Boston for gals? Any class to them?"

"Not enough for you," says Nate. "You'd be throwing yourself away! They's no doubt but that you could go down to Scollay Square or Revere Beach and take your pick, but you'd be a sucker to do it. New York's the place. And suppose you get tied up to some Boston countess and then went to New York and win a couple of big bouts and got invited round to some of them big mansions on Mott Street or the Tenderloin, and next thing you know, you'd probably meet a dozen gals that never even heard of Boston. Then you'd wished you'd of been more careful and not financed yourself to no bean shooter."

You read about the Igoe bout? I seen it. When they was all in the ring beforehand, Nate said to Igoe, he says: "Well, Bat, we've decided to let you stay three rounds. That'll be enough to give you a boxing lesson. But in the fourth round, you're going to hear music that'll rock you to sleep." Nate had heard that the Battler wasn't no lion heart and this kind of gab fretted him.

"I'll rock him to sleep himself," he said, but his teeth was shimmying.

Burke was just the same like in his other bouts. He wrote his name and address all over Igoe's pan, and convinced the Battler that any time he wanted to he could knock him for a row of stumps. That went on for three rounds, with Nate, as usual, begging the kid to put over a haymaker, and Burke paying no attention. So when the bell rung for the fourth, Nate hollered, "Good night, Bat!" and Igoe thought sure he meant business. And he wasn't named after Nelson. So the first time Burke hit him in this round he folded up like a bass singer's chin and flopped on the floor, yelling foul. Well, we all seen the blow; it landed just under the green spot where he parks his collar button. And besides that, they wasn't no force to it. But Igoe was through for the evening, and the kid had win another soft one. Personally I'd of rather took fifty socks on the jaw than the razzing the crowd give Bat.

Well, Nate was going to New York and stay a w'ile and he wanted to send Burke back to Chi to wait till they'd chose a date for the fight with Kemp. But Burkey said no; he could lay round New York as easy as Chicago and if Nate wouldn't take him there he was through. He says:

A Frame-up

"Here I am a coming champion, and what does it get me? I ain't having no fun. I want to meet some gals and dance with them and kid them."

"All right, come along," says Nate. "But I wished you'd remember one thing: When you do meet them swell East Side janes, don't treat them like toys. They've got feelings as well as riches and wealth, and I would rather see Kemp or Britton knock you lopsided than see you win fame and leave a trail of broken hearts."

"I'm no flirt!" says Burkey. "I can't help what they feel towards me, but I won't lead them on, not unlest I'm serious myself."

"Now you're talking like a man!" says Nate.

So they come to New York and stopped at the Spencer. Nate had a lot of business to tend to, and guys to see, and he didn't want this rube chasing round with him all the w'ile, so he turned him over to Jack Grace, the old lightweight. You know Jack, or at least you've heard of him. He'd kid Thomas A. Edison.

Nate had tipped off Jack about Burkey, and the second day they was in the Big Town, Jack took the boy for a walk. Every time they passed a car with a good-looking gal in it, Burke would ask, "Who's that?" And Jack pretended like he knew them all.

"That's Gwendolyn Weasel," he'd say. "Her old man owns part of the Grand Central Station—the Lower Level. And that one's Mildred Whiffletree, a niece of Bud Fisher, the ukulele king. And there's Honey Hives; she's a granddaughter of Old Man Bumble, the bee man. They got a big country place on Ellis Island."

"Where could a man meet these gals?" ast Burkey.

"Nowheres only at their home," said Jack. "And they's no chance of you getting invited round yet a w'ile. Nobody knows who you are. But wait till you've hung one on this Kemp guy's chin and I bet you'll have more invitations than a roach catcher."

Well, Nate landed the Kemp match sooner than he expected. Rickard said he'd put Burke on with Willie for the wind-up, three weeks from then. And he'd guarantee the winner a match with Britton.

Nate had got what he was after, but he was worried sick.

"I know he can beat Kemp if he fights," he says, "but I never yet been able to make him fight. And if he just babies along like he done in these other bouts, one of these New York referees is liable to say he ain't trying, and stop the bout. Or if it does go the limit, Kemp'll get the decision because he'll punch harder. And Kemp'll hit Burke too. He's far and away the best boy my kid's ever been against, too good to get showed up even by as fast and clever a boxer as Burkey.

A Frame-up

Our only chance is to make this little farmer slug
—tear in there and sock him like he did Porter.
But how we're going to do it is more than I know."

V

Jack Grace is the one that deserves the credit.
He went to work the night of Miss Morgan's big
show, when the receipts was turned over to dev-
astated France. Nate had to buy four tickets and
I and Jack and Burkey went with him.

Well, as you know, our best people was there
that night.

The old Garden was full of the folks that generally goes there to the horse show, not to boxing
bouts. The soup and fish was everywheres, and
gals that would knock your eye out, dressed
pretty near as warm as the fighters themselfs.

We couldn't keep Burke in his seat. He was
scared that he wouldn't see all the janes, and
just as scared that they wouldn't all see him.
The guys behind him was yelling murder and the
ushers bawled him out a dozen times.

Then all of a sudden, his eyes jumped right out
of his head and he gave a gasp and flopped down
in his chair. The three of us looked where he was
looking. And no wonder he'd wilted! What a
gal!

She was with a middle-aged man, probably her

dad, and she set in the row just ahead of us and
acrost the aisle. I guess it was the first time she'd
ever been to this kind of a party and she was all
flushed up with excitement. But she'd of been
pretty enough without that.

"There she is!" says Burke. "There's the
gal I want!"

"Who don't!" says Nate.

"Who is she?" Burke ast, and Nate was going
to tell him he didn't know. But Jack Grace cut in.

"It's Esther Fester," he said. "That's her
father with her, Lester Fester. He's the second
richest man in New York. They claim he made
three or four billion during the war, selling waffle
irons to Belgium. And she's his only kid. Every
young millionaire in town has proposed to her,
but she won't have nothing to do with them, calls
them all loafers.

"She says the man she marries will have to be
a champion of something, whether it's football
or boxing or halma. She don't care what, just
so's he's better in one line than anybody else."

"She's quite a boxing fan," says Nate. "I
seen her here several times before. She maybe
wants to look all the boys over and see which one
she likes the best."

"I understand she's a great admirer of Willie
Kemp," says Jack. "She's always here when he
boxes and she probably come to-night expecting

A Frame-up

to see him in the audience. Maybe he'll be introduced before the main bout, and if he is, we'll watch her close and see if she's interested."

"Why can't I get introduced?" ast Burke.

"You can," said Nate. "Wait till they're getting ready for the wind-up and then climb in the ring and tell Joe Humphreys who you are."

Well, he couldn't hardly wait till the preliminaries was over so's he could get up there and have her see him. And when he bowed, it was right at her.

"Young Burke, the Michigan Flash!" says Humphreys. "He is matched to box Willie Kemp in this ring two weeks from Friday night. The winner will meet Jack Britton for the welterweight title."

Coming back to his seat, Burkey had to pass the gal. He smiled right in her face and she smiled back. I guess it was all she could do to keep from laughing.

I don't suppose they's been more than three or four fights better than that Leonard-Mitchell scrap. It was certainly the best I ever seen. But I don't believe Burke knew they was fighting.

When it was over and the gang started out he would of overtook the gal and spoke to her only for Nate holding him.

"It'd make her sore and spoil everything," said Nate.

"How could it make her sore?" said Burke. "Didn't she smile at me?"

"Well, it'd make her old man sore," says Nate.

"What could he do?" says Burkey. "If he looked cross-eyed at me, I'd bust him."

"That'd be a sweet way to start a courtship!" said Jack. "Even New York gals ain't so far ahead of the times that they fall in love with every handsome young bud that introduces himself to their father with a smash in the jaw."

"But I just want her phone number," says the kid.

"You can get it at the hotel," says Jack. "The phone company got out a book three or four years ago that gives the names of a few of their rich subscribers, and what their number used to be, and if you call it up, they'll tell you what it's been changed to."

So as soon as we was back at the Spencer, Burkey run for the book. And he couldn't find no Lester Fester.

"I didn't think it'd be in there," says Jack. "They's very few New York millionaires has their number in the phone book. If they did, their wifes would bother them to death, calling up."

"But they must be some way to locate them," said the kid. "Somebody must know where they stay. A man as rich as him must have a big mansion somewheres. And you got to find out where it's at. If you don't find out for me to-

A Frame-up

morrow, why I'm through! I won't box Kemp or no one else."

And they knew he was cuckoo enough to mean it. But Jack Grace had his plans made already.

"I'll locate them to-morrow," he said, "that is, unlest you hear from the gal herself."

"But she don't know where I'm staying," says Burke.

"She might maybe call up Rickard and find out," says Jack.

So the kid went to bed and Nate and Jack set up and talked it over.

"It looks like we got him," said Jack. "If we can make him think him and Kemp is rivals, he'll fight."

"But that gal can't be framed," says Nate. "I don't know who she is, but she ain't the kind we could get any help from."

"We don't need her help," says Jack. "He'll get a special delivery to-morrow afternoon, with her name signed to it; that is, what he thinks is her name. I'll dope out the letter yet to-night. If necessary he'll get a letter every day till the day of the bout."

"And then what?" says Nate.

"Why, nothing," says Jack. "What do you care, if it does the work?"

"It don't seem right," said Nate. "I don't want to break the kid's heart."

"You got as much chance of breaking his

head!" says Jack. "What about the gal in Benton Harbor, that he was so stuck on and got over it in a day? But as far as that's concerned, we don't have to kill this gal off when we're through with Kemp. We can keep her going till he meets Britton. We'll have her tell him first that he's got to trim Kemp, and if that works, we'll send her to Europe or somewheres, leaving him a farewell note that she's been called away, but she'll be back in time to see him win the title."

"He's a sap," said Nate, "but I doubt if he's dumbbell enough to swallow this."

"You don't appreciate him," said Jack. "Where him and the fair sex is concerned, they's nothing so raw that he won't eat it up. But suppose he don't? You ain't got nothing to lose."

"Just him, that's all," says Nate.

"Well, he's no loss if he won't fight," said Jack. "And this may be the way to make him."

VI

Burke had started training at Daley's. When he got back from there the next afternoon, they was a special delivery waiting for him. It said:

DEAR MR. BURKE: You will probably be surprised getting a letter from one who you have never met, but still I suppose you get many let-

A Frame-up

ters from silly girls of my sex that has seen you and admires you. Hope you won't think bad of me for writing to you, but am a girl that acts on their impulse and sometimes am sorry afterwards that I done so and wished I was not so silly, but you know how girls are and especially in regards to affairs of the heart.

Well, Mr. Burke, you don't know me, but I was to the Garden last night with my daddy and set right near you and noticed you when I first come in, but didn't dast look at you and didn't know who you was till you was introduced from the ring. And then when you was returning to your seat I thought you smiled at me and I smiled back. Oh, Mr. Burke, was it me you was smiling at? If not I will feel very foolish for smiling at you and hope you won't think the worse of me for doing so.

Well, anyway, it's too late to mend and this A. M. I had my secretary get where you are staying from Mr. Rickard and am writing you this letter and suppose you will say it's just another fool girl writing mash notes, but I flatter myself that I am a little higher class than most girls as I am a society girl and don't write these kind of letters as a rule. So please don't think I am a fool and tear this up. Am just a girl that sometimes lets their feelings run away with them.

Am going to make pa take me to see the bout

How to Write Short Stories

between you and Willie Kemp, but am afraid you are going to be beaten that night, Mr. Burke, as have seen Mr. Kemp fight and believe he is going to be the champion. I admire him very much and up to last night, admired him more than any other man, but now am not so sure. There I am afraid I have been too bold and you will think I am a perfect fool.

Well, Mr. Burke, will not take up no more of your time though I don't suppose you have read this far, but hope you don't think I am a fool, but know you do. Pa don't approve of me writing to men to who I am not engaged and would be very angry was he to find out I had wrote to you, so can't let you answer this letter or call me up for fear he would find it out and be very angry. But maybe will write you again and certainly will see you fight Mr. Kemp and if you see me that night, please smile at me again so will not think you consider me a fool. But maybe you will not feel like smiling after you have boxed Mr. Kemp, as I think he is a wonder.

Well, Mr. Burke, good-by for this time and please don't think I am a fool.

> Your would-be friend,
> ESTHER FESTER.

Well, Jack Grace had guessed right. Burkey swallowed it whole. He begin reading it down in

A Frame-up

the lobby, but when he looked back and seen the name signed to it, he took it up to the room to finish it. And if he read it once, he read it twenty times—and looked sillier every time he read it. He surprised us one way, though. We was expecting he would show it to everybody. But he kept it to himself. Of course, we'd read it before it got to him. Jack had wrote it and had one of the phone gals copy it off.

Nate ast the kid at supper how he felt.

"Great!" he says.

"You want to keep working to improve your wind," says Nate. "This is your first fifteen-round bout and you may get tired."

"I won't have time to get tired," he says. "I'll knock him dead in a round!"

It was the first time he'd ever made a speech like that.

"Looks like you was right," says Nate to Jack, afterwards. "He's eat it up. The only thing now is to be sure and not overplay it. Just give him a couple more short notes between now and the bout."

"What shall I say in them?" says Jack.

"You don't need my advice," said Nate. "I think you wrote that one from memory. You must of got a few mash notes yourself."

"No," says Jack. "All the time I was boxing, I only got letters from one gal. And she always

How to Write Short Stories

said the same thing: 'If you're a man, you'll pay me back that eight dollars and sixty cents you stole.' "

Well, Burke pestered the clerks to death asking if they was sure no mail had came for him; and he went for the phone every time it rung, and was scared to go out for fear a call would come w'ile he wasn't there. Finally it got so that Nate couldn't hardly drag him to Daley's for his work-out, and they seen they'd have to spill another note or he'd worry himself out of shape. The second one was short and said:

DEAR MR. BURKE: It has been all as I could do to keep from writing you before this, but was afraid if I wrote too often you would think I was a fool.

Well, Mr. Burke, it's only five days now till your bout with Mr. Kemp and suppose you are excited. I know I am and can't hardly wait for the big event, though to be perfectly honest am in a funny position as I don't know if I want you or he to win. You see I am an admirer of the both of you. Suppose you will say to yourself I must be a funny girl to not know her own mind, but you see I have admired Mr. Kemp a long time and only seen you the other night for the first time, so don't know which I like best. Guess I will let you two decide the question for me and may the best man win.

A Frame-up

Pa is going to take me to the fight and only hope I will not faint or something with excitement. Suppose you will think me a fool for feeling this way in regards to two parties who I have never met, but as I told you before, am a girl that always lets their feelings get the best of them, though sometimes am sorry when it is too late. Hope you won't make me sorry, Mr. Burke. That is, if you win. Am afraid for your sake, however, that you are doomed with defeat, as Mr. Kemp has a punch and you are just a boxer that can't hit hard.

Well, Mr. Burke, must say ta ta for this time as am going to a toddle party at the Ritz.

Yours, ESTHER.

And the morning of the big day he got this one:

DEAR MR. BURKE: Just a line to let you know am thinking of you and if you beat Mr. Kemp, will call you up and see if we can't meet somewheres and have a dance, or maybe you don't care for la dance, but we can have a little chat if you don't think me too much a fool.

Well, Mr. Burke, I won't bother you when you must be already worried and nervous over the bout and will just say that I will be at the Garden and will see you even if you don't see me and wished I could tell you where I will set but don't know.

Well, Mr. Burke, good luck and may the best man win.

ESTHER.

On the way down from the hotel that night, Burkey ast Jack and I if we'd bet on him. We told him no. So he says:

"If you want to make some easy money, bet some of these wise crackers that I'll stop this bird in a round. I'll slap him dead!"

VII

So I and Jack did get down a couple of bets, fifty apiece. We bet the kid would win by a knock out and we got three to one. The smart guys had looked over his record and didn't see how he could stop Kemp.

But when they got in the ring, I wished for a minute I hadn't bet. Instead of paying any attention to what was coming off, Burkey was looking all over the house trying to locate the little peach. I was scared he'd still be doing it yet when the bout started, and Kemp'd sock him before he got down to business. But Jack Grace seen the danger, and leaned over and w'ispered to the kid:

"You remember that Fester gal? She's up in a box with her old man."

A Frame-up

"Where at?" ast Burke, all excited.

"It's pretty dark," says Jack, "but I'll try and point her out between rounds."

As you know, they wasn't no "between rounds." In the first two minutes Kemp made five trips to the floor, and he liked it so well the last time that he decided to sleep there.

And in the excitement, Jack pretended he'd lost sight of the gal.

VIII

Burkey staid in the room all the next day, waiting for the phone call. The papers had went nuts over him and said he was the Benny Leonard of the welters, and that it was just a question of the date when the title would change hands. But for all the effect it had on Burke, they might as well of said he'd opened a bird store.

Meanw'ile, Nate and Jack Grace talked it over and decided to go through with Jack's scheme— keep Esther alive till the Britton bout, but send her to Europe, where she wouldn't be so much trouble. So late in the evening, w'ile Burkey was still waiting for his call, a special delivery come for him that said:

DEAR MR. BURKE: Have bad news or at least hope you will agree with me and think it is bad. By the time you receive this note, will be on the

279

old pond with pa, bound for Europe. He got a cable this A. M. calling him to the other side and insisted on me going along. So we hustled round and got rooms on the ship that sails this P. M. I cried when he said I would have to go and hope you feel as bad as I do. But it's only for a short time and will be back in time to see you beat Britton and win the title. After that—well, Mr. Burke, I won't say no more.

You was wonderful last night and am proud of you. Wished I could tell you in person how much I admire you, but will do that later on. Will drop you a note just the minute we get back. In the mean time, don't forget one who is proud of you and wished I could meet my coming champion.

ESTHER.

Well, it was a blow to the kid, but it would of worked out all right only for the toughest kind of a break. Nate had to hurry back to Chi, but before he left he seen Rickard and closed for the Britton bout. Burke's end was to be $10,000.

So the second day after the Kemp bout, they was taking the Century home, and I and Jack Grace was over to see them off. They'd just shook hands and was starting through the gate when Burke seen her, the gal he'd went wild over at Miss Morgan's show! She was saying good-by to another pip.

A Frame-up

"Wait!" says Burkey, and before Nate could stop him, he'd grabbed the gal by the arm.

"Esther!" he says. "Miss Fester! You didn't go after all!"

The poor gal was speechless.

"Don't you know me?" said the kid. "I'm Burke, the boy that beat Kemp, the boy you been writing to."

She jerked her arm loose and found her tongue.

"I'm not interested in who you are," she said. "I don't know you and I don't believe I want to."

By this time, Nate had him.

"Come on, boy," he says. "You've made a mistake."

And he dragged him through the gate, w'ile the crowd stared goggle-eyed.

"Well," says our gal to her chum, "you're going to have a thrill—a trip with a crazy man!"

Burke was numb, Nate tells me, till the train was way out of New York. Then he said:

"Maybe she didn't recognize me. Or maybe she just didn't want her friend to know."

"That was probably it," says Nate.

"But why did she lie to me and say she was going to Europe?" says the kid.

After a w'ile he got up from his seat.

"Her friend's on this train," he said. "I'm going to find her and ask her something."

Nate tried to coax him out of it, but he wouldn't

listen. So Nate went with him to see that he didn't get in no trouble.

They found the gal's pal a couple of cars back. The kid stopped and said:

"I beg your pardon, lady, but I want to ask you just one question. That gal that seen you off, is her name Esther Fester?"

The jane laughed and says:

"I'm afraid it's nothing as poetical as that. Her name is plain Mary Holt."

Without another word, Burke followed Nate back to their own sleeper. He didn't open his clam again till they hit Albany. Then he made some remark about wanting some fresh air, and got off the train.

That's the last Nate seen of him till the other day, when he showed up in Chi, after money.

So you see why the Britton show had to be postponed. They's no plot for it.

HARMONY

When this story was first printed, the literary editor of the United Cigar Stores Premium Catalogue had the following to say: "The love story, half earthly, half spiritual, of a beautiful snare drummer and a hospital interne; unique for its word pictures of the unpleasant after effects of anæsthesia. It explains what radio is and how it works."

IX

HARMONY

Even a baseball writer must sometimes work.
Regretfully I yielded my seat in the P. G., walked
past the section where Art Graham, Bill Cole,
Lefty Parks and young Waldron were giving ex-
pert tonsorial treatment to "Sweet Adeline," and
flopped down beside Ryan, the manager.

"Well, Cap," I said, "we're due in Springfield
in a little over an hour and I haven't written a
line."

"Don't let me stop you," said Ryan.

"I want you to start me," I said.

"Lord!" said Ryan. "You oughtn't to have
any trouble grinding out stuff these days, with
the club in first place and young Waldron gone
crazy. He's worth a story any day."

"That's the trouble," said I. "He's been
worked so much that there's nothing more to
say about him. Everybody in the country knows
that he's hitting .420, that he's made nine home
runs, twelve triples and twenty-some doubles, that
he's stolen twenty-five bases, and that he can play
the piano and sing like Car*us*'. They've run his
picture oftener than Billy Sunday and Mary Pick-

ford put together. Of course, you might come through with how you got him."

"Oh, that's the mystery," said Ryan.

"So I've heard you say," I retorted. "But it wouldn't be a mystery if you'd let me print it."

"Well," said Ryan, "if you're really hard up I suppose I might as well come through. Only there's really no mystery at all about it; it's just what I consider the most remarkable piece of scouting ever done. I've been making a mystery of it just to have a little fun with Dick Hodges. You know he's got the Jackson club and he's still so sore about my stealing Waldron he'll hardly speak to me.

"I'll give you the dope if you want it, though it's a boost for Art Graham, not me. There's lots of people think the reason I've kept the thing a secret is because I'm modest.

"They give me credit for having found Waldron myself. But Graham is the bird that deserves the credit and I'll admit that he almost had to get down on his knees to make me take his tip. Yes, sir, Art Graham was the scout, and now he's sitting on the bench and the boy he recommended has got his place."

"That sounds pretty good," I said. "And how did Graham get wise?"

"I'm going to tell you. You're in a hurry; so I'll make it snappy.

Harmony

"You weren't with us last fall, were you? Well, we had a day off in Detroit, along late in the season. Graham's got relatives in Jackson; so he asked me if he could spend the day there. I told him he could and asked him to keep his eyes peeled for good young pitchers, if he happened to go to the ball game. So he went to Jackson and the next morning he came back all excited. I asked him if he'd found me a pitcher and he said he hadn't, but he'd seen the best natural hitter he'd ever looked at—a kid named Waldron.

" 'Well,' I said, 'you're the last one that ought to be recommending outfielders. If there's one good enough to hold a regular job, it might be your job he'd get.'

"But Art said that didn't make any difference to him—he was looking out for the good of the club. Well, I didn't see my way clear to asking the old man to dig up good money for an outfielder nobody'd ever heard of, when we were pretty well stocked with them, so I tried to stall Art; but he kept after me and kept after me till I agreed to stick in a draft for the kid just to keep Art quiet. So the draft went in and we got him. Then, as you know, Hodges tried to get him back, and that made me suspicious enough to hold on to him. Hodges finally came over to see me and wanted to know who'd tipped me to Waldron. That's where the mystery stuff started, because I

287

saw that Hodges was all heated up and wanted to kid him along. So I told him we had some mighty good scouts working for us, and he said he knew our regular scouts and they couldn't tell a ballplayer from a torn ligament. Then he offered me fifty bucks if I'd tell him the truth and I just laughed at him. I said: 'A fella happened to be in Jackson one day and saw him work. But I won't tell you who the fella was, because you're too anxious to know.' Then he insisted on knowing what day the scout had been in Jackson. I said I'd tell him that if he'd tell me why he was so blame curious. So he gave me his end of it.

"It seems his brother, up in Ludington, had seen this kid play ball on the lots and had signed him right up for Hodges and taken him to Jackson, and of course, Hodges knew he had a world beater the minute he saw him. But he also knew he wasn't going to be able to keep him in Jackson, and, naturally he began to figure how he could get the most money for him. It was already August when the boy landed in Jackson; so there wasn't much chance of getting a big price last season. He decided to teach the kid what he didn't know about baseball and to keep him under cover till this year. Then everybody would be touting him and there'd be plenty of competition. Hodges could sell to the highest bidder.

Harmony

"He had Waldron out practising every day, but wouldn't let him play in a game, and every player on the Jackson club had promised to keep the secret till this year. So Hodges wanted to find out from me which one of his players had broken the promise.

"Then I asked him if he was perfectly sure that Waldron hadn't played in a game, and he said he had gone in to hit for somebody just once. I asked him what date that was and he told me. It was the day Art had been in Jackson. So I said:

" 'There's your mystery solved. That's the day my scout saw him, and you'll have to give the scout a little credit for picking a star after seeing him make one base hit.'

"Then Hodges said:

" 'That makes it all the more a mystery. Because, in the first place, he batted under a fake name. And, in the second place, he didn't make a base hit. He popped out.'

"That's about all there is to it. You can ask Art how he picked the kid out for a star from seeing him pop out once. I've asked him myself, and he's told me that he liked the way Waldron swung. Personally, I believe one of those Jackson boys got too gabby. But Art swears not."

"That *is* a story," I said gratefully. "An old

How to Write Short Stories

outfielder who must know he's slipping recommends a busher after seeing him pop out once. And the busher jumps right in and gets his job."

I looked down the aisle toward the song birds. Art Graham, now a bench warmer, and young Waldron, whom he had touted and who was the cause of his being sent to the bench, were harmonizing at the tops of their strong and not too pleasant voices.

"And probably the strangest part of the story," I added, "is that Art doesn't seem to regret it. He and the kid appear to be the best of friends."

"Anybody who can sing is Art's friend," said Ryan.

I left him and went back to my seat to tear off my seven hundred words before we reached Springfield. I considered for a moment the advisability of asking Graham for an explanation of his wonderful bit of scouting, but decided to save that part of it for another day. I was in a hurry and, besides, Waldron was just teaching them a new "wallop," and it would have been folly for me to interrupt.

"It's on the word 'you,'" Waldron was saying. "I come down a tone; Lefty goes up a half tone, and Bill comes up two tones. Art just sings it like always. Now try her again," I heard him

Harmony

direct the song birds. They tried her again, making a worse noise than ever:

"I only know I love you;
  Love me, and the world (the world) is mine (the
    world is mine)."

"No," said Waldron. "Lefty missed it. If you fellas knew music, I could teach it to you with the piano when we get to Boston. On the word 'love,' in the next to the last line, we hit a regular F chord. Bill's singing the low F in the bass and Lefty's hitting middle C in the baritone, and Art's on high F and I'm up to A. Then, on the word 'you,' I come down to G, and Art hits E, and Lefty goes up half a tone to C sharp, and Cole comes up from F to A in the bass. That makes a good wallop. It's a change from the F chord to the A chord. Now let's try her again," Waldron urged.

They tried her again:

"I only know I love you——"

"No, no!" said young Waldron. "Art and I were all right; but Bill came up too far, and Lefty never moved off that C. Half a tone up, Lefty. Now try her again."

We were an hour late into Springfield, and it

was past six o'clock when we pulled out. I had
filed my stuff, and when I came back in the car
the concert was over for the time, and Art Graham
was sitting alone.

"Where are your pals?" I asked.

"Gone to the diner," he replied.

"Aren't you going to eat?"

"No," he said, "I'm savin' up for the steamed
clams." I took the seat beside him.

"I sent in a story about you," I said.

"Am I fired?" he asked.

"No, nothing like that."

"Well," he said, "you must be hard up when
you can't find nothin' better to write about than
a old has-been."

"Cap just told me who it was that found Waldron," said I.

"Oh, that," said Art. "I don't see no story in
that."

"I thought it was quite a stunt," I said. "It
isn't everybody that can pick out a second Cobb
by just seeing him hit a fly ball."

Graham smiled.

"No," he replied, "they's few as smart as that."

"If you ever get through playing ball," I went
on, "you oughtn't to have any trouble landing a
job. Good scouts don't grow on trees."

"It looks like I'm pretty near through now,"
said Art, still smiling. "But you won't never

catch me scoutin' for nobody. It's too lonesome a job."

I had passed up lunch to retain my seat in the card game; so I was hungry. Moreover, it was evident that Graham was not going to wax garrulous on the subject of his scouting ability. I left him and sought the diner. I found a vacant chair opposite Bill Cole.

"Try the minced ham," he advised, "but lay off'n the sparrow-grass. It's tougher'n a double-header in St. Louis."

"We're over an hour late," I said.

"You'll have to do a hurry-up on your story, won't you?" asked Bill. "Or did you write it already?"

"All written and on the way."

"Well, what did you tell 'em?" he inquired. "Did you tell 'em we had a pleasant trip, and Lenke lost his shirt in the poker game, and I'm goin' to pitch to-morrow, and the Boston club's heard about it and hope it'll rain?"

"No," I said. "I gave them a regular story to-night—about how Graham picked Waldron."

"Who give it to you?"

"Ryan," I told him.

"Then you didn't get the real story," said Cole, "Ryan himself don't know the best part of it, and he ain't goin' to know it for a w'ile. He'll maybe find it out after Art's got the can, but not

How to Write Short Stories

before. And I hope nothin' like that'll happen
for twenty years. When it does happen, I want to
be sent along with Art, 'cause I and him's been
roomies now since 1911, and I wouldn't hardly
know how to act with him off'n the club. He's a
nut all right on the singin' stuff, and if he was
gone I might get a chanct to give my voice a rest.
But he's a pretty good guy, even if he is crazy."

"I'd like to hear the real story," I said.

"Sure you would," he answered, "and I'd like
to tell it to you. I will tell it to you if you'll give
me your promise not to spill it till Art's gone.
Art told it to I and Lefty in the club-house at
Cleveland pretty near a month ago, and the
three of us and Waldron is the only ones that
knows it. I figure I've did pretty well to keep it
to myself this long, but it seems like I got to tell
somebody."

"You can depend on me," I assured him, "not
to say a word about it till Art's in Minneapolis,
or wherever they're going to send him."

"I guess I can trust you," said Cole. "But if
you cross me, I'll shoot my fast one up there in
the press coop some day and knock your teeth
loose."

"Shoot," said I.

"Well," said Cole, "I s'pose Ryan told you that
Art fell for the kid after just seein' him pop
out."

Harmony

"Yes, and Ryan said he considered it a remarkable piece of scouting."

"It was all o' that. It'd of been remarkable enough if Art'd saw the bird pop out and then recommended him. But he didn't even see him pop out."

"What are you giving me?"

"The fac's," said Bill Cole. "Art not only didn't see him pop out, but he didn't even see him with a ball suit on. He wasn't never inside the Jackson ball park in his life."

"Waldron?"

"No. Art I'm talkin' about."

"Then somebody tipped him off," I said, quickly.

"No, sir. Nobody tipped him off, neither. He went to Jackson and spent the ev'nin' at his uncle's house, and Waldron was there. Him and Art was together the whole ev'nin'. But Art didn't even ask him if he could slide feet first. And then he come back to Detroit and got Ryan to draft him. But to give you the whole story, I'll have to go back a ways. We ain't nowheres near Worcester yet, so they's no hurry, except that Art'll prob'ly be sendin' for me pretty quick to come in and learn Waldron's lost chord.

"You wasn't with this club when we had Mike McCann. But you must of heard of him; outside his pitchin', I mean. He was on the stage a

How to Write Short Stories

couple o' winters, and he had the swellest tenor voice I ever heard. I never seen no grand opera, but I'll bet this here C'ruso or McCormack or Gadski or none o' them had nothin' on him for a pure tenor. Every note as clear as a bell. You couldn't hardly keep your eyes dry when he'd tear off 'Silver Threads' or 'The River Shannon.'

"Well, when Art was still with the Washin'ton club yet, I and Lefty and Mike used to pal round together and onct or twict we'd hit up some harmony. I couldn't support a fam'ly o' Mormons with my voice, but it was better in them days than it is now. I used to carry the lead, and Lefty'd hit the baritone and Mike the tenor. We didn't have no bass. But most o' the time we let Mike do the singin' alone, 'cause he had us outclassed, and the other boys kept tellin' us to shut up and give 'em a treat. First it'd be 'Silver Threads' and then 'Jerusalem' and then 'My Wild Irish Rose' and this and that, whatever the boys ast him for. Jake Martin used to say he couldn't help a short pair if Mike wasn't singin'.

"Finally Ryan pulled off the trade with Griffith, and Graham come on our club. Then they wasn't no more solo work. They made a bass out o' me, and Art sung the lead, and Mike and Lefty took care o' the tenor and baritone. Art didn't care what the other boys wanted to hear. They could holler their heads off for Mike to sing a solo, but

Harmony

no sooner'd Mike start singin' than Art'd chime
in with him and pretty soon we'd all four be
goin' it. Art's a nut on singin', but he don't care
nothin' about list'nin', not even to a canary.
He'd rather harmonize than hit one past the
outfielders with two on.

"At first we done all our serenadin' on the train.
Art'd get us out o' bed early so's we could be
through breakfast and back in the car in time to
tear off a few before we got to wherever we was
goin'.

"It got so's Art wouldn't leave us alone in the
different towns we played at. We couldn't go to
no show or nothin'. We had to stick in the
hotel and sing, up in our room or Mike's. And
then he went so nuts over it that he got Mike to
come and room in the same house with him at
home, and I and Lefty was supposed to help keep
the neighbors awake every night. O' course we
had mornin' practice w'ile we was home, and Art
used to have us come to the park early and get in
a little harmony before we went on the field.
But Ryan finally nailed that. He says that when
he ordered mornin' practice he meant baseball
and not no minstrel show.

"Then Lefty, who wasn't married, goes and
gets himself a girl. I met her a couple o' times,
and she looked all right. Lefty might of married

297

her if Art'd of left him alone. But nothin' doin'.
We was home all through June onct, and instead
o' comin' round nights to sing with us, Lefty'd
take this here doll to one o' the parks or somewheres. Well, sir, Art was pretty near wild. He
scouted round till he'd found out why Lefty'd
quit us and then he tried pretty near everybody
else on the club to see if they wasn't some one who
could hit the baritone. They wasn't nobody.
So the next time we went on the road, Art give
Lefty a earful about what a sucker a man was to
get married, and looks wasn't everything and
the girl was prob'ly after Lefty's money and he
wasn't bein' a good fella to break up the quartette
and spoil our good times, and so on, and kept
pesterin' and teasin' Lefty till he give the girl
up. I'd of saw Art in the Texas League before
I'd of shook a girl to please him, but you know
these left-handers.

"Art had it all framed that we was goin' on the
stage, the four of us, and he seen a vaudeville
man in New York and got us booked for eight
hundred a week—I don't know if it was one week
or two. But he sprung it on me in September and
says we could get solid bookin' from October to
March; so I ast him what he thought my Missus
would say when I told her I couldn't get enough
o' bein' away from home from March to October,
so I was figurin' on travelin' the vaudeville cir-

cuit the other four or five months and makin' it unanimous? Art says I was tied to a woman's apron and all that stuff, but I give him the cold stare and he had to pass up that dandy little scheme.

"At that, I guess we could of got by on the stage all right. Mike was better than this here Waldron and I hadn't wore my voice out yet on the coachin' line, tellin' the boys to touch all the bases.

"They was about five or six songs that we could kill. 'Adeline' was our star piece. Remember where it comes in, 'Your fair face beams'? Mike used to go away up on 'fair.' Then they was 'The Old Millstream' and 'Put on Your Old Gray Bonnet.' I done some fancy work in that one. Then they was 'Down in Jungle Town' that we had pretty good. And then they was one that maybe you never heard. I don't know the name of it. It run somethin' like this."

Bill sottoed his voice so that I alone could hear the beautiful refrain:

"'Years, years, I've waited years
Only to see you, just to call you 'dear.'
Come, come, I love but thee,
Come to your sweetheart's arms; come back to me.'

"That one had a lot o' wallops in it, and we didn't overlook none o' them. The boys used to make us sing it six or seven times a night. But

How to Write Short Stories

'Down in the Cornfield' was Art's favor-ight. They was a part in that where I sung the lead down low and the other three done a banjo stunt. Then they was 'Castle on the Nile' and 'Come Back to Erin' and a whole lot more.

"Well, the four of us wasn't hardly ever separated for three years. We was practisin' all the w'ile like as if we was goin' to play the big time, and we never made a nickel off'n it. The only audience we had was the ball players or the people travelin' on the same trains or stoppin' at the same hotels, and they got it all for nothin'. But we had a good time, 'specially Art.

"You know what a pitcher Mike was. He could go in there stone cold and stick ten out o' twelve over that old plate with somethin' on 'em. And he was the willin'est guy in the world. He pitched his own game every third or fourth day, and between them games he was warmin' up all the time to go in for somebody else. In 1911, when we was up in the race for aw'ile, he pitched eight games out o' twenty, along in September, and win seven o' them, and besides that, he finished up five o' the twelve he didn't start. We didn't win the pennant, and I've always figured that them three weeks killed Mike.

"Anyway, he wasn't worth nothin' to the club the next year; but they carried him along, hopin' he'd come back and show somethin'. But he was pretty near through, and he knowed it. I knowed

Harmony

it, too, and so did everybody else on the club, only Graham. Art never got wise till the trainin' trip two years ago this last spring. Then he come to me one day.

" 'Bill,' he says, 'I don't believe Mike's comin' back.'

" 'Well,' I says, 'you're gettin's so's they can't nobody hide nothin' from you. Next thing you'll be findin' out that Sam Crawford can hit.'

" 'Never mind the comical stuff,' he says. 'They ain't no joke about this!'

" 'No,' I says, 'and I never said they was. They'll look a long w'ile before they find another pitcher like Mike.'

" 'Pitcher my foot!' says Art. 'I don't care if they have to pitch the bat boy. But when Mike goes, where'll our quartette be?'

" 'Well,' I says, 'do you get paid every first and fifteenth for singin' or for crownin' that old pill?'

" 'If you couldn't talk about money, you'd be deaf and dumb,' says Art.

" 'But you ain't playin' ball because it's fun, are you?'

" 'No,' he says, 'they ain't no fun for me in playin' ball. They's no fun doin' nothin' but harmonizin', and if Mike goes, I won't even have that.'

" 'I and you and Lefty can harmonize,' I says.

" 'It'd be swell stuff harmonizin' without no

301

tenor,' says Art. 'It'd be like swingin' without
no bat.'

"Well, he ast me did I think the club'd carry
Mike through another season, and I told him
they'd already carried him a year without him
bein' no good to them, and I figured if he didn't
show somethin' his first time out, they'd ask for
waivers. Art kept broodin' and broodin' about
it till they wasn't hardly no livin' with him. If
he ast me onct he ast me a thousand times if I
didn't think they might maybe hold onto Mike
another season on account of all he'd did for
'em. I kept tellin' him I didn't think so; but
that didn't satisfy him and he finally went to
Ryan and ast him point blank.

" 'Are you goin' to keep McCann?' Art ast
him.

" 'If he's goin' to do us any good, I am,' says
Ryan. 'If he ain't, he'll have to look for another job.'

"After that, all through the trainin' trip, he
was right on Mike's heels.

" 'How does the old souper feel?' he'd ask him.

" 'Great!' Mike'd say.

"Then Art'd watch him warm up, to see if he
had anything on the ball.

" 'He's comin' fine,' he'd tell me. 'His curve
broke to-day just as good as I ever seen it.'

Harmony

"But that didn't fool me, or it didn't fool Mike neither. He could throw about four hooks and then he was through. And he could of hit you in the head with his fast one and you'd of thought you had a rash.

"One night, just before the season opened up, we was singin' on the train, and when we got through, Mike says:

" 'Well, boys, you better be lookin' for another C'ruso.'

" 'What are you talkin' about?' says Art.

" 'I'm talkin' about myself,' says Mike. 'I'll be up there in Minneapolis this summer, pitchin' onct a week and swappin' stories about the Civil War with Joe Cantillon.'

" 'You're crazy,' says Art. 'Your arm's as good as I ever seen it.'

" 'Then,' says Mike, 'you must of been playin' blindfolded all these years. This is just between us, 'cause Ryan'll find it out for himself; my arm's rotten, and I can't do nothin' to help it.'

"Then Art got sore as a boil.

" 'You're a yellow, quittin' dog,' he says. 'Just because you come round a little slow, you talk about Minneapolis. Why don't you resign off'n the club?'

" 'I might just as well,' Mike says, and left us.

303

How to Write Short Stories

"You'd of thought that Art would of gave up then, 'cause when a ball player admits he's slippin', you can bet your last nickel that he's through. Most o' them stalls along and tries to kid themself and everybody else long after they know they're gone. But Art kept talkin' like they was still some hope o' Mike comin' round, and when Ryan told us one night in St. Louis that he was goin' to give Mike his chanct, the next day, Art was as nervous as a bride goin' to get married. I wasn't nervous. I just felt sorry, 'cause I knowed the old boy was hopeless.

"Ryan had told him he was goin' to work if the weather suited him. Well, the day was perfect. So Mike went out to the park along about noon and took Jake with him to warm up. Jake told me afterwards that Mike was throwin', just easy like, from half-past twelve till the rest of us got there. He was tryin' to heat up the old souper and he couldn't of ast for a better break in the weather, but they wasn't enough sunshine in the world to make that old whip crack.

"Well, sir, you'd of thought to see Art that Mike was his son or his brother or somebody and just breakin' into the league. Art wasn't in the outfield practisin' more than two minutes. He come in and stood behind Mike w'ile he was warmin' up and kept tellin' how good he looked, but the only guy he was kiddin' was himself.

Harmony

"Then the game starts and our club goes in and gets three runs.

" 'Pretty soft for you now, Mike,' says Art, on the bench. 'They can't score three off'n you in three years.'

"Say, it's lucky he ever got the side out in the first innin'. Everybody that come up hit one on the pick, but our infield pulled two o' the greatest plays I ever seen and they didn't score. In the second, we got three more, and I thought maybe the old bird was goin' to be lucky enough to scrape through.

"For four or five innin's, he got the grandest support that was ever gave a pitcher; but I'll swear that what he throwed up there didn't have no more on it than September Morning. Every time Art come to the bench, he says to Mike, 'Keep it up, old boy. You got more than you ever had.'

"Well, in the seventh, Mike still had 'em shut out, and we was six runs to the good. Then a couple o' the St. Louis boys hit 'em where they couldn't nobody reach 'em and they was two on and two out. Then somebody got a hold o' one and sent it on a line to the left o' second base. I forgot who it was now; but whoever it was, he was supposed to be a right field hitter, and Art was layin' over the other way for him. Art started with the crack o' the bat, and I never seen

305

a man make a better try for a ball. He had it
judged perfect; but Cobb or Speaker or none o'
them couldn't of catched it. Art just managed
to touch it by stretchin' to the limit. It went on
to the fence and everybody come in. They didn't
score no more in that innin'.

"Then Art come in from the field and what do
you think he tried to pull?

" 'I don't know what was the matter with me
on that fly ball,' he says. 'I ought to caught it in
my pants pocket. But I didn't get started till it
was right on top o' me.'

" 'You misjudged it, didn't you?' says Ryan.

" 'I certainly did,' says Art without crackin'.

" 'Well,' says Ryan, 'I wisht you'd misjudge all
o' them that way. I never seen a better play on a
ball.'

"So then Art knowed they wasn't no more use
trying to alibi the old boy.

"Mike had a turn at bat and when he come
back, Ryan ast him how he felt.

" 'I guess I can get six more o' them out,' he
says.

"Well, they didn't score in the eighth, and
when the ninth come Ryan sent I and Lefty out to
warm up. We throwed a few w'ile our club was
battin'; but when it come St. Louis' last chanct,
we was too much interested in the ball game to
know if we was throwin' or bakin' biscuits.

"The first guy hits a line drive, and somebody

Harmony

jumps a mile in the air and stabs it. The next
fella fouled out, and they was only one more to
get. And then what do you think come off?
Whoever it was hittin' lifted a fly ball to centre
field. Art didn't have to move out of his tracks.
I've saw him catch a hundred just like it behind
his back. But you know what he was thinkin'.
He was sayin' to himself, 'If I nail this one, we're
li'ble to keep our tenor singer a w'ile longer.'
And he dropped it.

"Then they was five base hits tnat sounded
like the fourth o' July, and they come so fast that
Ryan didn't have time to send for I or Lefty.
Anyway, I guess he thought he might as well
leave Mike in there and take it.

"They wasn't no singin' in the clubhouse after
that game. I and Lefty always let the others
start it. Mike, o' course, didn't feel like no
jubilee, and Art was so busy tryin' not to let nobody see him cry that he kept his head clear down
in his socks. Finally he beat it for town all alone,
and we didn't see nothin' of him till after supper.
Then he got us together and we all went up to
Mike's room.

" 'I want to try this here "Old Girl o' Mine," '
he says.

" 'Better sing our old stuff,' says Mike. 'This
looks like the last time.'

"Then Art choked up and it was ten minutes
before he could get goin'. We sung everything

307

we knowed, and it was two o'clock in the mornin'
before Art had enough. Ryan come in after midnight and set a w'ile listenin', but he didn't chase
us to bed. He knowed better'n any of us that it
was a farewell. When I and Art was startin' for
our room, Art turned to Mike and says:

" 'Old boy, I'd of gave every nickel I ever
owned to of caught that fly ball.'

" 'I know you would,' Mike says, 'and I know
what made you drop it. But don't worry about
it, 'cause it was just a question o' time, and if
I'd of got away with that game, they'd of mur-
dered some o' the infielders next time I started.'

"Mike was sent home the next day, and we
didn't see him again. He was shipped to Minneapolis before we got back. And the rest o' the
season I might as well of lived in a cemetery w'ile
we was on the road. Art was so bad that I thought
onct or twict I'd have to change roomies. Onct
in a w'ile he'd start hummin' and then he'd
break off short and growl at me. He tried out
two or three o' the other boys on the club to see if
he couldn't find a new tenor singer, but nothin'
doin'. One night he made Lefty try the tenor.
Well, Lefty's voice is bad enough down low.
When he gets up about so high, you think you're
in the stockyards.

"And Art had a rotten year in baseball, too.

Harmony

The old boy's still pretty near as good on a fly ball as anybody in the league; but you ought to saw him before his legs begin to give out. He could cover as much ground as Speaker and he was just as sure. But the year Mike left us, he missed pretty near half as many as he got. He told me one night, he says:

" 'Do you know, Bill, I stand out there and pray that nobody'll hit one to me. Every time I see one comin' I think o' that one I dropped for Mike in St. Louis, and then I'm just as li'ble to have it come down on my bean as in my glove.'

" 'You're crazy,' I says, 'to let a thing like that make a bum out o' you.'

"But he kept on droppin' fly balls till Ryan was talkin' about settin' him on the bench where it wouldn't hurt nothin' if his nerve give out. But Ryan didn't have nobody else to play out there, so Art held on.

"He come back the next spring—that's a year ago—feelin' more cheerful and like himself than I'd saw him for a long w'ile. And they was a kid named Burton tryin' out for second base that could sing pretty near as good as Mike. It didn't take Art more'n a day to find this out, and every mornin' and night for a few days the four of us would be together, hittin' her up. But the kid didn't have no more idea o' how to play the bag than Charley Chaplin. Art seen in a minute that he couldn't never beat Cragin out of his job, so what does he do but take him out and try and learn him to play the outfield. He wasn't no worse there than at second base; he couldn't of been. But before he'd practised out there three days they was bruises all over his head and shoulders where fly balls had hit him. Well, the kid wasn't with us long enough to see the first exhibition game, and after he'd went, Art was Old Man Grump again.

" 'What's the matter with you?' I says to him. 'You was all smiles the day we reported and now you could easy pass for a undertaker.'

" 'Well,' he says, 'I had a great winter, singin' all the w'ile. We got a good quartette down home and I never enjoyed myself as much in my life. And I kind o' had a hunch that I was goin' to be lucky and find somebody amongst the bushers that could hit up the old tenor.'

" 'Your hunch was right,' I says. 'That Burton kid was as good a tenor as you'd want.'

" 'Yes,' he says, 'and my hunch could of played ball just as good as him.'

"Well, sir, if you didn't never room with a corpse, you don't know what a whale of a time I had all last season. About the middle of August he was at his worst.

" 'Bill,' he says, 'I'm goin' to leave this old
310

Harmony

baseball flat on its back if somethin' don't happen. I can't stand these here lonesome nights. I ain't like the rest o' the boys that can go and set all ev'nin' at a pitcher show or hang round them Dutch gardens. I got to be singin' or I am mis'rable.'

" 'Go ahead and sing,' says I. 'I'll try and keep the cops back.'

" 'No,' he says, 'I don't want to sing alone. I want to harmonize and we can't do that 'cause we ain't got no tenor.'

"I don't know if you'll believe me or not, but sure as we're settin' here he went to Ryan one day in Philly and tried to get him to make a trade for Harper.

" 'What do I want him for?' says Ryan.

" 'I hear he ain't satisfied,' says Art.

" 'I ain't runnin' no ball players' benefit association,' says Ryan, and Art had to give it up. But he didn't want Harper on the club for no other reason than because he's a tenor singer!

"And then come that Dee-troit trip, and Art got permission to go to Jackson. He says he intended to drop in at the ball park, but his uncle wanted to borry some money off'n him on a farm, so Art had to drive out and see the farm. Then, that night, this here Waldron was up to call on Art's cousin—a swell doll, Art tells me. And

How to Write Short Stories

Waldron set down to the py-ana and begin to sing and play. Then it was all off; they wasn't no spoonin' in the parlor that night. Art wouldn't leave the kid get off'n the py-ana stool long enough to even find out if the girl was a blonde or a brunette.

"O' course Art knowed the boy was with the Jackson club as soon as they was interduced, 'cause Art's uncle says somethin' about the both o' them bein' ball players, and so on. But Art swears he never thought o' recommendin' him till the kid got up to go home. Then he ast him what position did he play and found out all about him, only o' course Waldron didn't tell him how good he was 'cause he didn't know himself.

"So Art ast him would he like a trial in the big show, and the kid says he would. Then Art says maybe the kid would hear from him, and then Waldron left and Art went to bed, and he says he stayed awake all night plannin' the thing out and wonderin' would he have the nerve to pull it off. You see he thought that if Ryan fell for it, Waldron'd join us as soon as his season was over and then Ryan'd see he wasn't no good; but he'd prob'ly keep him till we was through for the year, and Art could alibi himself some way, say he'd got the wrong name or somethin'. All he wanted, he says, was to have the kid along the last month

312

Harmony

or six weeks, so's we could harmonize. A nut?
I guess not.

"Well, as you know, Waldron got sick and
didn't report, and when Art seen him on the train
this spring he couldn't hardly believe his eyes.
He thought surely the kid would of been canned
durin' the winter without no trial.

"Here's another hot one. When we went out
the first day for practice, Art takes the kid off in
a corner and tries to learn him enough baseball
so's he won't show himself up and get sent away
somewheres before we had a little benefit from
his singin'. Can you imagine that? Tryin' to
learn this kid baseball, when he was born with a
slidin' pad on.

"You know the rest of it. They wasn't never
no question about Waldron makin' good. It's
just like everybody says—he's the best natural
ball player that's broke in since Cobb. They
ain't nothin' he can't do. But it *is* a funny thing
that Art's job should be the one he'd get. I
spoke about that to Art when he give me the
story.

" 'Well,' he says, 'I can't expect everything
to break right. I figure I'm lucky to of picked a
guy that's good enough to hang on. I'm in
stronger with Ryan right now, and with the old
man, too, than when I was out there playin'
every day. Besides, the bench is a pretty good

place to watch the game from. And this club won't be shy a tenor singer for nine years.'

" 'No,' I says, 'but they'll be shy a lead and a baritone and a bass before I and you and Lefty is much older.'

" 'What of it?' he says. 'We'll look up old Mike and all go somewheres and live together.' "

We were nearing Worcester. Bill Cole and I arose from our table and started back toward our car. In the first vestibule we encountered Buck, the trainer.

"Mr. Graham's been lookin' all over for you, Mr. Cole," he said.

"I've been rehearsin' my part," said Bill.

We found Art Graham, Lefty, and young Waldron in Art's seat. The kid was talking.

"Lefty missed it again. If you fellas knew music, I could teach it to you on the piano when we get to Boston. Lefty, on the word 'love,' in the next to the last line, you're on middle C. Then, on the word 'you,' you slide up half a tone. That'd ought to be a snap, but you don't get it. I'm on high A and come down to G and Bill's on low F and comes up to A. Art just sings the regular two notes, F and E. It's a change from the F chord to the A chord. It makes a dandy wallop and it ought to be a———"

Harmony

"Here's Bill now," interrupted Lefty, as he caught sight of Cole.

Art Graham treated his roommate to a cold stare.

"Where the h—l have you been?" he said angrily.

"Lookin' for the lost chord," said Bill.

"Set down here and learn this," growled Art. "We won't never get it if we don't work."

"Yes, let's tackle her again," said Waldron. "Bill comes up two full tones, from F to A. Lefty goes up half a tone, Art sings just like always, and I come down a tone. Now try her again."

Two years ago it was that Bill Cole told me that story. Two weeks ago Art Graham boarded the evening train on one of the many roads that lead to Minneapolis.

The day Art was let out, I cornered Ryan in the club-house after the others had dressed and gone home.

"Did you ever know," I asked, "That Art recommended Waldron without having seen him in a ball suit?"

"I told you long ago how Art picked Waldron," he said.

"Yes," said I, "but you didn't have the right story."

So I gave it to him.

How to Write Short Stories

"You newspaper fellas," he said when I had done, "are the biggest suckers in the world. Now I've never given you a bad steer in my life. But you don't believe what I tell you and you go and fall for one of Bill Cole's hop dreams. Don't you know that he was the biggest liar in baseball? He'd tell you that Walter Johnson was Jack's father if he thought he could get away with it. And that bunk he gave you about Waldron. Does it sound reasonable?"

"Just as reasonable," I replied, "as the stuff about Art's grabbing him after seeing him pop out."

"I don't claim he did," said Ryan. "That's what Art told me. One of those Jackson ball players could give you the real truth, only of course he wouldn't, because if Hodges ever found it out he'd shoot him full of holes. Art Graham's no fool. He isn't touting ball players because they can sing tenor or alto or anything else."

Nevertheless, I believe Bill Cole; else I wouldn't print the story. And Ryan would believe, too, if he weren't in such a mood these days that he disagrees with everybody. For in spite of Waldron's wonderful work, and he is at his best right now, the club hasn't done nearly as well as when Art and Bill and Lefty were still with us.

There seems to be a lack of harmony.

HORSESHOES

This is the kind of story which the reader can take up at any point and lay down as soon as he feels like it.   A trail of vengeance, ruthless and sinister, is uncovered to its hidden source by a flat-footed detective.

X

HORSESHOES

The series ended Tuesday, but I had stayed in Philadelphia an extra day on the chance of there being some follow-up stuff worth sending. Nothing had broken loose; so I filed some stuff about what the Athletics and Giants were going to do with their dough, and then caught the eight o'clock train for Chicago.

Having passed up supper in order to get my story away and grab the train, I went to the buffet car right after I'd planted my grips. I sat down at one of the tables and ordered a sandwich. Four salesmen were playing rum at the other table and all the chairs in the car were occupied; so it didn't surprise me when somebody flopped down in the seat opposite me.

I looked up from my paper and with a little thrill recognized my companion. Now I've been experting round the country with ball players so much that it doesn't usually excite me to meet one face to face, even if he's a star. I can talk with Tyrus without getting all fussed up. But this particular player had jumped from obscurity to fame so suddenly and had played such an im-

319

How to Write Short Stories

portant though brief part in the recent argument between the Macks and McGraws that I couldn't help being a little awed by his proximity.

It was none other than Grimes, the utility outfielder Connie had been forced to use in the last game because of the injury to Joyce—Grimes, whose miraculous catch in the eleventh inning had robbed Parker of a home run and the Giants of victory, and whose own homer—a fluky one—had given the Athletics another World's Championship.

I had met Grimes one day during the spring he was with the Cubs, but I knew he wouldn't remember me. A ball player never recalls a reporter's face on less than six introductions or his name on less than twenty. However, I resolved to speak to him, and had just mustered sufficient courage to open a conversation when he saved me the trouble.

"Whose picture have they got there?" he asked, pointing to my paper.

"Speed Parker's," I replied.

"What do they say about him?" asked Grimes.

'I'll read it to you," I said:

"'Speed Parker, McGraw's great third baseman, is ill in a local hospital with nervous prostration, the result of the strain of the World's Series, in which he played such a stellar rôle. Parker is in such a dangerous condition that no one is

Horseshoes

allowed to see him. Members of the New York team and fans from Gotham called at the hospital to-day, but were unable to gain admittance to his ward. Philadelphians hope he will recover speedily and will suffer no permanent ill effects from his sickness, for he won their admiration by his work in the series, though he was on a rival team. A lucky catch by Grimes, the Athletics' substitute outfielder, was all that prevented Parker from winning the title for New York. According to Manager Mack, of the champions, the series would have been over in four games but for Parker's wonderful exhibition of nerve and——'"

"That'll be a plenty," Grimes interrupted. "And that's just what you might expect from one o' them doughheaded reporters. If all the baseball writers was where they belonged they'd have to build an annex to Matteawan."

I kept my temper with very little effort—it takes more than a peevish ball player's remarks to insult one of our fraternity; but I didn't exactly understand his peeve.

"Doesn't Parker deserve the bouquet?" I asked.

"Oh, they can boost him all they want to," said Grimes; "but when they call that catch lucky and don't mention the fact that Parker is the luckiest guy in the world, somethin' must be wrong with 'em. Did you see the serious?"

How to Write Short Stories

"No," I lied glibly, hoping to draw from him the cause of his grouch.

"Well," he said, "you sure missed somethin'. They never was a serious like it before and they won't never be one again. It went the full seven games and every game was a bear. They was one big innin' every day and Parker was the big cheese in it. Just as Connie says, the Ath-a-letics would of cleaned 'em in four games but for Parker; but it wasn't because he's a great ball player—it was because he was born with a knife, fork and spoon in his mouth, and a rabbit's foot hung round his neck.

"You may not know it, but I'm Grimes, the guy that made the lucky catch. I'm the guy that won the serious with a hit—a home-run hit; and I'm here to tell you that if I'd had one-tenth o' Parker's luck they'd of heard about me long before yesterday. They say my homer was lucky. Maybe it was; but, believe me, it was time things broke for me. They been breakin' for him all his life."

"Well," I said, "his luck must have gone back on him if he's in a hospital with nervous prostration."

"Nervous prostration nothin'," said Grimes. "He's in a hospital because his face is all out o' shape and he's ashamed to appear on the street. I don't usually do so much talkin' and I'm ravin' a little to-night because I've had a couple o' drinks; but——"

"Have another," said I, ringing for the waiter, "and talk some more."

"I made two hits yesterday," Grimes went on, "but the crowd only seen one. I busted up the game and the serious with the one they seen. The one they didn't see was the one I busted up a guy's map with—and Speed Parker was the guy. That's why he's in a hospital. He may be able to play ball next year; but I'll bet my share o' the dough that McGraw won't reco'nize him when he shows up at Marlin in the spring."

"When did this come off?" I asked. "And why?"

"It come off outside the clubhouse after yesterday's battle," he said; "and I hit him because he called me a name—a name I won't stand for from him."

"What did he call you?" I queried, expecting to hear one of the delicate epithets usually applied by conquered to conqueror on the diamond.

"'Horseshoes!' " was Grimes' amazing reply.

"But, good Lord!" I remonstrated, "I've heard of ball players calling each other that, and Lucky Stiff, and Fourleaf Clover, ever since I was a foot high, and I never knew them to start fights about it."

"Well," said Grimes, "I might as well give you

all the dope; and then if you don't think I was justified I'll pay your fare from here to wherever you're goin'. I don't want you to think I'm kickin' about trifles—or that I'm kickin' at all, for that matter. I just want to prove to you that he didn't have no license to pull that Horseshoes stuff on me and that I only give him what was comin' to him."

"Go ahead and shoot," said I.

"Give us some more o' the same," said Grimes to the passing waiter. And then he told me about it.

Maybe you've heard that me and Speed Parker was raised in the same town—Ishpeming, Michigan. We was kids together, and though he done all the devilment I got all the lickin's. When we was about twelve years old Speed throwed a rotten egg at the teacher and I got expelled. That made me sick o' schools and I wouldn't never go to one again, though my ol' man beat me up and the truant officers threatened to have me hung.

Well, while Speed was learnin' what was the principal products o' New Hampshire and Texas I was workin' round the freighthouse and drivin' a dray.

We'd both been playin' ball all our lives; and when the town organized a semi-pro club we got jobs with it. We was to draw two bucks apiece

Horseshoes

for each game and they played every Sunday.
We played four games before we got our first pay.
They was a hole in my pants pocket as big as
the home plate, but I forgot about it and put the
dough in there. It wasn't there when I got home.
Speed didn't have no hole in his pocket—you can
bet on that! Afterward the club hired a good
outfielder and I was canned. They was huntin'
for another third baseman too; but, o' course,
they didn't find none and Speed held his job.

The next year they started the Northern Peninsula League. We landed with the home team.
The league opened in May and blowed up the
third week in June. They paid off all the out-
siders first and then had just money enough left
to settle with one of us two Ishpeming guys.
The night they done the payin' I was out to my
uncle's farm, so they settled with Speed and
told me I'd have to wait for mine. I'm still
waitin'!

Gene Higgins, who was manager o' the Battle
Creek Club, lived in Houghton, and that winter
we goes over and strikes him for a job. He give it
to us and we busted in together two years ago
last spring.

I had a good year down there. I hit over .300
and stole all the bases in sight. Speed got along
good too, and they was several big-league scouts
lookin' us over. The Chicago Cubs bought Speed

outright and four clubs put in a draft for me. Three of 'em—Cleveland and the New York Giants and the Boston Nationals—needed outfielders bad, and it would of been a pipe for me to of made good with any of 'em. But who do you think got me? The same Chicago Cubs; and the only outfielders they had at that time was Schulte and Leach and Good and Williams and Stewart, and one or two others.

Well, I didn't figure I was any worse off than Speed. The Cubs had Zimmerman at third base and it didn't look like they was any danger of a busher beatin' him out; but Zimmerman goes and breaks his leg the second day o' the season—that's a year ago last April—and Speed jumps right in as a regular. Do you think anything like that could happen to Schulte or Leach, or any o' them outfielders? No, sir! I wore out my uniform slidin' up and down the bench and wonderin' whether they'd ship me to Fort Worth or Siberia.

Now I want to tell you about the miserable luck Speed had right off the reel. We was playin' at St. Louis. They had a one-run lead in the eighth, when their pitcher walked Speed with one out. Saier hits a high fly to centre and Parker starts with the crack o' the bat. Both coachers was yellin' at him to go back, but he thought they was two out and he was clear round to third base when the ball come down. And Oakes muffs it! O' course he scored and the game was tied up.

Parker come in to the bench like he'd did something wonderful.

"Did you think they was two out?" ast Hank.

"No," says Speed, blushin'.

"Then what did you run for?" says Hank.

"I had a hunch he was goin' to drop the ball," says Speed; and Hank pretty near falls off the bench.

The next day he come up with one out and the sacks full, and the score tied in the sixth. He smashes one on the ground straight at Hauser and it looked like a cinch double play; but just as Hauser was goin' to grab it the ball hit a rough spot and hopped a mile over his head. It got between Oakes and Magee and went clear to the fence. Three guys scored and Speed pulled up at third. The papers come out and said the game was won by a three-bagger from the bat o' Parker, the Cubs' sensational kid third baseman. Gosh!

We go home to Chi and are havin' a hot battle with Pittsburgh. This time Speed's turn come when they was two on and two out, and Pittsburgh a run to the good—I think it was the eighth innin'. Cooper gives him a fast one and he hits it straight up in the air. O' course the runners started goin', but it looked hopeless be-

How to Write Short Stories

cause they wasn't no wind or high sky to bother anybody. Mowrey and Gibson both goes after the ball; and just as Mowrey was set for the catch Gibson bumps into him and they both fall down. Two runs scored and Speed got to second. Then what does he do but try to steal third—with two out too! And Gibson's peg pretty near hits the left field seats on the fly.

When Speed comes to the bench Hank says:

"If I was you I'd quit playin' ball and go to Monte Carlo."

"What for?" says Speed.

"You're so dam' lucky!" says Hank.

"So is Ty Cobb," says Speed. That's how he hated himself!

First trip to Cincy we run into a couple of old Ishpeming boys. They took us out one night, and about twelve o'clock I said we'd have to go back to the hotel or we'd get fined. Speed said I had cold feet and he stuck with the boys. I went back alone and Hank caught me comin' in and put a fifty-dollar plaster on me. Speed stayed out all night long and Hank never knowed it. I says to myself: "Wait till he gets out there and tries to play ball without no sleep!" But the game that day was called off on account o' rain. Can you beat it?

I remember what he got away with the next afternoon the same as though it happened yes-

terday. In the second innin' they walked him
with nobody down, and he took a big lead off
first base like he always does. Benton throwed
over there three or four times to scare him back,
and the last time he throwed, Hobby hid the ball.
The coacher seen it and told Speed to hold the
bag; but he didn't pay no attention. He started
leadin' right off again and Hobby tried to tag
him, but the ball slipped out of his hand and
rolled about a yard away. Parker had plenty o'
time to get back; but, instead o' that, he starts
for second. Hobby picked up the ball and shot it
down to Groh—and Groh made a square muff.

Parker slides into the bag safe and then gets up
and throws out his chest like he'd made the
greatest play ever. When the ball's throwed
back to Benton, Speed leads off about thirty foot
and stands there in a trance. Clarke signs for a
pitch-out and pegs down to second to nip him.
He was caught flatfooted—that is, he would of
been with a decent throw; but Clarke's peg went
pretty near to Latonia. Speed scored and strutted
over to receive our hearty congratulations. Some
o' the boys was laughin' and he thought they was
laughin' with him instead of at him.

It was in the ninth, though, that he got by with
one o' the worst I ever seen. The Reds was a run
behind and Marsans was on third base with two
out. Hobby, I think it was, hit one on the ground

right at Speed and he picked it up clean. The crowd all got up and started for the exits. Marsans run toward the plate in the faint hope that the peg to first would be wild. All of a sudden the boys on the Cincy bench begun yellin' at him to slide, and he done so. He was way past the plate when Speed's throw got to Archer. The bonehead had shot the ball home instead o' to first base, thinkin' they was only one down. We was all crazy, believin' his nut play had let 'em tie it up; but he comes tearin' in, tellin' Archer to tag Marsans. So Jim walks over and tags the Cuban, who was brushin' off his uniform.

"You're out!" says Klem. "You never touched the plate."

I guess Marsans knowed the umps was right because he didn't make much of a holler. But Speed sure got a pannin' in the clubhouse.

"I suppose you knowed he was goin' to miss the plate!" says Hank sarcastic as he could.

Everybody on the club roasted him, but it didn't do no good.

Well, you know what happened to me. I only got into one game with the Cubs—one afternoon when Leach was sick. We was playin' the Boston bunch and Tyler was workin' against us. I always had trouble with lefthanders and this was one of his good days. I couldn't see what he throwed up there. I got one foul durin' the afternoon's entertainment; and the wind was blowin' a hundred-mile gale, so that the best outfielder in the world couldn't judge a fly ball. That Boston bunch must of hit fifty of 'em and they all come to my field.

If I caught any I've forgot about it. Couple o' days after that I got notice o' my release to Indianapolis.

Parker kept right on all season doin' the blamedest things you ever heard of and gettin' by with 'em. One o' the boys told me about it later. If they was playin' a double-header in St. Louis, with the thermometer at 130 degrees, he'd get put out by the umps in the first innin' o' the first game. If he started to steal the catcher'd drop the pitch or somebody'd muff the throw. If he hit a pop fly the sun'd get in somebody's eyes. If he took a swell third strike with the bases full the umps would call it a ball. If he cut first base by twenty feet the umps would be readin' the mornin' paper.

Zimmerman's leg mended, so that he was all right by June; and then Saier got sick and they tried Speed at first base. He'd never saw the bag before; but things kept on breakin' for him and he played it like a house afire. The Cubs copped the pennant and Speed got in on the big dough, besides playin' a whale of a game through the whole serious.

How to Write Short Stories

Speed and me both went back to Ishpeming to
spend the winter—though the Lord knows it
ain't no winter resort. Our homes was there; and
besides, in my case, they was a certain girl livin'
in the old burg.

Parker, o' course, was the hero and the swell guy
when we got home. He'd been in the World's
Serious and had plenty o' dough in his kick. I
come home with nothin' but my suitcase and a
hard-luck story, which I kept to myself. I hadn't
even went good enough in Indianapolis to be sure
of a job there again.

That fall—last fall—an uncle o' Speed's died
over in the Soo and left him ten thousand bucks.
I had an uncle down in the Lower Peninsula who
was worth five times that much—but he had good
health!

This girl I spoke about was the prettiest thing
I ever see. I'd went with her in the old days, and
when I blew back I found she was still strong for
me. They wasn't a great deal o' variety in Ishpeming for a girl to pick from. Her and I went to
the dance every Saturday night and to church
Sunday nights. I called on her Wednesday evenin's, besides takin' her to all the shows that come
along—rotten as the most o' them was.

I never knowed Speed was makin' a play for
this doll till along last Feb'uary. The minute I
seen what was up I got busy. I took her out

Horseshoes

sleigh-ridin' and kept her out in the cold till she'd
promised to marry me. We set the date for this
fall—I figured I'd know better where I was at
by that time.

Well, we didn't make no secret o' bein' engaged; down in the poolroom one night Speed
come up and congratulated me. He says:

"You got a swell girl, Dick! I wouldn't mind
bein' in your place. You're mighty lucky to
cop her out—you old Horseshoes, you!"

"Horseshoes!" I says. "You got a fine license
to call anybody Horseshoes! I suppose you ain't
never had no luck?"

"Not like you," he says.

I was feelin' too good about grabbin' the girl
to get sore at the time; but when I got to thinkin'
about it a few minutes afterward it made me mad
clear through. What right did that bird have to
talk about me bein' lucky?

Speed was playin' freeze-out at a table near the
door, and when I started home some o' the boys
with him says:

"Good night, Dick."

I said good night and then Speed looked up.

"Good night, Horseshoes!" he says.

That got my nanny this time.

"Shut up, you lucky stiff!" I says. "If you
wasn't so dam' lucky you'd be sweepin' the
streets." Then I walks on out.

How to Write Short Stories

I was too busy with the girl to see much o'
Speed after that.   He left home about the middle
o' the month to go to Tampa with the Cubs.   I
got notice from Indianapolis that I was sold to
Baltimore.   I didn't care much about goin' there
and I wasn't anxious to leave home under the
circumstances, so I didn't report till late.

When I read in the papers along in April that
Speed had been traded to Boston for a couple o'
pitchers I thought: "Gee!   He must of lost his
rabbit's foot!"   Because, even if the Cubs didn't
cop again, they'd have a city serious with the
White Sox and get a bunch o' dough that way.
And they wasn't no chance in the world for the
Boston Club to get nothin' but their salaries.

It wasn't another month, though, till Shafer, o'
the Giants, quit baseball and McGraw was up
against it for a third baseman.   Next thing I
knowed Speed was traded to New York and was
with another winner—for they never was out o'
first place all season.

I was gettin' along all right at Baltimore and
Dunnie liked me; so I felt like I had somethin'
more than just a one-year job—somethin' I could
get married on.   It was all framed that the weddin'
was comin' off as soon as this season was over; so
you can believe I was pullin' for October to hurry
up and come.

One day in August, two months ago, Dunnie

Horseshoes

come in the clubhouse and handed me the news.

"Rube Oldring's busted his leg," he says, "and he's out for the rest o' the season. Connie's got a youngster named Joyce that he can stick in there, but he's got to have an extra outfielder. He's made me a good proposition for you and I'm goin' to let you go. It'll be pretty soft for you, because they got the pennant cinched and they'll cut you in on the big money."

"Yes," I says; "and when they're through with me they'll ship me to Hellangone, and I'll be draggin' down about seventy-five bucks a month next year."

"Nothin' like that," says Dunnie. "If he don't want you next season he's got to ask for waivers; and if you get out o' the big league you come right back here. That's all framed."

So that's how I come to get with the Ath-a-letics. Connie give me a nice, comf'table seat in one corner o' the bench and I had the pleasure o' watchin' a real ball club perform once every afternoon and sometimes twice.

Connie told me that as soon as they had the flag cinched he was goin' to lay off some o' his regulars and I'd get a chance to play.

Well, they cinched it the fourth day o' September and our next engagement was with Washin'ton on Labor Day. We had two games and I

How to Write Short Stories

was in both of 'em. And I broke in with my usual
lovely luck, because the pitchers I was ast to face
was Boehling, a nasty lefthander, and this guy
Johnson.

The mornin' game was Boehling's and he wasn't
no worse than some o' the rest of his kind. I only
whiffed once and would of had a triple if Milan
hadn't run from here to New Orleans and stole
one off me.

I'm not boastin' about my first experience with
Johnson though. They can't never tell me he
throws them balls with his arm. He's got a gun
concealed about his person and he shoots 'em up
there. I was leadin' off in Murphy's place and
the game was a little delayed in startin', because
I'd watched the big guy warm up and wasn't in
no hurry to get to that plate. Before I left the
bench Connie says:

"Don't try to take no healthy swing. Just
meet 'em and you'll get along better."

So I tried to just meet the first one he throwed;
but when I stuck out my bat Henry was throwin'
the pill back to Johnson. Then I thought: Maybe if I start swingin' now at the second one I'll
hit the third one. So I let the second one come
over and the umps guessed it was another strike,
though I'll bet a thousand bucks he couldn't see
it no more'n I could.

While Johnson was still windin' up to pitch

Horseshoes

again I started to swing—and the big cuss crosses me with a slow one. I lunged at it twice and missed it both times, and the force o' my wallop throwed me clean back to the bench. The Atha-letics was all laughin' at me and I laughed too, because I was glad that much of it was over.

McInnes gets a base hit off him in the second innin' and I ast him how he done it.

"He's a friend o' mine," says Jack, "and he lets up when he pitches to me."

I made up my mind right there that if I was goin' to be in the league next year I'd go out and visit Johnson this winter and get acquainted.

I wished before the day was over that I was hittin' in the catcher's place, because the fellers down near the tail-end of the battin' order only had to face him three times. He fanned me on three pitched balls again in the third, and when I come up in the sixth he scared me to death by pretty near beanin' me with the first one.

"Be careful!" says Henry. "He's gettin' pretty wild and he's liable to knock you away from your uniform."

"Don't he never curve one?" I ast.

"Sure!" says Henry. "Do you want to see his curve?"

"Yes," I says, knowin' the hook couldn't be no worse'n the fast one.

So he give me three hooks in succession and I

337

missed 'em all; but I felt more comf'table than when I was duckin' his fast ball. In the ninth he hit my bat with a curve and the ball went on the ground to McBride. He booted it, but throwed me out easy—because I was so surprised at not havin' whiffed that I forgot to run!

Well, I went along like that for the rest o' the season, runnin' up against the best pitchers in the league and not exactly murderin' 'em. Everything I tried went wrong, and I was smart enough to know that if anything had depended on the games I wouldn't of been in there for two minutes. Joyce and Strunk and Murphy wasn't jealous o' me a bit; but they was glad to take turns restin', and I didn't care much how I went so long as I was sure of a job next year.

I'd wrote to the girl a couple o' times askin' her to set the exact date for our weddin'; but she hadn't paid no attention. She said she was glad I was with the Ath-a-letics, but she thought the Giants was goin' to beat us. I might of suspected from that that somethin' was wrong, because not even a girl would pick the Giants to trim that bunch of ourn. Finally, the day before the serious started, I sent her a kind o' sassy letter sayin' I guessed it was up to me to name the day, and askin' whether October twentieth was all right. I told her to wire me yes or no.

I'd been readin' the dope about Speed all sea-

Horseshoes

son, and I knowed he'd had a whale of a year and that his luck was right with him; but I never dreamed a man could have the Lord on his side as strong as Speed did in that World's Serious! I might as well tell you all the dope, so long as you wasn't there.

The first game was on our grounds and Connie give us a talkin' to in the clubhouse beforehand.

"The shorter this serious is," he says, "the better for us. If it's a long serious we're goin' to have trouble, because McGraw's got five pitchers he can work and we've got about three; so I want you boys to go at 'em from the jump and play 'em off their feet. Don't take things easy, because it ain't goin' to be no snap. Just because we've licked 'em before ain't no sign we'll do it this time."

Then he calls me to one side and ast me what I knowed about Parker.

"You was with the Cubs when he was, wasn't you?" he says.

"Yes," I says; "and he's the luckiest stiff you ever seen! If he got stewed and fell in the gutter he'd catch a fish."

"I don't like to hear a good ball player called lucky," says Connie. "He must have a lot of ability or McGraw wouldn't use him regular. And he's been hittin' about .340 and played a

How to Write Short Stories

bang-up game at third base. That can't be all luck."

"Wait till you see him," I says; "and if you don't say he's the luckiest guy in the world you can sell me to the Boston Bloomer Girls. He's so lucky," I says, "that if they traded him to the St. Louis Browns they'd have the pennant cinched by the Fourth o' July."

And I'll bet Connie was willin' to agree with me before it was over.

Well, the Chief worked against the Big Rube in that game. We beat 'em, but they give us a battle and it was Parker that made it close. We'd gone along nothin' and nothin' till the seventh, and then Rube walks Collins and Baker lifts one over that little old wall. You'd think by this time them New York pitchers would know better than to give that guy anything he can hit.

In their part o' the ninth the Chief still had 'em shut out and two down, and the crowd was goin' home; but Doyle gets hit in the sleeve with a pitched ball and it's Speed's turn. He hits a foul pretty near straight up, but Schang misjudges it. Then he lifts another one and this time McInnes drops it. He'd ought to of been out twice. The Chief tries to make him hit at a bad one then, because he'd got him two strikes and nothin'. He hit at it all right—kissed it for three bases between Strunk and Joyce! And it was a wild

340

Horseshoes

pitch that he hit. Doyle scores, o' course, and
the bugs suddenly decide not to go home just yet.
I fully expected to see him steal home and get
away with it, but Murray cut into the first ball
and lined out to Barry.

Plank beat Matty two to one the next day in
New York, and again Speed and his rabbit's foot
give us an awful argument. Matty wasn't so
good as usual and we really ought to of beat him
bad. Two different times Strunk was on second
waitin' for any kind o' wallop, and both times
Barry cracked 'em down the third-base line like
a shot. Speed stopped the first one with his
stomach and extricated the pill just in time to
nail Barry at first base and retire the side. The
next time he throwed his glove in front of his face
in self-defense and the ball stuck in it.

In the sixth innin' Schang was on third base and
Plank on first, and two down, and Murphy combed
an awful one to Speed's left. He didn't have
time to stoop over and he just stuck out his foot.
The ball hit it and caromed in two hops right into
Doyle's hands on second base before Plank got
there. Then in the seventh Speed bunts one and
Baker trips and falls goin' after it or he'd of threw
him out a mile. They was two gone; so Speed
steals second, and, o' course, Schang has to make
a bad peg right at that time and lets him go to
third. Then Collins boots one on Murray and

341

they've got a run. But it didn't do 'em no good, because Collins and Baker and McInnes come up in the ninth and walloped 'em where Parker couldn't reach 'em.

Comin' back to Philly on the train that night, I says to Connie:

"What do you think o' that Parker bird now?"

"He's lucky, all right," says Connie smilin'; "but we won't hold it against him if he don't beat us with it."

"It ain't too late," I says. "He ain't pulled his real stuff yet."

The whole bunch was talkin' about him and his luck, and sayin' it was about time for things to break against him. I warned 'em that they wasn't no chance—that it was permanent with him.

Bush and Tesreau hooked up next day and neither o' them had much stuff. Everybody was hittin' and it looked like anybody's game right up to the ninth. Speed had got on every time he come up—the wind blowin' his fly balls away from the outfielders and the infielders bootin' when he hit 'em on the ground.

When the ninth started the score was seven apiece. Connie and McGraw both had their whole pitchin' staffs warmin' up. The crowd was wild, because they'd been all kinds of action. They wasn't no danger of anybody's leavin' their seats before this game was over.

Horseshoes

Well, Bescher is walked to start with and Connie's about ready to give Bush the hook; but Doyle pops out tryin' to bunt. Then Speed gets two strikes and two balls, and it looked to me like the next one was right over the heart; but Connolly calls it a ball and gives him another chance. He whales the groove ball to the fence in left center and gets round to third on it, while Bescher scores. Right then Bush comes out and the Chief goes in. He whiffs Murray and has two strikes on Merkle when Speed makes a break for home—and, o' course, that was the one ball Schang dropped in the whole serious!

They had a two-run lead on us then and it looked like a cinch for them to hold it, because the minute Tesreau showed a sign o' weakenin' McGraw was sure to holler for Matty or the Rube. But you know how quick that bunch of ourn can make a two-run lead look sick. Before McGraw could get Jeff out o' there we had two on the bases.

Then Rube comes in and fills 'em up by walkin' Joyce. It was Eddie's turn to wallop and if he didn't do nothin' we had Baker comin' up next. This time Collins saved Baker the trouble and whanged one clear to the woods. Everybody scored but him—and he could of, too, if it'd been necessary.

In the clubhouse the boys naturally felt pretty good. We'd copped three in a row and it looked

How to Write Short Stories

like we'd make it four straight, because we had
the Chief to send back at 'em the followin' day.

"Your friend Parker is lucky," the boys says to
me, "but it don't look like he could stop us now."

I felt the same way and was consultin' the
time-tables to see whether I could get a train out
o' New York for the West next evenin'. But do
you think Speed's luck was ready to quit? Not
yet! And it's a wonder we didn't all go nuts
durin' the next few days. If words could kill,
Speed would of died a thousand times. And I
wish he had!

They wasn't no record-breakin' crowd out when
we got to the Polo Grounds. I guess the New York
bugs was pretty well discouraged and the bettin'
was eight to five that we'd cop that battle and
finish it. The Chief was the only guy that warmed
up for us and McGraw didn't have no choice but
to use Matty, with the whole thing dependin' on
this game.

They went along like the two swell pitchers
they was till Speed's innin', which in this battle
was the eighth. Nobody scored, and it didn't
look like they was ever goin' to till Murphy starts
off that round with a perfect bunt and Joyce
sacrifices him to second. All Matty had to do
then was to get rid o' Collins and Baker—and
that's about as easy as sellin' silk socks to an
Eskimo.

Horseshoes

He didn't give Eddie nothin' he wanted to hit, though; and finally he slaps one on the ground to Doyle. Larry made the play to first base and Murphy moved to third. We all figured Matty'd walk Baker then, and he done it. Connie sends Baker down to second on the first pitch to McInnes, but Meyers don't pay no attention to him —they was playin' for McInnes and wasn't takin' no chances o' throwin' the ball away.

Well, the count goes to three and two on McInnes and Matty comes with a curve—he's got some curve too; but Jack happened to meet it and—Blooie! Down the left foul line where he always hits! I never seen a ball hit so hard in my life. No infielder in the world could of stopped it. But I'll give you a thousand bucks if that ball didn't go kerplunk right into the third bag and stop as dead as George Washington! It was child's play for Speed to pick it up and heave it over to Merkle before Jack got there. If anybody else had been playin' third base the bag would of ducked out o' the way o' that wallop; but even the bases themselves was helpin' him out.

The two runs we ought to of had on Jack's smash would of been just enough to beat 'em, because they got the only run o' the game in their half—or, I should say, the Lord give it to 'em.

Doyle'd been throwed out and up come Parker, smilin'. The minute I seen him smile I felt like

somethin' was comin' off and I made the remark
on the bench.

Well, the Chief pitched one right at him and
he tried to duck. The ball hit his bat and went on
a line between Jack and Eddie. Speed didn't
know he'd hit it till the guys on the bench wised
him up. Then he just had time to get to first
base. They tried the hit-and-run on the second
ball and Murray lifts a high fly that Murphy
didn't have to move for. Collins pulled the old
bluff about the ball bein' on the ground and Barry
yells, "Go on! Go on!" like he was the coacher.
Speed fell for it and didn't know where the ball
was no more'n a rabbit; he just run his fool head
off and we was gettin' all ready to laugh when
the ball come down and Murphy dropped it!

If Parker had stuck near first base, like he ought
to of done, he couldn't of got no farther'n second;
but with the start he got he was pretty near third
when Murphy made the muff, and it was a cinch
for him to score. The next two guys was easy
outs; so they wouldn't of had a run except for
Speed's boner. We couldn't do nothin' in the
ninth and we was licked.

Well, that was a tough one to lose; but we figured
that Matty was through and we'd wind it up the
next day, as we had Plank ready to send back at
'em. We wasn't afraid o' the Rube, because he
hadn't never bothered Collins and Baker much.

Horseshoes

The two lefthanders come together just like everybody'd doped it and it was about even up to the eighth. Plank had been goin' great and, though the score was two and two, they'd got their two on boots and we'd hit ourn in. We went after Rube in our part o' the eighth and knocked him out. Demaree stopped us after we'd scored two more.

"It's all over but the shoutin'!" says Davis on the bench.

"Yes," I says, "unless that seventh son of a seventh son gets up there again."

He did, and he come up after they'd filled the bases with a boot, a base hit and a walk with two out. I says to Davis:

"If I was Plank I'd pass him and give 'em one run."

"That wouldn't be no baseball," says Davis— "not with Murray comin' up."

Well, it mayn't of been no baseball, but it couldn't of turned out worse if they'd did it that way. Speed took a healthy at the first ball; but it was a hook and he caught it on the handle, right up near his hands. It started outside the first-base line like a foul and then changed its mind and rolled in. Schang run away from the plate, because it looked like it was up to him to make the play. He picked the ball up and had to make the peg in a hurry.

347

How to Write Short Stories

His throw hit Speed right on top o' the head and bounded off like it had struck a cement sidewalk. It went clear over to the seats and before McInnes could get it three guys had scored and Speed was on third base. He was left there, but that didn't make no difference. We was licked again and for the first time the gang really begun to get scared.

We went over to New York Sunday afternoon and we didn't do no singin' on the way. Some o' the fellers tried to laugh, but it hurt 'em. Connie sent us to bed early, but I don't believe none o' the bunch got much sleep—I know I didn't; I was worryin' too much about the serious and also about the girl, who hadn't sent me no telegram like I'd ast her to. Monday mornin' I wired her askin' what was the matter and tellin' her I was gettin' tired of her foolishness. O' course I didn't make it so strong as that—but the telegram cost me a dollar and forty cents.

Connie had the choice o' two pitchers for the sixth game. He could use Bush, who'd been slammed round pretty hard last time out, or the Chief, who'd only had two days' rest. The rest of 'em—outside o' Plank—had a epidemic o' sore arms. Connie finally picked Bush, so's he could have the Chief in reserve in case we had to play a seventh game. McGraw started Big Jeff and we went at it.

348

Horseshoes

It wasn't like the last time these two guys had hooked up. This time they both had somethin', and for eight innin's runs was as scarce as Chinese policemen. They'd been chances to score on both sides, but the big guy and Bush was both tight in the pinches. The crowd was plumb nuts and yelled like Indians every time a fly ball was caught or a strike called. They'd of got their money's worth if they hadn't been no ninth; but, believe me, that was some round!

They was one out when Barry hit one through the box for a base. Schang walked, and it was Bush's turn. Connie told him to bunt, but he whiffed in the attempt. Then Murphy comes up and walks—and the bases are choked. Young Joyce had been pie for Tesreau all day or else McGraw might of changed pitchers right there. Anyway he left Big Jeff in and he beaned Joyce with a fast one. It sounded like a tire blowin' out. Joyce falls over in a heap and we chase out there, thinkin' he's dead; but he ain't, and pretty soon he gets up and walks down to first base. Tesreau had forced in a run and again we begun to count the winner's end. Matty comes in to prevent further damage and Collins flies the side out.

"Hold 'em now! Work hard!" we says to young Bush, and he walks out there just as cool as though he was goin' to hit fungoes.

How to Write Short Stories

McGraw sends up a pinch hitter for Matty and Bush whiffed him. Then Bescher flied out. I was prayin' that Doyle would end it, because Speed's turn come after his'n; so I pretty near fell dead when Larry hit safe.

Speed had his old smile and even more chest than usual when he come up there, swingin' five or six bats. He didn't wait for Doyle to try and steal, or nothin'. He lit into the first ball, though Bush was tryin' to waste it. I seen the ball go high in the air toward left field, and then I picked up my glove and got ready to beat it for the gate. But when I looked out to see if Joyce was set, what do you think I seen? He was lyin' flat on the ground! That blow on the head had got him just as Bush was pitchin' to Speed. He'd flopped over and didn't no more know what was goin' on than if he'd croaked.

Well, everybody else seen it at the same time; but it was too late. Strunk made a run for the ball, but they wasn't no chance for him to get near it. It hit the ground about ten feet back o' where Joyce was lyin' and bounded way over to the end o' the foul line. You don't have to be told that Doyle and Parker both scored and the serious was tied up.

We carried Joyce to the clubhouse and after a while he come to. He cried when he found out what had happened. We cheered him up all we

could, but he was a pretty sick guy. The trainer
said he'd be all right, though, for the final game.

They tossed up a coin to see where they'd play
the seventh battle and our club won the toss; so
we went back to Philly that night and cussed
Parker clear across New Jersey. I was so sore
I kicked the stuffin' out o' my seat.

You probably heard about the excitement in
the burg yesterday mornin'. The demand for
tickets was somethin' fierce and some of 'em
sold for as high as twenty-five bucks apiece. Our
club hadn't been lookin' for no seventh game and
they was some tall hustlin' done round that old
ball park.

I started out to the grounds early and bought
some New York papers to read on the car. They
was a big story that Speed Parker, the Giants'
hero, was goin' to be married a week after the
end o' the serious. It didn't give the name o' the
girl, sayin' Speed had refused to tell it. I figured
she must be some dame he'd met round the circuit somewheres.

They was another story by one o' them smart
baseball reporters sayin' that Parker, on his way
up to the plate, had saw that Joyce was about
ready to faint and had hit the fly ball to left field
on purpose. Can you beat it?

I was goin' to show that to the boys in the clubhouse, but the minute I blowed in there I got some

news that made me forget about everything else. Joyce was very sick and they'd took him to a hospital. It was up to me to play!

Connie come over and ast me whether I'd ever hit against Matty. I told him I hadn't, but I'd saw enough of him to know he wasn't no worse'n Johnson. He told me he was goin' to let me hit second—in Joyce's place—because he didn't want to bust up the rest of his combination. He also told me to take my orders from Strunk about where to play for the batters.

"Where shall I play for Parker?" I says, tryin' to joke and pretend I wasn't scared to death.

"I wisht I could tell you," says Connie. "I guess the only thing to do when he comes up is to get down on your knees and pray."

The rest o' the bunch slapped me on the back and give me all the encouragement they could. The place was jammed when we went out on the field. They may of been bigger crowds before, but they never was packed together so tight. I doubt whether they was even room enough left for Falkenberg to sit down.

The afternoon papers had printed the stuff about Joyce bein' out of it, so the bugs was wise that I was goin' to play. They watched me pretty close in battin' practice and give me a hand whenever I managed to hit one hard. When I was out catchin' fungoes the guys in the bleachers cheered

Horseshoes

me and told me they was with me; but I don't
mind tellin' you that I was as nervous as a
bride.

They wasn't no need for the announcers to tip
the crowd off to the pitchers. Everybody in the
United States and Cuba knowed that the Chief'd
work for us and Matty for them. The Chief
didn't have no trouble with 'em in the first innin'.
Even from where I stood I could see that he had a
lot o' stuff. Bescher and Doyle popped out and
Speed whiffed.

Well, I started out makin' good, with reverse
English, in our part. Fletcher booted Murphy's
ground ball and I was sent up to sacrifice. I done
a complete job of it—sacrificin' not only myself
but Murphy with a pop fly that Matty didn't
have to move for. That spoiled whatever chance
we had o' gettin' the jump on 'em; but the boys
didn't bawl me for it.

"That's all right, old boy. You're all right!"
they said on the bench—if they'd had a gun they'd
of shot me.

I didn't drop no fly balls in the first six innin's—
because none was hit out my way. The Chief was
so good that they wasn't hittin' nothin' out o'
the infield. And we wasn't doin' nothin' with
Matty, either. I led off in the fourth and fouled
the first one. I didn't molest the other two.
But if Connie and the gang talked about me they

How to Write Short Stories

done it internally. I come up again—with Murphy on third base and two gone in the sixth, and done my little whiffin' specialty. And still the only people that panned me was the thirty thousand that had paid for the privilege!

My first fieldin' chance come in the seventh. You'd of thought that I'd of had my nerve back by that time; but I was just as scared as though I'd never saw a crowd before. It was just as well that they was two out when Merkle hit one to me. I staggered under it and finally it hit me on the shoulder. Merkle got to second, but the Chief whiffed the next guy. I was gave some cross looks on the bench and I shouldn't of blamed the fellers if they'd cut loose with some language; but they didn't.

They's no use in me tellin' you about none o' the rest of it—except what happened just before the start o' the eleventh and durin' that innin', which was sure the big one o' yesterday's pastime —both for Speed and yours sincerely.

The scoreboard was still a row o' ciphers and Speed'd had only a fair amount o' luck. He'd made a scratch base hit and robbed our bunch of a couple o' real ones with impossible stops.

When Schang flied out and wound up our tenth I was leanin' against the end of our bench. I heard my name spoke, and I turned round and seen a boy at the door.

Horseshoes

"Right here!" I says; and he give me a telegram.

"Better not open it till after the game," says Connie.

"Oh, no; it ain't no bad news," I said, for I figured it was an answer from the girl. So I opened it up and read it on the way to my position. It said:

"Forgive me, Dick—and forgive Speed too. Letter follows."

Well, sir, I ain't no baby, but for a minute I just wanted to sit down and bawl. And then, all of a sudden, I got so mad I couldn't see. I run right into Baker as he was pickin' up his glove. Then I give him a shove and called him some name, and him and Barry both looked at me like I was crazy—and I was. When I got out in left field I stepped on my own foot and spiked it. I just had to hurt somebody.

As I remember it the Chief fanned the first two of 'em. Then Doyle catches one just right and lams it up against the fence back o' Murphy. The ball caromed round some and Doyle got all the way to third base. Next thing I seen was Speed struttin' up to the plate. I run clear in from my position.

"Kill him!" I says to the Chief. "Hit him in the head and kill him, and I'll go to jail for it!"

355

How to Write Short Stories

"Are you off your nut?" says the Chief. "Go out there and play ball—and quit ravin'."

Barry and Baker led me away and give me a shove out toward left. Then I heard the crack o' the bat and I seen the ball comin' a mile a minute. It was headed between Strunk and I and looked like it would go out o' the park. I don't remember runnin' or nothin' about it till I run into the concrete wall head first. They told me afterward and all the papers said that it was the greatest catch ever seen. And I never knowed I'd caught the ball!

Some o' the managers have said my head was pretty hard, but it wasn't as hard as that concrete. I was pretty near out, but they tell me I walked to the bench like I wasn't hurt at all. They also tell me that the crowd was a bunch o' ravin' maniacs and was throwin' money at me. I guess the ground-keeper'll get it.

The boys on the bench was all talkin' at once and slappin' me on the back, but I didn't know what it was about. Somebody told me pretty soon that it was my turn to hit and I picked up the first bat I come to and starts for the plate. McInnes come runnin' after me and ast me whether I didn't want my own bat. I cussed him and told him to mind his own business.

I didn't know it at the time, but I found out afterward that they was two out. The bases was

Horseshoes

empty. I'll tell you just what I had in my mind:
I wasn't thinkin' about the ball game; I was de-
termined that I was goin' to get to third base and
give that guy my spikes. If I didn't hit one worth
three bases, or if I didn't hit one at all, I was
goin' to run till I got round to where Speed was,
and then slide into him and cut him to pieces!

Right now I can't tell you whether I hit a fast
ball, or a slow ball, or a hook, or a fader—but I
hit somethin'. It went over Bescher's head like
a shot and then took a crazy bound. It must of
struck a rock or a pop bottle, because it hopped clear over the fence and landed in the
bleachers.

Mind you, I learned this afterward. At the
time I just knowed I'd hit one somewheres and
I starts round the bases. I speeded up when I
got near third and took a runnin' jump at a guy
I thought was Parker. I missed him and sprawled
all over the bag. Then, all of a sudden, I come
to my senses. All the Ath-a-letics was out there
to run home with me and it was one o' them I'd
tried to cut. Speed had left the field. The boys
picked me up and seen to it that I went on and
touched the plate. Then I was carried into the
clubhouse by the crazy bugs.

Well, they had a celebration in there and it was
a long time before I got a chance to change my
clothes. The boys made a big fuss over me.

How to Write Short Stories

They told me they'd intended to give me five hundred bucks for my divvy, but now I was goin' to get a full share.

"Parker ain't the only lucky guy!" says one of 'em. "But even if that ball hadn't of took that crazy hop you'd of had a triple."

A triple! That's just what I'd wanted; and he called me lucky for not gettin' it!

The Giants was dressin' in the other part o' the clubhouse; and when I finally come out there was Speed, standin' waitin' for some o' the others. He seen me comin' and he smiled. "Hello, Horseshoes!" he says.

He won't smile no more for a while—it'll hurt too much. And if any girl wants him when she sees him now—with his nose over shakin' hands with his ear, and his jaw a couple o' feet foul— she's welcome to him. They won't be no contest!

Grimes leaned over to ring for the waiter.

"Well," he said, "what about it?"

"You won't have to pay my fare," I told him.

"I'll buy a drink anyway," said he. "You've been a good listener—and I had to get it off my chest."

"Maybe they'll have to postpone the wedding," I said.

"No," said Grimes. "The weddin' will take

358

Horseshoes

place the day after tomorrow—and I'll bat for Mr. Parker. Did you think I was goin' to let him get away with it?''

"What about next year?'' I asked.

"I'm goin' back to the Ath-a-letics," he said. "And I'm goin' to hire somebody to call me 'Horseshoes!' before every game—because I can sure play that old baseball when I'm mad."

Printed in the United States
103502LV00001B/27/A